The Tuning of the Word

The Musico-Literary Poetics
of the Symbolist Movement

DAVID MICHAEL HERTZ

Southern Illinois University Press
Carbondale and Edwardsville

90 89 88 87   4 3 2 1

Library of Congress Cataloging-in-Publication Data

Hertz, David Michael, 1954–
    The tuning of the word.

    Includes index.
    Bibliography: p.
    1. Music and literature.   2. Symbolism in literature.
I. Title.
ML3849.H39   1987   780'.08   86-3962
    ISBN 0-8093-1312-x

Permission to reproduce materials from copyright sources is acknowledged
on pp. ix–x.

To
my beloved family
and to
my students in *Crosscurrents in the Arts*

Contents

Acknowledgments

Permission to reproduce the following copyright materials is gratefully acknowledged:

Figures 1-1, 1-2, 1-3, 1-4, 1-5, 1-6, 1-7, 1-8, 1-13, 5-9, 5-20, 5-32, 5-34: Used by permission of G. Henle Verlag, Munich

Figure 19: From Beethoven *Sämtliche Lieder,* Breitkopf and Härtel, Wiesbaden.

Figure 1-10: From Schubert, *Gesaenge,* vol. 1: "Schaefers Klagelied." Used by permission of C. F. Peters Corporation

Figures 1-11, 2-3, 2-4, 2-5, 2-6, 2-7, 2-8, 2-9, 4-6, 5-14, 5-23, 5-28, 3-2, 3-3, 6-3: Used by special arrangement with G. Schirmer, Inc.

Figures 3-1, 3-4, 3-7, 3-8, 3-9, 6-1: From the Norton Critical Score of Claude Debussy, *Prélude à l'après-midi d'un faune,* edited by William W. Austin. Copyright © 1970. Used by permission of the publisher. W. W. Norton, Inc.

Figures 4-1, 4-2, 4-4, 4-5, 4-7, 4-8, 4-9, 4-10, 4-11, 4-12, 4-13, 4-14, 4-15, 4-16: From *Songs: 1880–1904,* music by Claude Debussy, edited by Rita Benton. Used by permission of Dover Publications, copyright © 1981.

Figures 4-3, 7-2, 7-3, 7-9, 7-10, 7-12, 7-13, 7-14, 7-15, 7-16, 7-17, 7-18, 7-19: From *Pelléas et Mélisande* piano/vocal score, copyright © 1907. Figures 7-11, 7-14, 7-20: From *Pelléas et Mélisande* orchestral score, copyright © 1904. Figures 4-17, 4-19, 4-20, 4-21, 4-22, 4-25, 4-26, 4-27, 4-29, 4-30, 4-31, 4-32, 4-33: From *Trois Poèmes de Stéphane Mallarmé,* copyright © 1913. Figure 4-34: From *Preludes,* book 2, copyright © 1913. Durand S. A. Editions Musicales. Used by permission of the publisher. Theodore Presser Company, sole representative U.S.A.

Figures 4-23, 4-24: *Historical Anthology of Music,* by Archibald T. Davison and Willi Apel. Copyright © 1949 by the President and Fellows of Harvard College; © 1977 by Alice Davison Hurnez and

Willi Apel. Reprinted by permission of Harvard University Press.

Figures 5-1, 5-2, 5-3, 5-4, 5-5, 5-6, 5-7, 5-8, 5-10, 5-11, 5-12, 5-13, 5-14, 5-15, 5-16, 5-17, 5-18, 5-19, 5-21, 5-22, 5-24, 5-25, 5-26, 5-27, 5-29, 5-30, 5-31, 5-33, 5-35, 5-36, 5-37, 5-38: Copyright 1914 by Universal Edition. Renewed 1941 by Arnold Schoenberg. Figure 6-4: Copyright © 1956, International Music Co. Used by permission of Belmont Music Publishers, Los Angeles, California 90049.

Figure 6-2: From *Famous Symphonic Poems in Score,* edited by Albert E. Weir, copyright © 1938. Used by permission of the publisher. Harcourt Brace Jovanovich, Inc.

Figures 6-5, 6-6: Copyright © 1908, Durand S. A. Editions Musicales, Editions Arima and Durand S. A. Editions Musicales Joint Publication. Used by permission of the publisher. Theodore Presser Company, sole representative U.S.A.

Figures 7-1, 7-4, 7-5, 7-6, 7-7, 7-8: From *Ariadne auf Naxos,* music by Richard Strauss, libretto by Hugo von Hofmannsthal. Copyright © 1912, 1913, 1916, 1922, 1924 by Adolph Furstner; renewed 1940, 1941, 1949, 1951. Copyright and renewal assigned to Boosey and Hawkes, Inc. Reprinted by permission.

Introduction

The Birth of Tragedy, Nietzsche's revolutionary study, originally had a much longer title when it appeared in 1872: *The Birth of Tragedy out of the Spirit of Music*.[1] Although Nietzsche does discuss the importance of *melos* in primitive Dionysian ritual, it is really his own book that grew out of the spirit of late German Romantic music. Symbolist poetics, which generated the subsequent development of modern poetry, was also born out of the spirit of music and largely nurtured in ideas of music. The Symbolists returned the favor to the art of music, though, for modern European music was partly gestated in the theories of Symbolist poetics. Developments in the fields of poetry and music in the late nineteenth century were also a result of purely linear influences. Musicians affected the work of later musicians and poetry written by influential figures had impact on subsequent poets. Nevertheless, the cultural ambience of the fin de siècle was one that lent itself to cross-fertilization between the arts. The object of this study is to unravel and retrace major strands in the complex pattern of interrelationships between the arts of music and literature in the late nineteenth century and to follow the manifestations of these substrata of interrelations in major works of art written in the early twentieth century.

John Hollander's *Untuning of the Sky: Ideas of Music in English Poetry* traces music as an image in English poetry from 1500 to 1700.[2] Hollander was especially interested in the gradual breakdown of the image of Christian world harmony. In the nineteenth century, the word of the poet was retuned, but this time to the actual sounds of music, for the Symbolists tried to approximate the textural flow of music. Furthermore, as the cogent system of organized sound—functional tonal harmony—gradually was stretched beyond its limitations, the art of music yielded, as Arnold Schoenberg observed, to literary influence. Music, then, attempted to tune itself to fit the word.

The innovative, rebellious, and revolutionary spirit of modern Western literature descends, in many respects, from Symbolist writings. The Symbolist moved language away from the task of the journalist, away from the emotive excess of the Romantic, and toward an ideal realm where the poet, freed from the necessity to describe reality, could create language that referred to itself, poetry chiefly about poetry. Accordingly, semioticians and deconstructionists have justifiably turned to Symbolist literature because of their natural inclination to study the complexity of poetic discourse. The paradoxical shoals and eddies of poetry show up with unusual clarity and brilliance in Symbolist poetry. Because of its importance for modern critics, Symbolism needs to be carefully studied in its original cultural context. This context cannot be fully revealed without a careful comparison of Symbolism with the historical development of nineteenth-century music, for ambiguity in Symbolist writing was a tendency that was linked to an interest in music as a pure art form. This book is a contribution to the uncovering and reevaluation of that context as it can be discerned from the study of historical documents such as the *Revue Wagnérienne* and the recognition of that context within specific works of art.

Any style or tendency in the arts is best defined through an examination of the ubiquitous dialectic between form and content, structure and meaning. Symbolism is characterized by two basic features in this universal dialectic. The first has to do with form. Symbolist style is marked by a hostility to periodic differentiation. The second has to do with content. Symbolist style features a kind of open-ended evocation of meanings. This is achieved by assembling unresolved actions and questions, as well as conflicting blocks of images, in the text. Tonal ambiguity in music parallels this literary tendency. These notions are developed throughout the seven essays of the book, but chapter 1 introduces and explains them in some detail.

Symbolist style successfully thwarts the feeling of periodicity in both poetry and music. I am convinced that the older ways of making music and poetry involved the linking of closed, symmetrical phrases. With High Romanticism we see the breaking of the rhythm of the phrase in music and poetry. Symbolist style is characterized by a continued inclination to form open-ended, fractured phrases, but the Symbolist phrase creates an aura of subtle mystery and expressive ambiguity, an introspective style that suggests rather than defines. The Symbolist phrase, indebted to High Romanticism but distinctly different from its precursors, characterizes the new style.

If the first step was to crack open the periodic phrase, the second had to do with Baudelaire's theory of correspondences and his way of perceiving the experience of listening to music. The discussion of his ideas in chapter 1 provides necessary historical perspective. Baudelaire understood how music could suggest possible meanings and psychological states rather than spell out specific concepts. His views had enormous importance for the Symbolists. Baudelaire's understanding of the power of music to suggest instead of explicate ties in with the creative approach to literature worked out by Barthes, a twentieth-century aesthete as sensitive to music and literature as Baudelaire, his nineteenth-century predecessor. Barthes was a taster of language, a literary gourmet whose joyful analysis of minute aspects of the word is far closer to the elegance of Mallarmé than to the much more conservative style of Balzac, the prose writer whom Barthes parses with such force and ingenious originality in his renowned *S/Z*. A Barthean view of poetic discourse helps to show, ultimately, how Mallarmé, following in the footsteps of Baudelaire, was able to create poetry that makes a unique music of its own.

These two main charactcristics, explained in chapter 1, are the chief clues that open up the secrets of the Symbolist style. The Symbolist poetic covers a great deal of terrain. Large and small forms show the traits of the new aesthetic. At various points in time, the lyric poem, the song, the cycle of poems, the song cycle, the tone poem, the lyric play, and the opera all show the important features of Symbolism. The influence of the new musico-literary aesthetic, chiefly engendered by Mallarmé, cuts across genres, media, and national boundaries. Chapter 2 traces the way in which Wagner's concepts of asymmetrical freedom and ambiguity were discussed in the *Revue Wagnérienne*. Gradually, however, the Romantic attitudes of Baudelaire and Wagner gave way to the new voice of Mallarmé within the pages of the *Revue Wagnérienne*. Claude Debussy was one of the very first important artists to appreciate the significance of Mallarmé. The relationships between the literary sensibility of Debussy, the composer's musical innovations, and the thought and verse of Mallarmé are examined in chapters 3 and 4. Mallarmé's importance emerges in greater detail in chapter 4. It becomes clear that Debussy's settings of Mallarmé's poems show far more affinity with Symbolist aesthetics than does the music he created for either his own verse or Verlaine's. Debussy's Baudelaire songs, as one might expect, are by far the most Wagnerian and Romantic in his oeuvre.[3] In chapter 5, the developing revolutionary modernism of Schoenberg is compared to the poems of Stefan George. *The Book of the Hanging Gardens* was an important step in Schoenberg's gradual evolution toward serialism. George, a poet influenced by the French Symbolists, helped to spark the innovations in this song cycle. Perhaps the most unique of the new subgenres of the late nineteenth century were the tone poem and the lyric play. They are discussed in terms of their remarkable similarities in chapter 6. Finally, the opera, the largest of the forms affected by Symbolism, is treated in chapter 7. Both Strauss and Debussy used Symbolist playwrights as librettists. Strauss formed a renowned partnership with Hofmannsthal, and Debussy worked with Maeterlinck. In the final analysis, however, Maeterlinck and Debussy, not Hofmannsthal and Strauss, formed the ideal collaboration between Symbolist playwright and composer.

A word of encouragement to both the general reader and the scholar with only a partial knowledge of this complex field. All of the quotations—whether excerpts from literature, critical sources, or musical scores—are carefully explained and justified in the body of my own text. Thus, someone without French, for example, can follow the general argument, and in the same way, someone who does not know music well (or cannot even read it) can ignore the musical examples without missing the key ideas. In addition, previously published English translations of long prose extracts in French and German have been included in the notes. As a result, the main thrust of this work is available to anyone who wishes to trace the origins of modern styles in art.

The Tuning of the Word

1. Periodicity and Correspondences in Poetry and Music

In the nineteenth century, the art of music was canonized. The influential author and aesthete Walter Pater summed up the high status of music in his seminal book on Renaissance art and poetry: "All art constantly aspires toward the condition of music."[1] The French Symbolists, however, wanted not only to aspire toward the condition of music but to take back some aspects of its nature for their own rightful use, to claim their own literary art as the supreme abstract art.[2] The Symbolists were, in effect, envious of the striking success of music as an art form and felt that their own art, the art of poetry, deserved equal and perhaps even greater recognition.

Music was a nineteenth-century symbol of art as an entity of priceless aesthetic value, purity, independence, universality, and truth. On the other hand, from the origins of musical Romanticism evident in Beethoven, who called himself a "tone poet" and not a "tone artist," through Wagner's view of the musician as a revealer of the unconscious, nineteenth-century musical thought displays a specific awareness of literary ideas and goals.[3] The interrelation of the two arts goes deeper, however, than an intense and mutual awareness in the nineteenth century. On a practical level, the interpenetration of music and literature in the nineteenth century involves parallel technical developments in the creation of works of art. Both arts moved toward freedom from all formalized constraints, both in organization and content, in syntax and semantics.

The mind tends to perceive art in terms of symmetrical groupings and simple repetitions. This was certainly known by Aristotle, as he clearly shows in both the *Rhetoric* and the *Poetics,* and has also figured largely in the thought of recent psychologists of perception such as Gombrich and Arnheim.[4] In terms of poetry and music, however, this tendency to form symmetrical units is not linked to the notion of static structures so much as it is linked to rhythm. Rhythm is a concept common to both music and poetry, but one that is extremely difficult to define. Most definitions, in dictionaries or in specialized reference books dealing with music or poetry, tend to describe rhythm as the symmetrical repetition of measurable units in time made up of both strong and weak elements, and with a strong degree of differentiation between the elements.[5] Symmetrical repetition facilitates the measurement of rhythm, but it is not a prerequisite for rhythm. Rhythm can also be asymmetrical in nature. For our purposes, rhythm is the sequential unfolding of discrete units in time. Symmetrical repetition is merely the most common rhythmic phenomenon.

The tendency to form symmetrical phrases in Western music is highly similar to the ancient and ubiquitous practice, in literary discourse, of organizing language in syntactical units of uniform length. Roland Barthes, who published an outline of rhetoric in *Communications,* credits Aristotle with designating a phrase that has a beginning and an end ("début et fin"), with at least two members ("élévation et abaissement") and at most four members, as a period.[6] A period for Aristotle is, in effect, a microcosm of his definition of a proper plot for a tragedy. Like a plot, it must have a beginning, an end, and a length that one can grasp easily. Like the plot, the period must be a complete, self-contained entity. Aristotle defines the period succinctly in the *Rhetoric*:

By a period I mean a portion of speech that has in itself a beginning and an end, being at the same time not too big to be taken in at a glance. Language of this kind is satisfying and easy to follow. It is satisfying, because it is just the reverse of indefinite; and moreover, the hearer always feels that he is grasping something and has reached some definite conclusion; whereas it is unsatisfactory to see nothing in front of you and get nowhere. It is easy to follow, because it can easily be remembered; and this because language when in periodic form can be numbered, and number is the easiest of all things to remember. That is why verse, which is measured, is always more easily remembered than prose, which is not . . .[7]

The structure of the period is dependent on divisions marked by systems of colons and commas. In general, the period has three or four colons, sometimes generating a tripartite phrase or sometimes generating a bipartite phrase with two smaller sections marked off by commas. The period, according to Barthes, is related to the "va-et-vient du souffle" (the inhalation and exhalation of breath).[8] The period, then, is the celebration, by an act of language, of the even pattern of human breathing.

The humanist tradition preserved the ancient concept of the period, and symmetrical balance, the major characteristic of the period, was an essential aspect of the ideal Renaissance sentence. In *Giotto and the Orators*, Michael Baxandall observes that "the pattern of the grand neo-classical sentence was the period: that is, the sentence containing a number of thoughts and statements in a number of balanced clauses."[9] Baxandall adds that in the more restrictive and conservative classical theorists "the first section of the periodic sentence (protasis) is seen as inducing suspense and a second sentence (apodosis) as resolving it: if A, then B; though A, yet B; as A, so to B and so on."[10] This idea of tension and resolution was intrinsic in the structuring of literary phrases throughout the humanist tradition. The period was the microcosm of the form of the work of art for the Renaissance. Baxandall states his case strongly: "The periodic sentence is the basic art form of the early humanists. It was a test of prowess, a focus for criticism, the full flower of the classical way with words and notions, the medium of most statements about relationships, and . . . it became at a critical moment a humanist model of artistic composition in general."[11]

From the sixteenth century on, music theorists transferred notions such as the period to music theory. In fact, they drew upon ideas of humanist rhetoric in general. The period, though, survives intact as rhetoric and music are compared in Dressler (1563), Burmeister (1606), and Mattheson (1737), until it surfaces in a tract by Heinrich Christoph Koch, *Versuch einer Anleitung zur Composition* (1787).[12] Harold S. Powers, who quotes Koch extensively in "Language Models and Musical Analysis," observes that Koch's concept of musical composition bears a remarkable similarity to the "hierarchic levels" conceived by his literary predecessors.[13] Koch argues that what holds true for speech is also valid for music.

By means of these more or less marked pauses in thought the products of these fine arts permit of being resolved into greater and lesser sections. Through the most marked, for example, speech falls into separate periods, and through the less marked in turn the periods fall into individual sentences and segments of speech. And as with speech, melody [is] resolved into periods, and these again into individual phrases and melodic segments by means of similar "pauses in thought."[14]

Momigny, writing in 1800, derived a notion of the period from the continuum of tension between "formal units."[15] By the time Schopenhauer wrote *Die Welt als Wille und Vorstellung* (1818), the musical period had become a formalized convention—the standard symmetrical phrase of music. The philosopher outlines the nature of the period in *Die Welt als Wille und Vorstellung*, clearly indicating that he understood its function as a structural code in early nineteenth-century music:

> Aus mehreren Takten besteht die musikalische Periode, welche ebenfalls zwei gleiche Hälften hat, eine steigende, anstrebende, meistens zur Dominante gehende, und eine sinkende beruhigende, den Grundton wiederfindende. Zwei, auch wohl mehrere Perioden machen einen Theil aus, der meistens durch das Wiederholungszeichen gleichfalls symmetrisch verdoppelt wird: aus zwei Theilen wird ein kleineres Musikstück, oder aber nur ein Satz eines grössern; wie denn ein Konzert oder Sonate aus dreien, eine Symphonie aus vier, eine Messe aus fünf Sätzen zu bestehen pflegt. Wir sehen das Tonstück, durch die symmetrische Eintheilung und abermalige Theilung, bis zu den Takten und deren Brüchen herab, bei durchgängiger Unter-, Über- und Neben-Ordnung seiner Glieder, gerade so zu einem Ganzen verbunden und abgeschlossen werden, wie das Bauwerk durch seine Symmetrie: nur dass bei diesem ausschliesslich im Raume ist, was bei jenem ausschliesslich in der Zeit.[16]

For Schopenhauer, the part determines the nature of the whole. The part, the periodic unit, is a molecule of musical structure. This molecule is made up of specific components, some of them purely linear, that is to say, taking place in measured time, some of them horizontal. The horizontal components are simultaneous soundings of pitches that are best described as harmonic events. The molecule of musical structure is divided into two large parts, the first part featuring a move away from a tonality, which is described by Schopenhauer as featuring a "rising" or "striving" towards the dominant, the second part featuring a move back to the tonic, which Schopenhauer refers to as a sinking yet soothing feeling. Harmonic events are thus linked to phrase lengths.

Schopenhauer argues that this unit is more important than the larger musical form in which it appears or than the kind of instruments required to execute a musical work. A sonata, a symphony, a concerto, a mass are all built with periods. For Schopenhauer, the most important identifying feature of an entire musical style is not a matter of larger issues of form, genre, medium, or scope, but a small symmetrical unit of musical thought. Schopenhauer, in terms of his own musical culture—that of the early nineteenth century—is perfectly justified in his claims. The most dominant feature of early nineteenth-century music is the norm of the period.

Theoreticians who paved the way for the explosion of creativity that was Haydn, Mozart, and Beethoven had transferred the metaphor of the period into a musical fact. For the great composers of the early nineteenth century, the period had become a code of orientation that allowed a point of departure, but by the time they inherited it, the standard period was what Wagner disparagingly called the "quadratic phrase."[17] It was a four-part unit of musical syntax. The four smaller portions fit into two equally larger portions—the antecedent and consequent clauses. The antecedent clause opens the phrase; the consequent closes it. Beethoven, Wagner's idol, rarely escapes from the rule of the quadratic phrase. Beethoven relied on it throughout his creative life (see figures 1-1 to 1-6).

1-1. Beethoven, Piano Sonata in F Minor, Opus 2, No. 1 (1795), measures 1–8

1-2. Beethoven, Piano Sonata in D Major, Opus 10, No. 3 (1796–98), measures 1–16

1-3. Beethoven, Piano Sonata in F Minor, *Appassionata*, Opus 57 (1804–5), measures 1–8

1-4. Beethoven, Piano Sonata in E Minor, Opus 90 (1814), Nicht zu geschwind und sehr singbar vorgetragen, measures 1–8

1-5. Beethoven, Piano Sonata in E Major, Opus 109, (1820), measures 1–8

1-6. Beethoven, Piano Sonata in C Major, Opus 111 (1821–22), measures 1–8

There is nothing mysterious about these musical periods for the trained musician—for a musician trained, that is, in the European tradition. Each idea is presented in a complete, cogent, clear form. Each excerpt has a clearly defined tonality that marks the point of departure and the point of return, and a simple complement of chords—dominant and tonic—that are evenly spaced and politely expose the aural possibilities of the tonality. Beethoven, moreover, provides in these excerpts the basic architectonic unit that simultaneously generates and fits into the overall structure of an entire movement. We expect to hear these periods repeated as we listen. If we do not, we are surprised; if we do, we are satisfied. This amounts to a cultural code of expectations that is mutually understood by the composer and his listener. As Schopenhauer points out, the period is a microcosm of a style. It is a basic unit of musical thought in Beethoven, implying not only a specific symmetrical length but also harmonic movement, tonal unity, and co-ordination of these linear and horizontal features.

For Hugo Riemann, the structure of music was dependent upon the measure of the period. Walter Dürr and Walter Gerstenberg, in a recent article on rhythm, call Riemann's *System der musikalischen Rhythmik und Metrik* (1903), "the most significant document on Classical-Romantic rhythmic theory."[18] By the time Riemann published his study, however, the once coherent styles of European music were in a shambles. Riemann was looking back into the past to justify his theories and thus chose to illustrate his arguments with composers who had written a century earlier—Haydn, Mozart, and Beethoven. The musical beat, for Riemann, culminated in the "eight-bar period." Riemann called it a "normative basic schema."[19] The eight-bar period could be extended by augmentation or shortened by diminution.[20] (See, for example, the opening bars of Beethoven's Opus 10, No. 3.) The complete musical period for Riemann was characterized by a proposition (*Aufstellung*) and response (*Beantwortung*).[21] It was a perfectly symmetrical unit of musical thought, even more rigidly fixed in Riemann's theories than in its original classical conception.

What might periodization be in modern poetics? S. R. Levin has used the term, and Sandra Bermann has constructed an argument that would be enhanced by the use of such a term in strictly literary poetics.[22] For Levin, poetry is characterized by a higher degree of "unity" than that found in prose or ordinary speech. Levin calls the structures creating this unity *couplings*. Couplings have to do with the deep structure of a poem as well as the surface qualities that enable us to identify a poem.[23] Levin differentiates between the "natural equivalences" that may bind a poem together and the systematic use of equivalences created by "conventional matrices" of poetic organization.[24] "This new matrix is one which derives not from the syntagmatic system of languages, but rather from the body of conventions which a poem, as an organized literary form, observes."[25] English poetry, Levin adds, practices two significant conventions—rhyme and meter: "As conventions, these two features result in incorporating into the poem a periodicity of equivalences."[26] Systematic repetitions for Levin make up the "periodicity of equivalence."[27] Periodicity is involved with the manner in which the pulse falls on every foot in iambic meter, for example. Or, with rhyme, "the periodicity involves line-ends, in certain combinations, depending on the rhyme scheme employed in the poem. Thus, in the rhyme scheme *abab,* the ends of the alternate lines are equivalent on the axis of rhyme."[28] All repetitions are "periodic." Helmholtz, in his tract on the sensations of tone, argues that what distinguishes music from noise is the presence of even periodic waves.[29] Nevertheless, both this concept and Levin's are too far-reaching to embrace the mainstream of European poetic practice. Periodicity would better serve our purposes if we confined it to conventionalized phrase structure in poetry. Periodization in poetry is the tendency to structure poetry into organized stanza forms.

Bermann hints at this in her article on the sonnet:

> What makes a sonnet? The usual response announces the repetition of its fixed verse form: fourteen hendecasyllabic lines rhyming ABBA ABBA CDE CDE (the most common Italian form) or fourteen iambic pentameters rhyming ABAB CDCD EFEF GG (the Shakespearean). Clearly, the principle behind such a description is, in turn, the frequency and the complexity of repetition. Meter is that regular return of accent and syllable by which we mark the temporal movement of a text, and rhyme the repetition of sound tying one word to another, usually at the end point of the line. Stanzas organize repetitions of rhyme and meter into larger units. And the sonnet tradition, with its repetition of a recognizable form in the course of some seven centuries of lyric practice only reenacts the same poetic principle.[30]

Stanzas, the "larger units" to which Bermann refers, are periodic structures. The quatrain of the sonnet form, moreover, exactly mirrors in poetry the shape of the "quadratic phrase" in music. Both are divisible by units of two into eight small parts (as differentiated by the caesura in poetry and the bar line in music), into four parts (by the measured line in poetry), and into antecedent and consequent clauses.

Consider the opening quatrain of Baudelaire's famous poem "Correspondances," to which we will return again later for other reasons, with the last movement of Beethoven's Opus 13, (figures 1–7 and 1–8).

> La Nature est un temple où de vivants piliers
> Laissent parfois sortir de confuses paroles;
> L'homme y passe à travers des forêts de symboles
> Qui l'observent avec des regards familiers.

1-7. Beethoven, Piano Sonata in C Minor, *Pathétique*, Rondo, measures 1–8

The basic correspondence between the periodic form of these two excerpts may be represented as in figure 1-8. In the music, the antecedent clause is set apart by the harmonic movement from tonic chord to dominant chord. In the quatrain, "piliers," which arrives at the point where it is rhythmically expected (at the end of the alexandrine), is contrasted by "paroles," which arrives at the same point in the next line. Beethoven, a practitioner of classical form but never a pedant, pulls against the regulatory force of the bar line with continual upheavals that anticipate the first beat of the bar. Each bit of the phrase begins either on or after the third beat of the bar (the second main pulse if we observe the call for cut time strictly).

La Nature est un temple où de
vivants piliers

Laissent parfois sortir de confuses
paroles

L'homme y passe à travers des
forêts de symboles

Qui l'observent avec des regards
familiers

1-8. Periodic form in Baudelaire's "Correspondances," lines 1–4,
compared with Beethoven, Opus 13, measures 1–8

Baudelaire, on the other hand, is far more conservative. Aside
from the the subtle bonding of "piliers" and "paroles" with the repetition of the letter *p,* there is no flirtation with the dominating regularity of his periodic structure. The first thought of the poem—
"nature is a temple of living pillars allowing sometimes the
emission of confused words"—comes to a close politely marked by
a semicolon. The rhyming of "symboles" with "paroles" links the
antecedent and consequent clauses together and also signifies the
point of greatest distance from the first line by obscuring the memory of "piliers" as it reinforces our memory of the "oles" sound.
The thought of the consequent clause—"man passes there across
the forest of symbols that observe him with familiar glances"—is
closed with a sense of return. "Piliers," rhyming with "familiers,"
signifies the end of the thought by providing a unifying factor
achieved through sound. The reader is signaled that the thought is
over because the rhyme with the earlier word is completed. Rhyme
is thus an external factor forced on the syntagmatic chain of words.
As Jakobson has observed, "the poetic function projects the principle of equivalence from the axis of selection on the axis of combination."[31]

In the same way, external factors define the nature of the
eight-bar period, especially those of tonal harmony and tonality.
Tonality, in its broader sense, means organizing musical pitches by
observing a loyalty to a single dominating pitch. It is perhaps a phenomenon that is identifiable as a musical universal, since this kind
of tonality has appeared in so many mutually exclusive corners of
the world. Yet, tonality was not used to specify the notes of a key
until 1821, when Castil-Blaze employed the term *tonalité.*[32] Tonal-

ity, from the seventeenth century through most of the nineteenth century, referred to the major-minor system of keys worked out in a set of twenty-four possibilities and practically symbolized by the twelve pitches of the European keyboard. Each of the twenty-four possibilities could function as a *tonalité* for Castil-Blaze in 1821, or Fetis, in 1844, who called tonality the "necessary, successive or simultaneous" relationships between keys.

Beethoven's period is built in the context of the key of C minor. This external function of the axis of selection is as important for comprehending a Beethovenian period as it is for understanding the symmetrically organized, rhythmic division of parts within it. The period is constructed around the "tonic" pitch of C and the fifth above it—the pitch of G. The pitch of G, which convention labels as a "dominant" in relation to C, is richer in overtones (in relation to C) than any other except the octave above C itself. Around this relationship of "tonic" and "dominant," conventions generated the twin concepts of *harmonic tonality* and *tonal harmony*, both of which are fixed by the specific chordal interrelations of a specific tonality.[33]

Tonal harmony was built on the notion that the simultaneous grouping of notes spaced in thirds forms an entity. For example, the tonic chord of the period is C–E-flat–G. It is the primary chordal entity of the period. It appears in bar one, bar two, bar three, bar six, bar seven, and bar eight. Moreover, it begins and closes the period. The chords of bars four and five represent the remaining pitch possibilities in the key of C minor. These remaining pitches are organized in layers of thirds that rise from the dominant pitch of G: G, B, D, F, and A-flat. Together they form the dominant pole of C minor. The dominant pole of C minor makes up a dialectical opposite and complement to the pitches of the tonic chord. This other pole of the key of C minor is the dissonant pole, the unresolved pole. The conventions of periodization call for the swing away from the tonic to harmonic tension in the heart of the period. A resolution marks the close of the period. Thus, dissonance is conveniently housed within the embrace of consonance.

Beethoven's period firmly enclosed within a harmonic tonality, encased by conventions forced on its syntagmatic axis and contingent upon the frequent repetitions of C in the melody itself, is a hypotactic structure, that is to say, a structure made up of a hierarchy of dominant and subordinate parts. In the same way, Baudelaire's quatrain is built around a pair of subjects—one for each half of the complete thought: "la nature" and "l'homme." The poetry flows semantically and syntactically from these two subjects. "L'homme" is a reply to "la nature." It is a contrasting subject that emphasizes the poetic quality of the text because it is a noun occupying a position grammatically parallel to "la nature."

According to Levin, the coupling of linguistic phenomena in equivalent positions is the predominant unifying element of poetry, and in our study we shall borrow Levin's notion of "coupling" to denote any signifiers in poetry or music in structurally parallel and symmetrical positions.[34] Any grouping of signifiers, whether it is a surface feature such as alliteration, or a parallel pair of grammatical structures, or musical cadences arriving at corresponding moments in different phrases, is a kind of coupling. Coupling is the result of the inclination of the mind to make symmetries. In art, the desire to organize form by constructing couplings seems to be a dominant force. In fact, a stylistic propensity for asymmetry may be as much an urge to escape from regularity as anything else. Musical serialism, for example, was the result of a need to escape from the practice of grouping tones in organized couplings—the convention of systematized tonality. Yet even in the absence of couplings, one senses their implied presence. The rebellious search for freedom is haunted by the authoritarian call of order.

In the specific case of this Baudelaire excerpt, the parallel position of the subjects "l'homme" and "la nature" is more significant than, say, the alliterations on *p* between "piliers" and "paroles." "La nature" is the anchor of the antecedent part of the phrase. The other subject, "l'homme," is the anchor of the reply. On this coupling, the symmetry of the entire phrase depends. Baudelaire's period, too, is a hypotactic structure.

The quadratic period is the most common unit of differentiation of the traditional means of organizing poetry practiced by Baudelaire. To illustrate this further, let us consider another example from *Les Fleurs du mal*, one commonly attached to the various critical interpretations of Baudelaire's supposed *modernité*.

> Quand le ciel bas et lourd pèse comme un couvercle
> Sur l'esprit gémissant en proie aux longs ennuis,
> Et que de l'horizon embrassant tout le cercle
> Il nous verse un jour noir plus triste que les nuits . . .[35]

One clearly evolved, complete idea holds this quatrain together. As

E. Auerbach has observed, the imagery here is startling, even frightening.[36] The image of the sky, ordinarily befitting a pastoral setting, or a Romantic hymn of praise to nature, is connected with the notion of the lid, which evokes the sensations of death, captivity, finality, and closure. The sky weighs on the groaning spirit with the power of a giant lid. The horrible image is developed in the second half of the quatrain: "And when the horizon embraces the whole circle (of the lid of the sky) it pours out on us a black day sadder than nights." This is an extraordinary personal vision of deep human agony, yet it is set forth with pristine clarity. The alexandrines, once again, are politely divided into eight even parts by the caesuras. As in the quatrain from "Correspondances," this is parallel to the usual eight-bar length of the musical period. The equivalents of the antecedent and consequent halves in the music are clearly marked off by the clauses beginning "when the sky" and "and when the sky embracing" as well as by the rhymes. The whole is conveniently housed within the lowest common denominator of two. This quatrain is also a natural counterpart in poetry of the periodic phrase in music, and the flow of the disturbing message within the poem is neatly housed within it. Moreover, we are able to follow the development of the image of the lid-sky as it develops through each of four lines into a clear depiction of a distraught emotional state.

For both poetry and music of the early nineteenth century, then, the period is a norm, and we may use the term *norm* here in the sense called for by René Wellek in his *Theory of Literature*, which is as much a work of aesthetics as a work of literary criticism.[37] To understand the interpenetration of the periodic form in early nineteenth-century music and poetry, one has only to turn to the myriad songs set by composers like Beethoven and Schubert. In almost any song by either composer, the music and the poem are organized together by the principle of periodicity. Consider the way in which the symmetrical form of the poetry generates the symmetrical period in the following excerpts (see figures 1-9 and 1-10). According to Bermann, hypotactic structures can "undermine" the "repetitive form" of a sonnet. This is not at all the case in our examples. Here, hypotactic sentences emphasize and complement the surface conventions of periodization with deeper sources of unity.

Parataxis (placing side by side) is a far different means of organization from hypotaxis (arranging under). Hypotaxis requires a clear hierarchy of events in either poetry or music. Parataxis is

1-9. Beethoven, *Ich liebe dich*, measures 1–8. From Beethoven, *Sämtliche Lieder*, Breitkopf and Härtel, Wiesbaden.

1-10. Schubert, *Schäfer's Klagelied*, measures 1–8

characterized by a lack of expected coordinating elements. Mallarmé's "Salut," his toast of elusive elegance, is built from a poetics of parataxis. "Salut," unlike the sonnets of Baudelaire, truly does pull against the externally imposed form of the sonnet's conventionalized fourteen-line structure.

> Rien, cette écume, vierge vers
> A ne désigner que la coupe;
> Telle loin se noie une troupe
> De sirènes mainte à l'envers.
>
> Nous naviguons, ô mes divers
> Amis, moi déjà sur la poupe
> Vous l'avant fastueux qui coupe
> Le flot de foudres et d'hivers;
>
> Une ivresse belle m'engage
> Sans craindre même son tangage
> De porter debout ce salut
>
> Solitude, récif, étoile
> A n'importe ce qui valut
> Le blanc souci de notre toile.[38]

The startling enjambments in the two quatrains play against the expected flow of verse. The poem, in fact, begins with what feels aurally like an enjambment—the displaced "rien." Which is the subject in the first sentence: "rien," "cette écume," or "vierge vers"? Actually, all three are the subject. The nominative function here is a highly complex, tripartite metaphorical construct. All three are key concepts that are intermingled thematically throughout the poem. Mallarmé, accordingly, strikes the eye and the ear with the three of them in the first line. How different from the clear syntactic and semantic hierarchy of Baudelaire!

The real difficulties, though, begin in the sestet. After "ce salut," the words "solitude," "récif," and "étoile" are placed side by side without explanatory connectives that might lead us to construct a facile hierarchy of meaning. Mallarmé's syntactic innovations create considerable semantic ambiguity. First of all, "ce salut" arouses our expectations as we wish to discover what kind of "salut" is called for. As readers, we expect adjectives after "salut." Instead, Mallarmé provides a chain of nouns, each of which is an image from a different sphere of experience. "Solitude," "reef," and "star" are juxtaposed without explanation or preparation. Of course, there is a semantic link between the nouns, but the reader must intuit it for himself. "Solitude" is an abstract noun; it is a condition which evokes a psychological context. "Reef" is a lonely bit of land jutting out of the sea. "Star" is a solitary glimmer of light in the blackness of the night sky. Meaning can be unraveled here, but the syntax, the structure, does little to guide us along the path leading towards meaning.

The sestet of a sonnet, when formed in the Petrarchan fashion, is made up of two tercets. If quatrains are quadratic periods, tercets are tripartite periods. In the poetry of Baudelaire, conventions of rhyme and meter wed with syntax to form hypotactic, periodic phrases. In the Mallarmé sestet quoted above, the paratactic structure actually does pull against the conventions of sonnet writing. The difference will be clarified if we compare the sestet of the Mallarmé poem with the sestet of Baudelaire's "Correspondances."

> Il est des parfums frais comme des chairs d'enfants,
> Doux comme les hautbois, verts comme les prairies,
> —Et d'autres, corrompus, riches et triomphants,
> Ayant l'expansion des choses infinies,
> Comme l'ambre, le musc, le benjoin et l'encens,
> Qui chantent les transports de l'esprit et des sens.[39]

Here, "Il est des parfums frais" and "Et d'autres . . . / Ayant l'expansion des choses infinies" subordinate the imagery in the single sentence that makes up the sestet. Baudelaire, who introduced an entire vocabulary into literature, did little to rebel against the usual practice of structuring poetry. Over half the poems in the first edition of *Les Fleurs du mal* are sonnets. In the sonnets, moreover, hypotactic syntax does not undermine the periodic organization of the poetry; rather, it underscores and enhances it. For Baudelaire, as well as for Beethoven, conventional hypotactic phrase structures provided the linguistic anchors upon which the line of syntactic tensions secured the dramatic sense of the work of art. Mallarmé, drawing upon his uniquely personal ideas of music, created a far more complex kind of poetry, a poetry that loosens the conventional line of connection between syntax and sense.

Mallarmé's obfuscation of the syntactic hierarchy of a poetic line rivals the revolutionary fracturing of the musical period in Wagner. The opening of Wagner's *Tristan* prelude (see figure 1-11) is also a paratactic structure. No clear tonality houses the three-bar motif. Instead of a complete periodic idea, Wagner begins the prelude with a chain of fragments, each one freely bonded to the next.

1-11. Wagner, *Tristan und Isolde,* Prelude, measures 1–20.
Used by special arrangement with G. Schirmer, Inc.

Here Wagner abandons the symmetrical unit of the period with its traditional coupling of antecedent and consequent clauses housed within the limits of a clear tonality. Beethoven, on the contrary, rarely abandons the period. From Opus 1 through the late quartets, the period gives Beethoven's musical language coherence and clarity. But Wagner begins *Tristan* with a process that was carried out, in Beethoven's music, at a much later point in musical composition. Wagner takes a small motive, a mere fraction of a normal musical period, and begins to develop it sequentially. Instead of a period, one finds a series of small ideas that are linked together until they have huge repercussions. Here harmonic movement obfuscates the establishment of a tonality. The dominant seventh chords in measures three, seven, and eleven are thwarted by another sonority, a half-diminished seventh in measures two, six, and ten. How we are to interpret these half-diminished seventh chords, known as "Tristan" chords because of their famous usage in this passage, is a musicological issue as old as the opera itself. Whether the "Tristan" chord of measure two is a misplaced supertonic seventh chord in D-sharp minor or an inverted dominant of a dominant (the dominant on E in measure three) is less important than its new context. Wagner slips from the "Tristan" chord to a seventh chord three times. A periodic resolution of the chord and the phrase in which it is housed would look very different (see figure 1-12). Such a working out of the phrase would place the "Tristan" chord in a clear hierarchy of tones relating to A minor.

1-12. A periodic resolution of the "Tristan" chord

Since the small phrase of measures one through three is not closed but open-ended, Wagner is able to attach as many repetitions of it as he needs to fit his dramatic requirements. A full period is signified by a clear closure. Wagner dispenses with closure and thus rids himself of the need either to repeat the old period or to begin a new idea expressed in the form of another periodic structure. Even in measures sixteen to seventeen, where cadential tension rises toward a cadence on an A-minor chord, Wagner writes a deceptive cadence on an F-major chord. The deceptive cadence, a pattern of incomplete closure that thwarts all expectations, is a Wagnerian norm from *Lohengrin* through *Parsifal*. Thus, it loses its value as a moment of great significance and tension, which it always possessed in earlier periodic music. Here, Wagner sews a new motif into the heart of the cadence, thus overlapping the ideas and creating a seamlessness in the music. Musical punctuation is defunct at the expense of organic continuity.

Mallarmé and Wagner achieve an antiperiodic sensibility that is valid for their art forms. Wagner extended and stretched European harmonic tonality by relying more on the few sonorities with more mobility and less on the greater number of chords with less mobility. Schoenberg acknowledges this distinction in *Structural Functions of Harmony*: "There exist only three diminished chords and four augmented triads. Accordingly every diminished seventh chord belongs to at least eight tonalities or regions, and every augmented triad belongs, in the same manner, to six tonalities or regions."[40] Diminished seventh chords and augmented triads are fewer in number but they can lead anywhere, to almost any tonality, and they contributed to the demise of the old tonal conventions precisely because of their mobility. Wagner extended the possibilities of signification of the tonal system, then, in his use of the diminished seventh chords in *Tristan,* for example. These sonorities are available to more tonalities than, say, an ordinary major triad.

This technique is also employed by Liszt, who weaves a small and dissonant motif into a huge structure in the B-minor Sonata. The motive of the B-minor Sonata outlines diminished seventh chords and is free of the usual tonic-dominant sensibility of a periodic theme (see figure 1-13). Liszt's theme consequently fits into a strikingly varied number of tonal contexts.

1-13. Liszt, *Sonata* in B Minor, measures 8–13

The first kind of ambiguity infused into both poetry and music in the nineteenth century is syntactic in nature and involves the replacement of the old periodic manner of building forms with a new parataxis. The older style required a clear differentiation of ideas housed in tabular blocks. Externally imposed conventions helped to clarify the distinctions between the blocks. In music, a strong tonic-dominant sensibility was imposed on the formation of themes. In poetry, rhyme and meter combined to organize poetic utterances in stanzas and thereby reinforce the hypotaxis and couplings inherent in the language itself.

When the strong tendency toward periodicity and closure was removed from both poetry and music, syntactic structures tended to allow for a high degree of metonymy. The free bonding of parts generated a new organism, for in the structure of the syntax itself, ideas were free to combine and separate in novel ways. This is largely because phrase structures in music and poetry after Wagner became open-ended, paratactic, and elliptical and were self-consciously set apart from older structures that reeked of artificial symmetry.

The second major expression of a fresh sense of freedom in music and literature was semantic in both origin and nature, although it was facilitated by the stylistic changes in syntax that we have been considering. For influential nineteenth-century writers, music came to stand for an art that was free of the requirements of logic and explanation, art unfettered by ratiocinative development. Important nineteenth-century poets admired, above all, the evocative power of music. Music apparently was able to suggest seemingly unconnected progressions of percepts to the mind of a listener. These percepts could not be explained logically. Furthermore, they did not need to be explained logically. They were valid in themselves.

Music obviously had tremendous ability to generate intense involuntary mental activity. For this reason, too, music fascinated the writers. Undoubtedly, the most significant literary figure to single out the unique nature of music was Charles Baudelaire. Baudelaire's ideas on music were ubiquitous in France in the late nineteenth century. They were reprinted numerous times in important literary journals, and they had seminal influence on an entire generation of poets, both in France and beyond its borders. Although Baudelaire was not a specialist in music, his conceptions cannot be dismissed as the notions of an uninformed amateur. His views were shared by the best musical minds of his time.

Baudelaire's idea of music was rooted in his awareness that the human mind tends to experience synesthesia. Baudelaire believed that the senses intermingle as the mind encounters phenomena. In "Correspondances," Baudelaire observed that man is prone to acts of symbol making as he wanders in the "temple of nature":

> Comme de longs échos qui de loin se confondent
> Dans une ténébreuse et profonde unité,
> Vaste comme la nuit et comme la clarté,
> Les parfums, les couleurs et les sons se répondent.[41]

This symbol making, though, is only possible because of the ability of the mind to experience sensations synesthetically. Baudelaire's simile here is based on an aural orientation. "As far-off echoes dissolve together in a shadowy and profound unity," so do "perfumes, colors and sounds correspond." Correspondences intermingle as sounds combine. Baudelaire was not so naive as to think that sound had to indicate specific literary programs, but he knew that the sounds of music have tremendous power to suggest and evoke acts of mind beyond the notes themselves. He knew that music has a great ability to induce the human mind to make psychological substitutions.[42]

As E. H. Gombrich has shown, the mind has a boundless capacity to make substitutions:

> The possibility of metaphor springs from the infinite elasticity of the human mind; it testifies to its capacity to perceive and assimilate new experiences as modifications of earlier ones, of finding equivalences in the most disparate phenomena and of substituting one for another. Without this constant process of substitution neither language nor art, nor indeed civilized life would be possible.[43]

Gombrich argues that synesthesia, which was so vital to the theories of the great mid-nineteenth-century Romantics such as Wagner and Baudelaire, has deep-seated roots in the ordinary functioning of the brain.

> The metaphors of daily speech may provide a convenient starting point for the study of these equivalences, particularly those which "transfer" qualities from one sensory experience to another. These so-called synesthetic metaphors which make us speak of a "velvet tone," and "black bass," a "loud colour," etc., are specially interesting for us, because here no conscious transfer takes place. . . . Somehow in the centre of our minds the qualities of blackness and of a bass voice converge and meet.[44]

Synesthesia must be cultivated beyond the level of ordinary experience to be an act of poetry. Nevertheless, in that "place" in the "center of the mind" described by Gombrich, a place common to us all, Baudelaire's poetics begins. Baudelaire's poetics, and, indirectly, his notion of music, rest on the assumption that the mind can mesh diverse impressions taken in by the senses.

The new interest in music developed in conjunction with a suspicion of the logical and didactic aspects of literary expression. Roland Barthes, who unravels *Sarrasine* in *S/Z*, has touched upon a distinction between the "texte classique" and the "texte moderne" that helps to clarify the novel musical attitude of the literary Symbolists, an attitude vitally important in the formation of their writings.[45] In classical prose, Barthes argues, the twin codes of actions and questions coordinate and orient the reader. According to Barthes, just as melody and harmony orient the ear, the working out of actions and the resolution of questions provide firm semantic limitations in a traditional literary text. A traditional literary text, because it is easy to understand, might be referred to as a "readerly text" or a "tonal text." Unity in this kind of traditional writing is preserved by the careful ordering of hermeneutic problems and presented events. We learn to hear music in a tonal way. In the same fashion, we learn to read in a tonal way—through the systematized ordering of questions and actions. These organizing elements have a limiting or constraining influence. They reduce the potential meanings of a work of literature. Barthes argues that "it is precisely this constraint which limits the plural of the classical text." The modern text, for Barthes, has a greater "plural"; the symbolic components of its texture are less limited by the logical progression of actions and questions. Barthes proposes that the origins of modern writing lie in the cracks between the orderly progression of the classical text, in the exploitation of ambiguity in the act of signification.

In general, ordering in art limits possibilities. Ordering reduces the symbolic potential of signifiers. Although Barthes is not writing about traditional poetry, it is clear that poetry in the conventional sense has more extensive stylized limitations, which in turn place even greater constraints on a literary pattern. In traditional poetry, the classical constraints of actions and questions are also present, but they are augmented by the confining norms of periodic and hypotactic patterns. The Symbolists, who valued music as an emblem of freedom, systematically challenged these ordering constraints. For Baudelaire, music did not need to tell a specific story or revolve around specific problems. It merely suggested changing emotional states in the realm of sound. His attempts to describe the experiencing of music in language are inextricably bound up with the eventual development of a new school of poetry.

In Mallarmé's poetry, which evolved from Baudelaire's theories, polyvalent signifiers are formed from recurrent symbols that are freed from the dominance of hypotactic structures. "Rien," "écume," "musique," "rêve," "éventail," "dentelle" are some of the isolated images wrenched from banal contexts and juxtaposed against other images in order to create an open-ended pattern of meaning. But the words that recur are few in number and carefully controlled and regulated. Thus, when we see them, they touch off the vibration of recognition. Metaphors in Mallarmé are no longer held strictly within the limits of the orderly ratiocinative process of the tonal text—the answering of questions and the relating of actions outlined by Barthes. Once the old regulating structures of poetry are cracked open, imagery is freed from constraint and opened up to greater possibilities of meaning. But it was Baudelaire who found a new freedom of expression in the art of music and who paved the way for Mallarmé's aesthetic ambiguities.

Baudelaire works out his ideas systematically in the influential essay "Richard Wagner et Tannhäuser à Paris" (1861). Baudelaire writes that in music, just as in the arts of painting and poetry, "il y a toujours une lacune complétée par l'imagination de l'auditeur."[46] In music, the "lacune" is far greater than in the other arts. To illustrate the way the imagination fills in the lacuna, Baudelaire compares three responses to Richard Wagner's *Lohengrin* overture. Listening to music in the nineteenth century amounted to creating a subsidiary work of art—a prose poem of suggestions, percepts, symbols, and concepts arising out of the auditory experience of musical performance. Such prose poems are nothing more than glorified versions of those synesthetic transferences identified by Gombrich as intrinsic to even the simplest linguistic acts.

Baudelaire first considers Wagner's own response, which was originally printed to accompany the concert as a typical Romantic *programme.*

Dès les premières mesures, l'âme du pieux solitaire qui attend le vase sacré *plonge dans les espaces infinis.* Il voit se former peu à peu une apparition étrange qui prend un corps, une figure. Cette apparition se précise davantage, et *la troupe miraculeuse des anges,* portant au milieu d'eux la coupe sacrée, passe devant lui. Le saint cortège approche; le coeur de l'élu de Dieu s'exalte peu à peu; il s'élargit, il se dilate; . . . *il cède à une béatitude croissante,* en se trouvant toujours rapproché de *la lumineuse apparition,* et quand enfin le Saint-Graal lui-même apparaît au milieu du cortège sacré, *il s'abîme dans une adoration extatique, comme si le monde entier eût soudainement disparu.* Cependant le Saint-Graal répand ses bénédictions sur le saint en prière et le consacre son chevalier. Puis *les flammes brûlantes adoucissent progressivement leur éclat;* dans sa sainte allégresse, la troupe des anges, souriant à la terre qu'elle abandonne, regagne les célestes hauteurs. Elle a laissé le Saint-Graal à la garde des hommes purs, *dans le coeur desquels la divine liqueur s'est répandue,* et l'auguste troupe s'évanouit *dans les profondeurs de l'espace,* de la même manière qu'elle en était sortie.[47]

Wagner provides an abstraction of the content of the opera. (The italics are Baudelaire's, and they are intrinsic to his argument.) It is as if the dramatic movement of the plot had been sifted out by a centrifuge and all that is left is a series of interacting images. No specific mention is made of the hero, Lohengrin, and heroine, Elsa, the villains, Frederick and Ortrud, other major characters, or other definite features of dramatic importance in the opera that is to follow (for example, the overwhelming symbol of the swan). We have something far more abstract.

A wanderer "plunges into infinite space." "Little by little" an apparition that takes the form of a body and a face appears in the void. The vision becomes "the miraculous troop of angels," which floats by in the midst of infinite space. Wagner tends to link his exotic images with words that describe the ebb and flow of the music (for example verbs, adverbs). The vision takes form "peu à peu," just as the "heart of God's elect" stirs "peu à peu." It "swells." It "dilates." It "gives way to a new impulse" of blissful peace. The Holy Grail is "swallowed up." The burning flames "progressively" lose their brilliance after the Holy Grail "blesses" the knight. The angels leave the grail with "pure men" and vanish in the same way they came. The music, for Wagner, renders in motion the abstract symbolic content of the opera.

Liszt, who conducted the premiere of the opera, provides a description of the overture that tends to concern itself less with the flow of the musical events as they fade into each other and more with the individual symbols suggested by the music. He also tells us more about what really goes on in the actual overture—the divided desks of violins that provide the harmonic richness, the brilliant eruptions of the brass, the pianissimos, the horns, and so on.

Cette introduction renferme et révèle *l'élément mystique*, toujours présent et toujours caché dans la pièce. . . . Pour nous apprendre l'inénarrable puissance de ce secret, Wagner nous montre d'abord *la beauté ineffable du sanctuaire*, habité par un Dieu qui venge les opprimés et ne demande qu'*amour et foi* à ses fidèles. Il nous initie au Saint-Graal; il fait miroiter à nos yeux le temple de bois incorruptible, aux murs odorants, aux portes d'*or*, aux solives d'*asbeste*, aux colonnes *d'opale*, aux parois de *cymophane*, dont les splendides portiques ne sont approchés que de ceux qui ont le coeur élevé. . . . Il ne nous le fait point apercevoir dans son imposante et réelle structure, mais, comme ménageant nos faibles sens, il nous le montre d'abord reflété dans *quelque onde azurée* ou reproduit par *quelque nuage irisé*.

C'est au commencement *une large nappe dormante* de mélodie, un *éther vaporeux qui s'étend*, pour que le tableau sacré s'y dessine à nos yeux profanes; effet exclusivement confié aux violons, divisés en huit pupitres différents, qui, après plusieurs mesures de sons harmoniques, continuent dans les plus hautes notes de leurs registres. Le motif est ensuite repris par les instruments à vent les plus doux; les cors et les bassons, en s'y joignant, préparent l'entrée des trompettes et des trombones, qui ré pètent la mélodie pour la quatrième fois, avec un *éclat éblouissant de coloris*, comme si dans cet instant unique l'édifice saint *avait brillé* devant nos *regards aveuglés, dans toute sa magnificence lumineuse et radiante*. Mais *le vif étincellement*, amené par degrés à *cette intensité de rayonnement solaire*, s'éteint avec rapidité, comme une lueur céleste. La *transparente vapeur* des nuées se referme, la vision disparaît peu à peu dans le même encens *diapré* au milieu duquel elle est apparue, et le morceau se termine par les premières six mesures, devenues *plus éthérées encore*. Son caractère d'*idéale mysticité* est surtout rendu sensible par le *pianissimo* toujours conservé dans l'orchestre. . . . Telle est l'image qui, à l'audition de ce sublime *adagio*, se présente d'abord à nos sens émus.[48]

Wagner, Liszt says, protects us from the overwhelming beauty of the grail. Wagner veils it. He disguises it by showing it as reflected in an "azure wave" or a "rainbowed cloud." The grail transforms as the music transforms. It becomes a vast "lake of melody," a "vaporous ether." As the motif is taken up by different instruments, the grail continues its transformations, eventually bursting into full view with the trumpets and trombones. The mystical elusiveness of the grail is preserved, however, as the tumult of the orchestra quickly ebbs. Vaporous clouds and iridescent incense stimulate Liszt's senses as the vision fades away. Liszt's prose poem has less action and concentrates on the shifting visions of the central symbol—the grail. There is no host of angels, no pious knight, but a phantasmagoria of views of that single *élément mystique* supposedly presented by Wagner's music. What ties Liszt's phantasmagoria together? The flow of the music.

As Baudelaire notes, the music suggests the free evocation of symbols in different listeners. Sounds suggest colors, images, odors. Both sound and color can function as media for the transmission of ideas. The lacuna that is filled in by different minds as they enter the world of sound can be measured and compared. "The reader knows what goal we pursue," Baudelaire writes. He is illustrating how true music "suggests analogous ideas in different minds."[49] Baudelaire, the practitioner of the old Swedenborgian theory of correspondence, argues that this should not be surprising.

> D'ailleurs, il ne serait pas ridicule ici de raisonner a priori, sans analyse et sans comparaisons; car ce qui serait vraiment surprenant, c'est que le son *ne pût pas* suggérer la couleur, que les couleurs *ne pussent pas* donner l'idée d'une mélodie, et que le son et la couleur fussent impropres à traduire des idées; les choses s'étant toujours exprimées par une analogie réciproque, depuis le jour où Dieu a proféré le monde comme une complexe et indivisible totalité.[50]

Once Baudelaire has established this point with great care, he is ready to present his own "reading" of Wagner's overture.

> Dès les premières mesures, je subis une de ces impressions heureuses que presque tous les hommes imaginatifs ont connues, par le rêve, dans le sommeil. Je me sentis délivré *des liens de la pesanteur*, et je retrouvai par le souvenir l'extraordinaire volupté qui circule dans les *lieux hauts* (notons en passant que je ne connaissais pas le programme cité tout à l'heure). Ensuite je me peignis involontairement l'état délicieux d'un homme en proie à une grande rêverie dans une solitude absolue, mais une solitude avec *un immense horizon* et une large *lumière diffuse*; *l'immensité* sans autre décor qu'elle-même. Bientôt j'éprouvai la sensation d'une clarté plus vive, *d'une intensité de lumière* croissant avec une telle rapidité, que les nuances fournies par le dictionnaire ne suffiraient pas à exprimer *ce surcroît toujours renaissant d'ardeur et de blancheur*. Alors je conçus pleinement l'idée d'une âme se mouvant dans un milieu lumineux, d'une extase *faite de volupté et de connaissance*, et planant au-dessus et bien loin du monde naturel.[51]

These are the three specimens—all literary descriptions of the *Lohengrin* overture—that Baudelaire presents for careful scrutiny.

Baudelaire's rendering, as he himself tells us, is simpler, more abstract, and we can now clearly see his purpose. Where Wagner sees a "host of angels," Liszt sees a "monument." Baudelaire himself does not see, he *feels* sensations—the pleasure of the dream, release from all bonds of weight and gravity, limitless height, absolute solitude, pure immensity (as a pure, unadorned sensation, as an absolute essence), brightness that goes beyond the limits of the descriptive powers of the dictionary (Baudelaire is probably indebted to Delacroix for this idea), wisdom (*connaissance*), and joy (*volupté*).

Is this merely a triple dose of shoddy Romantic emotionalism? What have we learned about the ability of words to tell us about the overture from these seemingly vague reveries? How do we know what all three listeners actually heard? (Baudelaire claims that he had not read either description before he wrote his own.) As Baudelaire informs us, the important issue here is not the individuation of each version of the music, but the similarities between them: "Mais l'important est ici de s'attacher aux ressemblances." Baudelaire is awed by the penetrating power of music to suggest the essence of ideas. The preconstructed nature of the music has caused a kind of overlap in the various lacunae filled in by the auditors. Music, Baudelaire realized, is at once open-ended and structured, bounded and boundless. Each "traduction" from music to words has its uniqueness, but they are all connected by the singular generating power of the overture.

Dans les trois traductions nous trouvons la sensation de *la béatitude spirituelle et physique*; de *l'isolement*; de la contemplation de *quelque chose infiniment grand et . . . beau; d'une lumière intense* qui réjouit *les yeux et l'âme jusqu'à la pâmoison*; et enfin la sensation de *l'espace étendu jusqu'aux dernières limites concevables.*[52]

Baudelaire has clearly demonstrated how music communicates without a narrative and without the mere imitation of an action. Wagner, Liszt, and Baudelaire have all understood, as the poet articulately shows us, some essential aspect of the music and each is able to express it in his own way. Baudelaire has identified six abstract states of mind that have to one degree or another been substituted as equivalents for the music in the minds of the listeners: (1) physical and spiritual beauty; (2) isolation; (3) something infinitely grand and handsome; (4) intense light; (5) sensation of the swoon; and (6) infinite space. Schopenhauer would argue that these sensations are the result of the direct communications of the will. They are the result of an expressive act unadulterated by reason (*Vernunft*), or ideas, or the practices of imitation (*Nachahmung*).

As Gombrich observes, to say that "upright poles are phallic symbols" is not as accurate a statement as "upright poles lend themselves so well to use as phallic symbols that their use for this (conscious or unconscious) purpose is exceedingly widespread."[53] The availability of a signifier for the act of *metapherein* determines its most likely use. A sign is not an absolute but depends on a context.

> In an erotically charged atmosphere the merest hint of formal similarity with sexual functions creates the desired response and the same is true of the dream symbols investigated by Freud. The hungry man will be similarly attuned to the discovery of food—he will scan the world for the slightest promise of nourishment. The starving may even project food into all sorts of dissimilar objects—as Chaplin does in *Gold Rush* when his huge companion suddenly appears to him as a chicken.[54]

The kinds of correspondences constructed between the music and the minds of Wagner, Liszt, and Baudelaire involves the most primitive, direct acts of substitution. The three men are giving free reign to their imaginations, feasting on the sensation of the music as though they were starving for musical sound.

Wagner and Liszt form a perception housed in the context of watered-down Christianity and medieval myth ("des anges," "le saint cortège," "l'élu de Dieu," "le Saint Graal"). Baudelaire, in his own perpetual state of self-conscious self-examination, bases his entire discussion of the overture in terms of the *je*: "je subis," "je me sentis," "je me peignis." The Symbolists will not forget the importance of music as outlined by Baudelaire, but they will turn against this kind of obviously emotive, personal response to it as they search for a more refined, concrete, and reserved poetry.

Baudelaire's poetic vision at large was rooted in Swedenborgian doctrine, a particularly superstitious brand of Catholicism, tremendous personal agony, and an overwhelming sense of guilt. His was a poetry of direct, immediate responses to sensation. Walter Benjamin has argued that Baudelaire had "placed the shock experience at the very center of his artistic work."[55] Like all powerful sensations, the experiencing of music seizes Baudelaire's *je* with the assurance and seductiveness of a powerful lover. Consider his de-

scription of this process in the poem "La Musique," which originally bore the title "Beethoven":

> La musique souvent me prend comme une mer!
> Vers ma pâle étoile,
> Sous un plafond de brume ou dans un vaste éther.
> Je mets à la voile;
> La poitrine en avant et les poumons gonflés
> Comme de la toile,
> J'escalade le dos des flots amoncelés
> Que la nuit me voile;
> Je sens vibrer en moi toutes les passions
> D'un vaisseau qui souffre;
> Le bon vent, la tempête et ses convulsions
> Sur l'immense gouffre
> Me bercent.—D'autres fois, calme plat, grand miroir
> De mon désespoir![56]

Music instigates a series of shocks, a series of powerful sensations in Baudelaire's mind, and that immediate encounter with
music is the subject of the poem. He renders a personal reaction to
music, a description of the experience of music. This is more important than a specific meaning of music for Baudelaire. First music takes him and sweeps him up like a great sea. He is "under a fog"
or in "a vast ether." His stimulated chest heaves forward as his
lungs swell (with the ether or fog?). He shudders as his being vi-
brates with great passions (like a groaning ship). The wind and the
convulsions of a tempest rock the *je* along in the "immense gouf-
fre." At other times, the poet feels the overwhelming calm of the
sea of sound that reflects his great despair.

Baudelaire's theory of synesthetic correspondences gave his
verse startling originality. Nevertheless, he uses synesthesia to give
his poetry descriptive power. Whether he is telling us about his own
emotional tumult, his sensations as he listens to music, or the wind-
ing streets of Paris, he uses language to make us experience as intensely as possible what he is experiencing. Baudelaire's is a poetry
in which signifiers, safe in their contexts, are laden with new meanings; but as we have seen, his signifiers are embedded in verse of
syntactic clarity. Imagery in Baudelaire is gripping because of its
powerful immediacy, because of its assault on our sensibilities as
readers. Language is used to create startling, arresting effects.

Synesthetic correspondence in Baudelaire meant new expressive freedom, but Baudelaire's liberties were taken in the semantic field, not in the syntactic field. Wagner and Liszt, though, changed the patterns of both syntax and semantics in music as they exploited dissonance to gain new expressivity. For all three artists, each an archetypal Romantic in his own way, music could freely suggest colors, ideas, images, touches, even smells. Wagner, Liszt, and Baudelaire expanded the vocabulary of art. They paved the way for an uninhibited exploration of the senses. Total indulgence, however, leads to surfeit, and the enthusiastic abandon of the Romantics eventually gave way to an attitude of greater restraint, even in the way in which music, the Romantic art par excellence, was understood.

Baudelaire's reading of Wagner's overture to *Lohengrin* is not as far from Hanslick's view of absolute music as one might think. True, one must admit that we are never given precise details about the music. Baudelaire never tells us that the piece is in A major, that the lugubrious tempo contributes to the sensation of limitless space and time, that the incessant deceptive cadences create the very concrete aural experience of denial and expectation, that the overture is little more than the ceaseless unfolding of an A-major chord, that the small amount of periodic differentiation in the piece creates the ethereal floating quality noted by the three commentators. But Baudelaire has shown that music is a kind of disinterested language that merely suggests certain concepts and percepts and does not necessarily describe anything specifically.

The poet recognized the power of the pattern in Wagner's music. He realized that the overture is not telling a story; it is not prefiguring the action of the opera. He sees his efforts, along with the program of Wagner and the description of Liszt, as translations of the centripetal pattern of music. There is no pictorial pattern developed by Baudelaire, although there is far more of one in Wagner's program. The images are suggested independently and do not refer to one static picture. Baudelaire recognized that music is essentially ambiguous and mysterious in its inherent nature, that its power to communicate is great but that it is difficult to identify just what kind of information is communicated by music. French poets, following the thought of Baudelaire, continued to view music in this way throughout the reign of Symbolism as a dominating literary movement.

2. Wagner and the French

In *Lohengrin,* an opera of transition for Wagner, the periodic unit is still a structural norm. This is not true in the later music dramas, where the period becomes the mere residue of the older style and serves little structural purpose. Here, however, the motive ♩♩.. ♪ | (♩) is expanded into the proper length of a period when Elsa finally shares her vision of the knight with the entire company:

> Mit züchtigem Gebaren,
> gab Tröstung er mir ein;
> des Ritters will ich wahren,
> er soll mein Streiter sein![1]

These lines of Wagner conform exactly with the periodic structure of the verse forms used by the great lyric poets (Goethe, Eichendorff, and Heine, for example) who furnished the ideal texts for *Lieder* composers such as Schubert and Schumann. Moreover, they are equivalent to the standard quadratic period form used in Baudelaire's sonnets, although the unit of verse is not the French alexandrine, but a rather ordinary, *völkisch,* German iambic trimeter. Elsa has changed in mood from her dreamlike, clairvoyant state to "excited ecstasy," as Wagner indicates in the score: "Elsa's Mienen gehen von dem Ausdruck träumerischen Entrücktseins zu dem schwärmerischer Verklärung über."[2] She responds to the questioning of the king by recounting, in Wagner's own words, nothing but "ein mit süssem Vertrauen erfüllendes Traumgebild."[3]

Now, Wagner says that she moves from her dream to the expectation of "fulfillment in reality" ("der Erfüllung in der Wirklichkeit").[4] To show this passage from "Traumgebild" to "Wirklichkeit," Wagner chooses to house his musical information in the length of a standard eight-bar period, the length of Riemann's musical norm (figure 2-1). Is it an ordinary period, though? Absolutely not. By the time Elsa sings the word "Tröstung," Wagner has already slipped into the key of D major. D major bears a precarious relationship to A-flat major. A-flat and D are separated by a tritone. The tritone, within the old system of musical conventions, was a tonally unstable interval. It most often occurred *within* the context of a dominant or secondary dominant chord. In the Wagner excerpt, the tritone is *outside* the context of the interlocking pattern of dominant/tonic harmonies. The tritone, in fact, establishes a new harmonic context itself, for the harmonies are now generated by the tonally unstable outline of the A-flat/D tritone. Debussy worked the harmonic and tonal ambiguity of the tritone into a fresh musical pattern—the whole-tone scale (see figure 2-2)—just a few decades later. Although Wagner would probably have detested Debussy's innovations, the creator of the *Gesamtkunstwerk* provided an important precedent for the French composer by stretching the old musical language with freer usages of dissonant intervals such as the tritone.

2-1. Wagner, *Lohengrin*, act 1, scene 2, measures 108–15

tritone   whole-tone scale

2-2. Tritone and whole tone scale in figure 2–1

The first segment of Wagner's antecedent clause (*Aufstellung*) is in A-flat major. The second segment, on the words "gab Tröstung er mir ein," is in the foreign key of D major. The consequent clause (*Beantwortung*), which sets the words "des Ritters will ich wahren," is marked by yet another modulation—to F major. F major happens to be a key that is built on a chord which does not exist at all in A-flat major. Finally, with the words "er soll mein Streiter sein," the return to A-flat major is effected, and we should say *affected* as well, for the bewildering phantasmagoria of different tonal orientations has obscured the original key. The return to A-flat is not inevitable and expected. It is a miraculous surprise that Wagner can pull it off at all! The modulations, which sounded far more eerie to the nineteenth-century ear than to our twentieth-century ears, signify the passage from "Traumgebild" to "Wirklichkeit." It is the establishment of the cadence and the rounding out of the full musical thought with the sound of the old norm that shows that Elsa has returned to reality. Wagner admits, as we have already noted, that the context of the poetry, the literary material, enables the passage to function effectively.

Arnold Schoenberg, who also happens to analyze this excerpt from *Lohengrin* in *Structural Functions of Harmony,* was the composer who finally divorced musical signs from the confines of conventional European tonal orientation. Schoenberg was aware that Wagner's innovations stemmed from the need to render dramatic concepts in musical terms:

> Drama and poetry are greatly inspiring to a composer. But much of what they evoke on the one hand, they revoke on the other. A melody, if it followed the dictates of its musical structure alone, might develop in a direction different from that in which a text forces it. It might become shorter or longer, produce its climax earlier or later—or dispense with it entirely—requires less striking contrasts, much less emphasis, or much less accentuation. Besides the text is frequently so overwhelming in itself as to conceal the absence of value in a melody.[5]

However, Wagner himself realized that his individualistic modulations were dependent on extramusical influences and did not belong in conventional music. The old couplings of the Beethoven period no longer apply to Wagner. Wagner insisted that his music, together with his streamlined texts, portrayed "pure soul events" and "the inner springs of action."[6] They also gave him tremendous dramatic mobility. For example, the opening scenes of *Götterdäm-merung* and *Siegfried* are bound to the entire *Ring* cycle by the frag-mentary phrases of the leitmotifs. Here periodic structure is out-moded by the bonding power of smaller, more open-ended units like the tiny "Rheingold" motive (figure 2-3), the "ring" motive (figure 2-4), or the "Nothung" motive (figure 2-5). Although tonic and dominant chords are either present or implied in these small fragments, less of a firm dominant sensibility exists here than in the older periods, and the fragments are small enough to be squeezed into any mass of musical material, at the precise moment when they are dramatically needed throughout the *Ring*.

In *Tristan und Isolde,* too, the smaller leitmotifs combine to cre-ate a concatenation of psychological states embodied in music. For example, at the end of act 2, scene 3, Isolde finishes her melody first (figure 2-6). Then, instead of a formal cadence, we hear the chromatic meandering of the "Tristan" motive (figure 2-7). Next, Wagner attaches the "transfiguration of love" motive (figure 2-8). Finally, with the entrance of Melot, we hear Melot's own sinister motive (figure 2-9).

Rhein - - - gold! Rhein - - - gold! hei - a - ja - hei - a! hei - a - ja - hei - a!

2-3. Wagner, *Das Rheingold,* act 1, scene 1, measures 554–57.
Used by special arrangement with G. Schirmer, Inc.

2-4. *Das Rheingold,* act 1, scene 1, measures 743–44: the "ring" motive.
Used by special arrangement with G. Schirmer, Inc.

No - thung! No - thung! Neid - lich - es Schwert!

2-5. Wagner, *Siegfried,* act 1, scene 3, measures 551–14: the "Nothung" motive. Used by special arrangement with G. Schirmer, Inc.

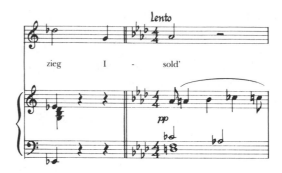

2-6. Wagner, *Tristan und Isolde*, act 2, scene 3, measures 370–71.
Used by special arrangement with G. Schirmer, Inc.

2-7. *Tristan und Isolde*, act 2, scene 3, measures 371–74: the "Tristan" motive.
Used by special arrangement with G. Schirmer, Inc.

2-8. *Tristan und Isolde*, act 2, scene 3, measures 375–76: the "transfiguration of
love" motive. Used by special arrangement with G. Schirmer, Inc.

2-9. *Tristan und Isolde*, act 2, scene 3, measures 377–79: Melot's motive.
Used by special arrangement with G. Schirmer, Inc.

Wagner has made these astonishingly varied transformations
in musical syntax in only nine measures, without the structuring
norm of the period and without a strong sense of a tonal hierarchy
or harmonic rhythm. In Wagner's operas, the small motives function as signifiers for characters, thematic ideas, aural symbols for
objects, emotions, actions. Wagner, who became disgusted with the
dictatorship of the periodic sensibility, called it "quadratic compositional construction."[7] For Wagner, it was up to poetry to fertilize
music (he saw poetry as a virile, masculine force and music as a fertile feminine element) and save it from the oppressive boredom of
pointless symmetry and repetition.[8] Wagner was convinced that
words, freed from the requirements of formal musical phrase
structure, can generate a naturally flowing music that organically
reflects the "inner depths of soul-events" ("die Tiefen der inneren
Seelenvorgänge").[9] This new freedom from repetition, as Wagner
tells us in *Zukunftsmusik,* is the essential difference between *Der
fliegende Holländer* and his later and superior *Tristan und Isolde.*[10]

Music, Wagner writes in *Beethoven,* cannot lead the search into
the "mystic ground" of "the unconscious" if it is to revel in the artificial "systematization of rhythmic structure."[11] This systematization of the periods fostered the false and superficial analogy between music and architecture suggested by Goethe. In Palestrina's
music, there is no false symmetry, Wagner argues. Palestrina, without the artificial *Periodenbau,* achieves the most successful realization of the "inmost dream image of the world."[12] Harmonic movement makes up the only audible rhythm in Palestrina, according to
Wagner.[13] "Succession" (*Zeitfolge*) is connected only to the subtlest

variation in harmonic movement.[14] This interest of Wagner's in the convention-free rhythm in earlier, unspoiled music is taken up by Debussy, but for different reasons. Only Beethoven, of the classical masters, had been able to overcome the artificial framework of periodic *Gerüste* ("scaffoldings").[15] The unconscious had been hidden in composers like Haydn by *Vernunft* (reason).

> Der "Vernunft" seiner Kunst begegnete er nur in dem Geiste, welcher den formellen Aufbau ihres äusseren Gerüstes ausgebildet hatte. Das war denn eine gar dürftige Vernunft, die aus diesem architektonischen Periodengerüste zu ihm sprach, wenn er vernahm, wie selbst die grossen Meister seiner Jugendzeit darin mit banaler Wiederholung von Phrasen und Floskeln, mit den genau eingeteilten Gegensätzen von Stark und Sanft, mit den vorschriftlich rezipierten gravitätischen Einleitungen von so und so vielen Takten, durch die unerlässliche Pforte von so und so vielen Halbschlüssen zu der seligmachenden lärmenden Schlusskadenz sich bewegten. Das war die Vernunft, welche die Opernarie konstruiert, die Anreihung der Opernpiècen aneinander diktiert hatte, durch welche Haydn sein Genie an das Abzählen der Perlen seines Rosenkranzes fesselte.[16]

Wagner borrows from Schopenhauer's *Parerga und Paralipomena* the notion that the musician performs a function analogous to the "vision of the clairvoyant somnambulist."[17] Thus, he can directly transmute the inner "true dream" (*Wahrtraum*) into musical shape. The more a musician follows his instinctual need to perform this act of correspondence between soul and sound, the less likely he will tend to compose periods that are mere "architectonic symbols."[18] In this concept lies the birth of Wagner's notion of free verse and his use of "musical prose" in his music dramas.[19]

Wagner's *Oper und Drama* takes on new significance in the light of *Beethoven*. In *Oper und Drama*, Wagner argues that vowels are the roots of speech and originally served as "man's first emotional language."[20] *Stabreim*, made up of consonants, enables verbal expression of emphasis and concentrated feeling. *Stabreim* provides articulation of the primal music of the vowels. The open sound of the vowels, only providing subjective realization of the feelings generated by an object, furnished the crude origins of both music and language. Here Wagner theorizes about the first substitutions of tone and language that result in the arts of music and literature. For Wagner, human need and not the tendency of man to imitate (mimesis, *Nachahmung*) was the cause of the early connections between man's utterances in tones, words, and images and the world around him. *Stabreim* gave the primitive tone-language shape and was, therefore, the first conventionalizing force in music and literature. Thus, melody in music should not be "ready-made." It should grow with the emotion. By allowing for this, *Vernunft* and understanding will be circumvented and the feelings can be directly expressed. In short, Wagner wants to regain something of the primal power of the open vowels used within the first crude *Stabreim* in his own music. A musical phrase, he says, should be uttered in "one breath."[21] It should be simplified by cutting out "superfluous words."[22] Thus, the word can be united with feeling. Artificial poetry, typified by the French couplet, has been "sucked dry" of this "feeling," and Wagner himself equates the stupifying boredom of the French couplet with the artificial period.[23]

The impact of this idea certainly did not escape the French theorists of Symbolism, as we shall see, when they formulated their own poetics. For Wagner, however, asymmetry was a way of rendering the emotions in music and poetry in a more gripping and realistic way. This, perhaps, is why Wagner was first praised by the Realists, even before the Symbolists.[24] Wagner, simply, was trying to make the emotions real by cutting out the artifice of convention. Too much symmetry in phrase structure, for Wagner, was unnatural, undesirable, and perhaps even impossible to achieve.[25] By cutting away words that shaped the music into standard periodic forms, Wagner was performing the same task as Flaubert, who used to shout out his prose in his apartment—much to the consternation of his neighbors—to make sure that his words did not have the old symmetrical rhythm of poetry.

In *Beethoven,* Wagner argues that the sound world is to the light world as dreaming is to waking.[26] Therefore, music is as the dream in relation to the mind.[27] Both music and the dream recover from the mind information that would otherwise be lost. In his effort to cut away the conventional habits of symmetrical, tabular organization, Wagner wanted to recover the primordial power and purity of the dream. To realize this goal, Wagner felt it necessary to crack open the formalized norm of the periodic phrase and build his huge operas out of tiny fragmented ideas, which we know as leitmotifs. Nietzsche understood the significance of this important innovation; that is why, after the philosopher became disenchanted with Wagner, he branded the composer not as a creator of great operas but as music's "greatest miniaturist."[28] The leitmotif is really a detached, open-ended signifier that is free to bond with any number of compositional possibilities. Carl Dahlhaus observes that "musical verse-form, the regular period composed symmetrically of antecedent and consequent clauses, was dissolved in Wagner's music dramas from *Das Rheingold* on, if not into prose, then into a kind of *vers libre*."[29]

Wagner's music becomes continuously developmental as his small sequences accrue greater and greater ramifications of meaning throughout his lengthy music dramas. Wagner achieves comprehensibility with his small, fractured musical ideas by repeating them frequently. Repetition of a tonal center facilitated the comprehension of the older symmetrical periods. By repeating the smaller, incomplete motives, Wagner kept the ordering and unifying qualities afforded by repetition, but he no longer needed the formal nature of the older symmetry. The leitmotif, a fragmented musical unit, replaced periodization and fixed conventions of tonality (tonality and periodization were interlocking conventions) to make comprehension possible in Wagner's operas. In the same way, the freed signifiers of the Symbolists liberated modern poetry from the kind of comprehension through convention that had been practiced earlier: a comprehensibility that was achieved through the use of rhyme and rhythmic repetitions in verse structures that functioned in conjunction with the orderly semantic development of ideas.

Wagner's idea of the dream had little to do with the actual biological dream. Instead, to the composer of the music drama, the dream was a symbol. It symbolized truth as opposed to the artificial "ausseres Gerüste," which supposedly hid expressivity in older music. By invoking the notion of the dream, Wagner attempted to justify the loosening of the signifiers of music and poetry from the old symmetrical contexts.

Both the credo of asymmetry and a distrust of artificial reason (*Vernunft*) were exported from Germany to France and transmuted from music to literature in an important literary periodical, the *Revue Wagnérienne,* published in Paris from February 1885 to July 1888. It is in the *Revue Wagnérienne* that nineteenth-century ideas of music and literature were intermingled and intermarried in a novel and heady mixture. Although the *Revue Wagnérienne* was published for only three years, it managed to cover an enormous amount of material pertinent to the important changes in the interdisciplinary aesthetics of music and literature in France in the 1880s. In the *Revue Wagnérienne,* despite its short life, Wagner's critical and artistic output was thoroughly discussed, Schopenhauer's philosophy evaluated, Tolstoy's impact on letters considered in relation to Wagner's, Beethoven and German music in general honored as subjects of serious critical discussions, the interrelations of Wagnerian music and French painting outlined, the state of French literature, music, and art assessed. Since the *Revue Wagnérienne* also published important poems and essays by Merrill, Ghil, Verlaine, Mallarmé, narratives by Huysmans, and articles by Villiers de l'Isle Adam and Swinburne, it was read, discussed or at least known by the entire Parisian literary intelligentsia of the era.

For a sampling of Wagner's impact on the literature of the 1880s, one can turn to the eight sonnets printed in the 8 January 1886 issue of the *Revue*: Mallarmé's "Hommage à Wagner," de Wyzewa's "Siegfried-Idyll," Verlaine's "Parsifal," René Ghil's "Hymne à la Musique," and sonnets by Stuart Merrill, Charles Morice, Charles Vignier, and Edouard Dujardin.[30]

Wagner's ideas are in the souls of these poets. "Go to sleep," begins de Wyzewa's poem. "Abolish the visions of the vain world: sleep," he continues, "here is the profound threshold of the lulling wave." Ghil exclaims that "my grand dream in half-voice rises in the starry air, veiled by the afternoon of the desert sleep, when he puts alcohol into wine, this Wagner." Merrill speaks in almost the same voice as Ghil: "At the auroral moment, the vague hymn of alarm where the flutes of all modulate their murmurs." Ghil praises Wagnerian heroes: "Lohengrin, Tannhäuser, and Parsifal the chaste, whose flags of purple undulate with pageantry, ride in the clamor of bronze symbols." Morice continues the Wagnerian kudos: "To give life a mirage of the sky, he [Wagner] plunges it and enpurples it in torrential blood of the exulting joy of a divine tumult." Only Mallarmé's poem clearly departs from the stock images of Wagner worship and embarks on a new course, toward a poetry of abstraction, while Verlaine's is distinguished by its sheer superiority. The rest, although rather conventional sonnets, are important as documents that record the high-pitched intensity of the French interest in Wagner in the 1880s.

The primary lesson from Wagner's operas which was transposed from operatic to strictly literary affairs was the notion that, as Fourcaud puts it in the first pages of the review, Wagner's union of "active drama and symphonic expressivity" enabled a departure from "the formalities and requirements of earlier formal opera."[31] Formality in poetry, too, came to be regarded with suspicion by the Symbolists, and Wagner, who singled out the couplet and alexandrine as a cause of stagnation in French poetry, was quoted on the subject in an 1885 issue of the *Revue*: "Sous la même influence, la Poésie Française classique, oeuvre de mort intellectuelle, et dont les lois examinées présentent une précise analogie avec les lois de l'Opéra et de la Sonate."[32] These words were rendered into French by Dujardin's literary *confrère* Theodor de Wyzewa, who published his translation of large portions of Wagner's *Beethoven* in the *Revue Wagnérienne*.[33] From the excerpts of *Beethoven* alone, Wagner's ideas on the dream and his hatred of the formalized periodic sensibility were communicated to French writers and musicians. Fourcaud, writing in the first pages of the review, singles out the stagnant nature of the older, pre-Wagnerian opera as too symmetrical, as chopped into artificial sections, as having nothing to do with "true action" or the *mise en jeu* of the passions and everything to do with merely satisfying the desires of the singers.[34] Theodor de Wyzewa knew that the pathway to truth, according to Wagner, was to allow "la volonté," in the Schopenhauerean sense, to flow freely in music. Thus, he felt it was necessary to sum up Schopenhauer's ideas on music in order to prepare the reader for an intelligible introduction to *Beethoven*:

> Schopenhauer distingue la musique des autres arts, par ce qu'elle donne l'Idée de l'univers sans l'intermédiaire d'aucun concept concret. Mais il ajoute que cette intuition de l'Idée dans la musique ne serait pas possible, si l'on n'avait, déjà, par la conscience, une intuition subjective de cette Idée. Or, la conscience renferme deux parties: la conscience de soi-même—qui est la Volonté et la conscience des autres choses, qui est la Représentation.
>
> La musique, pure de tout concept concret, répond évidemment, à ce côté de la conscience qui est tourné vers le dedans, Le Rêve: où l'esprit parvient au plein éveil de cette conscience intérieure, peut donner l'idée de ce qu'est la musique.[35]

As the Wagner-Schopenhauer link is interpreted by de Wyzewa, music, free from "concrete concepts" responds to "that side of consciousness" which "turns inwards." The dream, which turns toward the "interior consciousness," is able to provide some idea of what music is really like. De Wyzewa's interest in Schopenhauer can be traced throughout his numerous contributions in the *Revue*

Wagnérienne, and Schopenhauer's view of music as an ideal art form is often brought into discussions of Wagnerian aesthetics by the other commentators in the review as well.

On the whole, the writers of the review believed that music operated in the Schopenhauerean sense—that it recorded the interior movements of the soul. Certainly the Symbolist hostility to reality had an affinity with Schopenhauer's view of the condition of music. Music typified an art that shunned the exterior world, which created nothing but pain for the individual, for the interior world of the unconscious. Charles and Pierre Bonnier, in their "Documents de critique experimentale," decided that there are two stages of comprehension: "La compréhension provenant de la perception, et la compréhension qui s'opère quand l'esprit n'est plus sous l'impression de l'atmosphère acoustique et optique. Il s'agit, en un mot, de comprendre le 'symbole' contenu dans cette oeuvre."[36] The two essayists grapple with German terminology as they attempt to define these stages. Combined, the two levels of comprehension form the "Gefühlswerdung des Verstandes" (understanding turning into feeling).[37] Without "feeling," *Verstand* gets in the way of the direct communicative ability of the *symbole.* Elsewhere the Bonniers continue to distinguish the importance of *Gefühle* and *Verstand,* both in relation to Schopenhauer and the Wagnerian aesthetic. *Gefühl* is translated into French as "sensation" and *Verstand* as "comprehension."[38] Continually, *Gefühl* is praised as more vital and essential than *Verstand* or *Vernunft.* Clearly this distinction is a gloss on Wagner's speculations in *Beethoven.* In fact, Wagner in general, throughout his writings, tends to speak of *Vernunft* or *Verstand* or any kind of ratiocinative activity in relation to music in a pejorative sense.

In other portions of the *Revue Wagnérienne,* de Wyzewa, who was as enthusiastic about Beethoven as Wagner, discusses the "soul" as rendered in music in Beethoven's String Quartet, opus 135. De Wyzewa writes in very abstract language, which surely could have impressed the poets of his circle, even those who knew little or nothing about music: "Quelque douce brise de jouerie, l'émoi d'un léger rêve consolant. Et malgré les souvenirs parfois du mal, la discrète joie s'affermit . . . un large flot d'angoisse; il se gonfle, il se devise; oh! combien toujours impitoyable!"[39] Here, Schopenhauer's view of music's ability to translate the will into sounds becomes the notion of the music's ability to perform "la traduction des émotions." "Each note is a word," says de Wyzewa, but a note is a "mot" more expressive than the "vocables" of verbal language.[40]

Dujardin's account of the prelude to *Parsifal* reverberates with echoes of Symbolist style. Although it is like Baudelaire's response to the *Lohengrin* prelude in that it is a literary description of a specific piece of music, it is not as marked by deeply personal emoting as Baudelaire's: "Le Prélude:—Une vague initiation à des lointains, un effort calme à des lointains, et des prières; et la recherche plus âpre, l'aspiration plus douloureuse, et l'attente plus triste; et la consolation de quelque promesse, sous l'entrouvrement d'un voile au spectacle d'âme."[41] Dujardin clearly heard the feeling of timelessness and spacelessness given by Wagner to music, an effect that was achieved in a strictly musical sense by Wagner's continual thwarting of the rhythmic dominance of the bar-line as a general metric unit. It is highly possible that the lugubrious sonorities in Wagner clearly led to the sense of the "void" and the vastness of the "azure," so characteristic of the Symbolist mentality. The opening melody of *Parsifal,* as directed by the Bonniers, "rises out of the obscurity." Music that did not dance, but ebbed and flowed in undulating waves was a key inspiration to the new literary stylists:

Du silence et de l'obscurité profonde s'élève très lentement, comme un grave énoncé symbolique, la mélodie fondamentale du drame.—Les notes se succèdent simplement sans commentaire harmonique, la phrase semble parfaite et inaltérable dans sa forme comme dans sa signification; le silence qui la précédait peut revenir après elle. Cette phrase suffirait à nous induire profondément dans l'essence même de cette vie musicale qui désormais nous initiera à la vie dramatique plus intimement encore que la poésie et la mimique.[42]

Much of the language used here in the literary descriptions of the experiences of music shows traces of a vocabulary that was later honed, refined, and made abstract by the great poets of Symbolism. For example, the "essaim des fleurs" described by Wagner himself as he discusses a *Parsifal* scene appears as the "essaim éternel du désir" in Mallarmé's "Après-midi d'un faune." Catulle Mendès, describing the prelude to *The Flying Dutchman,* hears wind, lightning, and the sea on a black night. The waves "stand on end." They form "vortexes" that "hollow out." Mendés constructs a vision of a ship overcome by the sea:

Tout d'abord, l'orchestre éclate avec fureur. Le vent, l'éclair, la mer combattent dans la nuit noire. Les vagues se hérissent, des tourbillons se creusent. Mêlée par instants aux bruits de la tempête, s'exhale une clameur puissante et triste, une clameur qui est, à la fois un sanglot et un appel. Oh! de quelle douleur, de quelle espérance cent fois déçue, ce cri est-il la plainte? Tout le prodigieux fracas de l'Océan ne peut couvrir la voix qui gémit et qui désire.[43]

Mallarmé, later, will create the "naufrage" absent from all seas, just as he created the flower "absente de tous bouquets."[44] Rarefied, purified into abstraction by Mallarmé, the image of the ship troubled by stormy seas is passed along in a rich literary heritage that stretches from the early Romantic poets to Wagner to Mallarmé and finally to Yeats, Maeterlinck, and Hofmannsthal in the nineties. Undoubtedly the impact of Wagner's *Flying Dutchman* on the sensibilities of Mendès aided in the passage of the ship through nineteenth-century literary imagery, and the sea voyages of *Tristan* as well as the final shipwreck in *Götterdämmerung* were no less important.

For the writers of the review, the prose poem account of music was a "traduction" from one artistic medium into another. Thus, Dujardin describes his attempt to paraphrase the final movement of *Die Walküre* in a small corner of an 1886 issue of the review as "an attempt at translating" the music "into words," as a "transcription" of the music.

J'ai vu le fier sommet rocheux,—la forêt de sapins,—les pointes aigües,—et la garde des précipices où git le monde,—les grands cortèges, solennels, des nuages,—la désolatrice vastitude des Walküréens refuges:—et, sous la lance du Terrible, la flamme crépitante jaillissait, courait, nageait, volait, le feu, aux tintinnabulants éclats, aux dansantes furies, universel. . . . Oh! Brünnhilde ma forte, dors couchée en les ruissellements du rouge sonore, dors en la très haute paix des divins embrasements, sommeille, calme, sommeille, bonne: Brünnhilde, espère à Lui: Héros viendra, le réveilleur. Noble viendra, vainqueur des Dieux, superbe et roi . . . sur le roc transfulguré, ô Brünnhilde, en l'indubitable attente, sommeille dors, bien aimée, parmi la jubilante flamme: je te sens, et je te pense, et dans les majestueux gais épanouissements du feu avec toi je rêve aux Crépuscules futurs, ô dormeuse des divinités passées.[45]

The words "crépitante," "jaillissait," "courait," "nageait," "volait," seem to typify Dujardin's reactions to what he hears. The imperfect tense for Dujardin is undoubtedly a tense that best communicates the idea of the flow of Wagner's music. Wagner's music seems to pulsate with the flux of life, of the here and now, for the litterateurs of the *Revue*. It is far from the fossilized time schemes of formalized French writings. It is an art of the present, and, of course, of the future. In *Der Fall Wagner,* Nietzsche argues that Wagner's music no longer "dances" but "oozes." Clearly, the writers working on the review were fascinated by Wagner's ability to bathe listeners in what seemed to be giant, oozing waves of sound. Wagner's music was the music of the dream to them, and not the music of the dance, and the dream tended to connect itself to imagery of the sea, of undulating waves, of great spaces.

Even if they never heard a note of Wagner, the writers of the review were aware of his great claims for music as a gateway to the unconscious mind, as an analogue to the dream. Wagner's letter to F. Villot, printed in an 1885 issue, states that everything, including the exterior world, is dependent on "des mouvements intérieurs de l'âme." Thus, his idea of how the antilogical activity of the mind communicates information through music appears in French before the Paris coterie:

> Lorsque je composai mon *Tristan,* je me plongeai avec une entière confiance dans les profondeurs de l'âme, de ses mystères; et de ce centre intime du monde je vis s'épanouir sa forme extérieure. . . . La vie et la mort, l'importance de l'existence du monde extérieur, tout dépend uniquement des mouvements intérieurs de l'âme. L'action qui vient à s'accomplir dépend d'une seule cause de l'âme qui la provoque, et cette action éclate au jour telle que l'âme s'en est formé l'image dans ses rêves.[46]

The dream was passed as a thematic symbol and poetic model from Wagner to the Symbolists. It was in listening to Wagner's music of dream states that the Symbolists became aware of an art that was not only magically timeless and spaceless, but also seemed to be time and space encompassing. From their descriptions of what they heard, we realize that they perceived Wagner's circumventing of rigid delineations of time and space in his music.

The writers of the review often use the French imperfect tense or gerunds and present participles to describe Wagner's music, as Dujardin does when responding to *Die Walküre.* Eventually their poetry, too, turned away from the more formalized, distancing verb tenses like the *passé simple* to the present tense or the *imparfait.*

They wanted to claim for their art the same quality of *mystère* they sensed when they listened to music. Wagner, above all, stood for the antithesis of a view of the past as seen through traditional situations. He stood for the immediate present. His music embodied all that was modern, revolutionary, uninhibited, and innovative. Through Wagner, the litterateurs of the review became interested in all European music, but it was Wagner's music that caught their attention.

Catulle Mendés, in his imitation of Socratic dialogue "Le jeune Prix de Rome et le vieux Wagnériste," detected an aspect of the Wagnerian opera that was to reach a new fruition in the fin-de-siècle Symbolist theater. Wagner's operas, says Mendès's "Wagnériste," "évite la vivacité de l'action." The Wagnerian opera, he asserts, avoids action by delaying the plot with long narratives and soliloquies, which are sprawled in vast developments of characters or passions and are idealized by the *symboles* until they become unreal. Character and emotion are more important than plot:

> Son drame—non pas toujours mais quelquefois . . . s'attarde à de longs récits, s'étale en de vastes développements de caractères ou de passions, s'idéalise par la recherche des symboles jusqu'à devenir irréel, et n'en est pas moins poignant au point de vue de peuple pour lequel il a été conçu, n'en doit pas paraître moins admirable au critique loyal qui fait la part des nationalités. Mais vous, créateur, n'empruntez rien à une personnalité qui n'est pas, qui ne peut pas être la vôtre.[47]

Indeed there is little action in the Wagnerian opera, few dramatic murders, few battles, duels, or rapes. In fact, the most erotic moment in *Tristan und Isolde* is not an emphatic kiss but a lazy embrace amidst a bower of flowers. The important events in the Wagnerian narrative often take place offstage and are frequently summed up in long sections of review that are conducted by stock characters like the "Norns" of *Götterdämmerung* and are aided by the revamping of leitmotifs. A grail, sword, magic helmet (the *Tarnhelm*), ring, circle of fire, spear, gigantic swan become symbols that take on new semantic weight as great dramatic tension is concentrated on them and in the music that signifies them. Thus, they replace the need for action. The old Aristotelian convention of a cogent plot no longer applies in Wagner. This is what Catulle Mendès senses so acutely. Wagner became a model for the Symbolist dramatist and was, in a way, the first Symbolist dramatist himself.

Mendès's clever little dialogue is written in a style that is prefigured in the history of music criticism by Schumann's essays. The article is an important part of the *Revue Wagnérienne,* however, for it is one of the few places where a critic tries to take on the issue of Wagnerism in relation to French sensibilities. The true subject of French music, chides the "Wagnériste," must be, in essence, purely French and the French musician must recover the essential quality of French melody and thus develop the pure musical soul of France. Ignore the old Italian models used by Rameau, the "Wagnériste" argues, and adapt "the dramatic system of Richard Wagner," for the old "cadre théâtrical" has been broken by the "drama that we dream."[48]

The "Prix de Rome" retorts that arguing for "pure French music" and adopting Wagner's dramatic system at the same time sounds like a contradiction. "Not in the least," answers the "Wagnériste." Wagner's double genius as poet and musician carries over from "the uniqueness of his race" and "the originality of his nature" into theoretical ideas that have universal applications. The author of *Opera and Drama* has discovered an America in dramatic art, and it is not imitating Christopher Columbus to travel to New York."[49] The "double atmosphere" of music and poetry permeating French *légendes* and *chansons* must be uncovered by a corresponding French musician of genius, the "Wagnériste" concludes.[50] Alone or aided by a poet, this uniquely French artist will "deliver" our opera from "des entraves anciennes, ridicules ou démodées."[51] He will unify "poetry and music by renouncing the old forms—'récitatifs,' 'arias,' 'strettes.' "[52] The "Wagnériste" clearly sees the significance of Wagner's hatred of "square" periodic phrasing, for the new French genius will also break the scaffolding of the old "square" melody, and without "Germanizing" it, the French genius will prolong melody according to the "poetic rhythm."[53] Music will become "la parole" but a "parole" that will nevertheless be music as well. And the orchestra will be a "vast vat" in which all the "elements of drama" will boil "in fusion."[54]

Harmony and *symphony* become important literary symbols as well as musical terms in the *Revue Wagnérienne.* The notion of harmony comes to suggest ideas of resonating meanings, of mysterious contexts, of breaking laws with sensuous sounds. Even tone-deaf poets understood that harmony as an idea was important. De Wyzewa, grossly oversimplifying musical matters, argues that music, in the case of Beethoven and his precursors, was melody, and in the case of the Romantics and Wagner, it was harmony.[55] Nevertheless, there were more detailed accounts of Wagnerian approaches to harmony in the *Revue Wagnérienne*.

Among the most perceptive commentaries on harmony is "Le Système harmonique de Richard Wagner" by Albert Soubies and Charles Malherbe. Soubies and Malherbe conclude that if "harmony is only a science, then Wagner's is bad, if harmony is artistic adventure, then Wagner's is good."[56] The authors of the short article maintain that a history of the *basse* amounts to a history of music.[57] With Palestrina, the bass was "pure," unadorned by harmonic regulations. Clearly, they are aware not only of the way music was constructed before the functional harmonic system of Rameau, but also of the ideas Wagner expressed on Palestrina in *Beethoven*. Bach embodied the concept of the figured bass, they add. With Haydn, Mozart, and Beethoven, the bass still conserves its utilitarian function, for one can determine a specific harmonic function from it.[58] Wagner, they maintain, discarded this yoke of the bass because he wanted to make everything melodic.[59] With Wagner, they say, there are no more connections between the rules of harmony and the actual practice of forming an accompaniment.[60] This results in the impression of "harmonic vagueness," the sense of the "indefinite" which one detects upon first hearing a Wagner score.[61] The "perfect chord" is most often "set aside."[62] The sense of precision of the "final cadence" is not predominant. Instead, Wagner prefers to write a *cadence rompue*.[63] Clearly, those writers and readers of the *Revue* who were less musically versed and possessed a primarily literary orientation could have understood this in a more abstract sense: the new music and the new poetry ought to replace the feeling of cadential closure provided by the expected with the sensation of continuity provided by the unexpected.

Soubies and Malherbe summarize by noting that Wagner shows a "hatred of elementary chords," a love of "complex ones," a predilection for "seventh chords," "enharmonics," and "pedal points," and a facility in modulation that "blurs tonality."[64] Wagner takes away all restraints, they conclude. Parallel fifths, false relations, contrary motions in the wrong contexts—all subvert the old standards.[65]

The purity of lines in the "musical science" of the seventeenth century was already blurred by the rise of instrumental polyphony. Eighteenth-century composers began to free music from "laws." By the mid-nineteenth century, "liberty" became complete. The "entanglement of parts," "complicated designs," and "extraordinary variety of timbres" led to a music dwelling more and more in "overall impressions" and less on purity of principles, which the ear can discern.[66] Musical sound, in other words, became free from didactic laws.

While the remarks of Soubies and Malherbe are obviously perfunctory and general by the analytical standards of the twentieth century, they are of great historical interest. The two critics clearly understood, even at this early date (1885), the implications of Wagner's musical innovations in terms of the history of music, and at times they sound as if they are already describing the achievements of Debussy, who was still forming as an artist at the very moment that these writers composed their small article for the *Revue Wagnérienne*. Finally, when the litterateurs of the review speak of *obscurité* or ambiguity in music or literature, we can be sure that at least two contributors to the *Revue Wagnérienne* had a very good idea of what they might mean in a strictly musical sense, for Soubies and Malherbe knew what Wagner stood for in relation to the development of modern music at the end of the nineteenth century.

In "Notes sur la littérature Wagnérienne," Theodore de Wyzewa sounds like a twentieth-century semiotician when he discusses the connections he discerns between the arts and the domain of the sensations: "Art recreates life by the means of signs."[67] "Words," he adds, create "notions." The "ideas" are at first vague and then "define themselves and multiply." There is a "law of attenuation" and a "law of simplication" of signs in the "compilation" of ideas. The literature of Hugo, Balzac, Dickens, Flaubert, Goncourt, and Zola wanted to create a "reality more real than and superior" to "artistic life."

De Wyzewa identifies the emergence of Symbolism, on the other hand, with what he calls "symphonic poetics." Symphonic poetics was an alternative to the literature of realism. First, Lamartine instilled the "slow and *monotone* symphony" of noble sentiments. Hugo created romantic poetry that evoked emotion only from sensual life. While the Parnassians treated "vague," indefinite subjects, Mallarmé was the first who wrote (de Wyzewa uses the musical term *composer*) with respect to "total emotion." The Parnassians, he argues, were more like laborers than poets. Not one of them provides a true *symphonie* in which the "progression of an emotion is analyzed and developed." Mallarmé was the first one who adapted for a subject the emotion produced ("émotion produite") by the creation and contemplation of "philosophical dreams." He sought pure emotions but at the same time indicated "the reason of emotions." Mallarmé does not go against conventions of musical verse any more than Wagner does. Wagner, de Wyzewa argues, does not "annul" the old musical language, but he gives it a special sense and produces only certain emotions. Mallarmé's *"musique* verbale" accomplishes the same thing as Wagner's "musique instrumentale." The free nuance of emotion of the new poetry furnishes a new "musique des mots," a kind of musical prose.

Perhaps the most important statement in de Wyzewa's aesthetic discussion is his definition of *émotion produite*. It is a rapid flux of images, ideas so dense and tumultuous that the mind cannot discern the elements but only the total effect. Sometimes words fail:

> L'émotion est ainsi un état très instable et très rare de l'esprit: elle est un rapide afflux d'images, de notions, un afflux si dense et tumultueux que l'âme n'en peut discerner les éléments, toute à sentir l'impression totale. Parfois l'émotion escorte un raisonnement, ou quelques paroles prononcées: alors elle est un accompagnement sonore et continu à de très poignantes idées. Parfois elle envahit tout l'être, et les paroles cessent comme les notions.[68]

Thus, "le son musical" is the special "sign" for translating "l'émotion" and the rhythm of images can increase, decrease, hover, and rush forward as the emotional content of the "images" changes.

It is impossible to "translate" the emotions with "precise words." There is always some degree of ambiguity. "To suggest the emotions," one needs the "musical tone."

> Traduire l'émotion par des mots précis était évidemment impossible: c'était la composer l'émotion, donc la détruire. L'émotion, plus encore que les autres modes vitaux, ne peut être traduite directement, mais seulement suggérée. Pour suggérer les émotions, mode subtil et dernier de la vie, un signe spécial a été inventé: le son musical.[69]

All art, he concludes, pursues a common end: "the creation of a superior life through the means of precise signs." The new music for de Wyzewa is a literary one, a "musique des mots." It will be even more direct than Wagner's music because it will not need the intermediary of "voice" or "tone."

> Mais déjà l'heure approche où les sons musicaux ne pourront plus produire l'émotion, s'ils sont directement entendus: leur caractère propre de sons empêchera l'âme de les considérer comme de purs signes d'émotions. Une musique nouvelle deviendra nécessaire, écrite, non jouée; suggérant l'émotion sans l'intermédiaire de sons entendus. La suggérant meilleure et plus intime. La musique des mots, qui est la poésie, avait d'abord le besoin pour émouvoir, d'être dite: aujourd'hui nous la lisons: et ses sonorités nous procurent plus entièrement l'émotion, sans l'intermédiaire de la voix.[70]

Finally, the *symphonie littéraire* has little or nothing to do with nineteenth-century symphonic practices in the technical sense of musical composition. De Wyzewa is calling for a kind of poetry which has a greater emotional range because it does not have to tell a story. Thus, it will equal the expressive powers of the symphony.

In the *Revue Wagnérienne*, the first indications of a maturation from the practices of Wagner worship are noticeable in the French suspicion of Wagner's call for *völkische* poetry. The acceptance of Wagner's ideas on German nationalism is never complete and unconditional. For example, Philippe Gille, writing in the 8 March 1886 issue, expresses his reservations about the nationalistic ideas behind the conception of Bayreuth.[71]

One can easily comprehend the transition from Wagnerism to Symbolism by considering an early article on Wagner by the Romantic poet Nerval, which was printed in an 1887 issue. Nerval heard Wagner as only a Romantic heard music. "The Holy Grail" was "a cup filled with the blood running from out of the wound that Christ received on the cross."[72] Nerval's reaction is filled with immediate, violent, gripping imagery. Likewise, Wagner was interested in the most direct, emotive kind of poetic language. As Wagner himself quite clearly shows in *Opera and Drama*, the closer a word is bound to the thing it signifies, the more it suits his purposes. Sound, meaning, and function are to be unified in the most direct relationships possible according to the Wagnerian poetics.

Symbolist aesthetics set out to do precisely the opposite of this. Sound, meaning, and function, whether in poetry or music, exist in a subtle balance of interrelationships. It is these interrelationships themselves that the true Symbolist contemplates. The narrations and descriptions of primal passions are repugnant to the Symbolist. For the Symbolist, the human emotion is a pure, abstract entity that deserves the attention of poetic contemplation. Anything that intrudes upon this contemplative link is unwanted ballast. It is not surprising then that the Symbolists begin to turn away from the Wagnerian aesthetic as they begin to understand it and that this change can be traced in the very review which celebrates the greatness of the German composer.

An early example of the reservations of the French is a "chronique" by Dujardin himself. The editor singles out Villiers de l'Isle Adam's *Akedysseril* as another "art of the future," as an art resulting from the precursor of Wagnerian music. Here Wagner's works become a source of a new development in literature and not ends in themselves. The new goal is the literary one of Villiers de l'Isle Adam. The "poem in prose,"[73] *Akedysseril,* is a "simple story," "very human" and philosophical, a work of "real dream," like *Tristan.*[74] "Here the Wagnerian work must be saluted," adds Dujardin, but the author has only dreamt in agreement with the "poems" of Wagner.[75] Villiers, Dujardin proposes, has given us something completely new. Wagnerian literature is "absolutely suggestions," "less simple, less precise, less grand than the art of Wagner," and "more hermetic."[76] Dujardin could be describing not only the *Akedysseril* of Villiers but also the work of Mallarmé, whose essay "Richard Wagner: Rêverie d'un poète français," begins on the following page of the review.

The Mallarmé "Rêverie" is similar in tone, content, and style to the prose-poem responses to music that are so numerous in the *Revue Wagnérienne,* and, in fact, dominate the journal as the most characteristic method by which the French writers recorded their reactions to music. The only differences, aside from the literary superiority of Mallarmé's "Rêverie," are that Mallarmé's essay is not a direct response to a specific piece of music but a general musing on the idea of Wagner in an abstract sense, and that Mallarmé is highly suspicious of Wagnerian pomp. The French poet prefers, rather than the specificity of a hero like Siegfried, the universality of "la Figure que Nul n'est."[77] Nevertheless, in Mallarmé's passages of praise (not his theoretical moments in the essay), the precedents of de Wyzewa, Dujardin, and Mendés are discernible:

Maintenant, en effet, une musique [Wagner's] qui n'a de cet art que l'observance des lois très complexes, seulement d'abord le flottant et l'infus, confond les couleurs et les lignes du personnage avec les timbres et les

thèmes en une ambiance plus riche de Rêverie que tout air d'ici-bas, dé-
ité costumée aux invisibles plis d'un tissu d'accords; ou va l'enlever de sa
vague de Passion, au déchaînement trop vaste vers un seul, le précipiter,
le tordre: et le soustraire à sa notion, perdue devant cet afflux surhu-
main pour la lui faire ressaisir quand il domptera tout par le chant, jailli
dans un déchirement de la pensée inspiratrice.[78]

Mallarmé, though, senses something in Wagner that is contradictory to Symbolist taste, and as the issues of the review continue
to appear, it becomes clear that he is not alone. Even Dujardin, the
avid Wagnériste, begins to take a more skeptical view of the *Gesamtkunstwerk* in the latter portion of the *Revue*. In a tone recalling
the voice of the "Wagnériste" in the article by Catulle Mendès, Dujardin denounces the general practice of "nationalistic prejudices"
while at the same time bemoaning the sterility of the French composers.[79] The nationalism of Bayreuth has become unattractive to
him. There should be an "ideal" Bayreuth, protected by Symbolist
language, bathed in obscurity with "a sonorous silence," a "formi-
dable sanctuary of inaccessibility." This, he says, will be an "open
page" of the "all powerful symphony," stretching out like "an infinity."[80] Dujardin could be describing the effect Mallarmé wanted
to create in "Un Coup de dés." The *symphonie,* which obviously
made a great impression on the Symbolists when they heard it in a
concert hall, is now reclaimed as an abstract symbol that stands for
the way words interact on the pages in a book.

In the last pages of the *Revue,* Dujardin criticizes Wagner's
middle operas. Wagner's music, Dujardin says, was impure in this
developing stage. Only in the last stage of his career, after the
Beethoven essay and especially in *Parsifal* (his "finest work"), did
Wagner achieve "pure" music.[81] Here Dujardin's comments mark
the sea-change in French views of Wagner that were echoed later
by Debussy.

In the January 1887 issue, Dujardin discusses the decision to
engage Alfred Ernst as an addition to the staff of the *Revue Wagnérienne.* Dujardin states that Ernst's task will be to uncover new composers who followed routes opened by Wagner. Ernst, though, will
be looking for French composers who can say something uniquely
French in nature. Following the principles uncovered by Wagner,
with Ernst's new purpose as specified by Dujardin, the overall tone
of the *Revue* changes from one of "blind adulation" to one of critical reflection. Ernst, who wrote an important early book on

Wagner entitled *Richard Wagner et le trend contemporain*, becomes critical of Wagner by the last 1888 issue of the *Revue*: "Au point de vue de l'Art wagnérien, la période 'héroïque' est close, admirer Wagner est devenu banal. La période pratique, commerciale, si vous voulez, ne tardera point à s'ouvrir en France, étant déjà ouverte ailleurs depuis pas mal d'années."[82] The "heroic" period had reached its zenith and by the end of the decade, Wagner then could be dismissed by Ernst as "banal." The critical shift in taste had begun.

De Wyzewa has the last word in Dujardin's review, and for de Wyzewa, it is time to reassess Wagnerism. Mere imitation is no longer acceptable: "Nos Wagnériens savent tous, je le jurerais, qu'il faut chercher à comprendre Wagner et non à imiter ses petits procédés de modulation."[83] Wagner loomed as a museum piece. The governing voice is suddenly now that of Mallarmé, who saw the likelihood of Wagner's art degenerating into a "frisson familier."[84] In his effort to cut away unnecessary symmetry and repetition, Wagner attempted to attain the primordial power and purity of the dream state. Mallarmé and the other writers of the *Revue Wagnérienne,* even those who were not trained musicians, understood this and were able to apply the lesson to their own creative activity. Mallarmé also understood the difference between his own temperament and Wagner's, though. As he says in his sonnet "Hommage à Wagner," the study of secret truths of the "grimoire" should not be spread about until they become familiar to the multitude but instead belong carefully covered and preserved in an armoire. And toward the end of his essay on Wagner, published in the *Revue,* Mallarmé expresses his general reservations about the composer. The "house" of Wagner's art becomes only a temple with a lovely "parvis" in which the poet can rest, half-way up the mountain, as he climbs to reach the Absolute.

With the final edition of the *Revue Wagnérienne* in 1888, the initial phase of Wagnerism was over, but the transition from this initial phase is subtle and gradual. The passage from Wagner's art of the *Volk* to a new and secret art of the elite is recorded, issue by issue, in the pages of Dujardin's *Revue.*

3. Mallarmé and Debussy

Debussy's music and the ideal poetry of Mallarmé are created from a poetics of negation, whereas in Wagner's music and Baudelaire's poetry, anything and everything is allowed in order to reinforce dramatic expressivity. Wagner and Baudelaire want us to understand their art as quickly and easily as possible. Mallarmé and Debussy are intentionally difficult and tease us by denying easy access to their works. In Mallarmé and Debussy, dramatic expressivity is kept at bay. This explains Mallarmé's hatred of narration and description, which he viewed as banal tasks beneath the real purpose of words. In Wagner, tonal harmony is exploited to serve the needs of drama. In Debussy, tonal harmony, symmetrical periodization, and other accoutrements of Western music are carefully shunned.

Mallarmé built upon Baudelaire's work with the possibilities of correspondences, but he wanted to bypass the pressures of logical discourse and to establish a new link between poetry and the mind. Thus, he turned to the idea of music as expounded by Schopenhauer. Mallarmé wanted to show that poetry, too, had a direct correspondence to the will. Schopenhauer and Mallarmé turned away from simple correspondences between words and things. Schopenhauer did this in his praise of music, Mallarmé in his innovations in poetry.

Both the philosopher and the poet practiced a substitution of restraint that rivals the great critical shift initiated by Leone Battista Alberti at the start of the Renaissance. As Gombrich has argued, gold gained easy prominence as a sign of value because of our innate love of glitter and light.[1] Alberti, however, rejected the glitter and sparkle of gold in favor of a new symbol of purity.

When in the fifteenth century, Leone Battista Alberti discussed the decoration suitable for places of worship, he considered the use of gold only to reject it. Quoting the authority of Plato and of Cicero he advocated the use of plain white, as he was convinced that the divine powers loved purity best in life and art.[2]

Alberti, then, turned to white because of its lack of unwanted content, because of its lack of opulent signification. The white wall had the presence of absence for Alberti. In other words, the white wall was conspicuous and noteworthy because of what was absent from it. Its emptiness made it meaningful. The emptiness of the wall forced it to bear the sign of purity in contradistinction to the gaudy, decorative walls of medieval design.

> The difference lies precisely in the fact that Alberti rejects the gratification of outward splendour in favour of something more "dignified." He values the white wall not only for what it is, but for what it is not. . . . Art now stands in a cultural context in which an expectation aroused and denied can by itself become expressive of values.[3]

Just as medieval man loved gold as a signifier of value and beauty, the central symbol of Wagner's *Ring* is one that is based upon man's innate attraction to light and glitter—the ubiquitous, omnipresent symbol of the ring itself. Just as Alberti chose the understated quality of white, Mallarmé preferred the silence of the "blank space" on the white page to the bombast of Wagner. The critical shifts in taste are highly similar, even though hundreds of years separate them. Certainly the medieval church rivaled the *Gesamtkunstwerk* of Wagner. Either the nobleman or the peasant who entered the church was as assaulted by his own senses as the devout Wagnerian who entered the darkened hall of Bayreuth. The decorative, embellished religious scenes painted on the walls, the majestic heights of the cathedral itself, the smell of incense, and the Gregorian chanting of the monks combined to lift the worshiper away from his mundane, daily existence. His senses were to seize him as music seized Baudelaire—in powerful waves of synesthesia. For Alberti, such excess was no longer desirable.

Like Alberti, Mallarmé realized his need to purge art by ridding it of overabundant, unwanted meanings. Moreover, it is certainly not coincidental that Mallarmé and Debussy both turned to the contextual values of silence to restore integrity and purity in art. For Debussy, the rejuvenating presence of absence was made by asymmetrical blank spaces in time—the haunting silences in his music. For Mallarmé, the blank white space on the page meant as much as the white space on the wall meant to Alberti.

Mallarmé admits that since Wagner, it had become possible to "hear" light ("ouïr l'indiscutable rayon").[4] Nevertheless, although Mallarmé hoped to write for the theater and lauded the *Gesamtkunstwerk*, he clearly intended poetry to achieve the purity of the most austere musical forms:

> Décadente, Mystique, les Écoles se déclarent ou étiquetées en hâte par notre presse d'information, adoptent, comme rencontre, le point d'un Idéalisme qui (pareillement aux *fugues*, aux *sonates*) refuse les matériaux naturels, et, comme brutale, une pensée exacte les ordonnant; pour ne garder de rien que la suggestion. Instituer une relation entre les images exactes, et que s'en détache un tiers aspect fusible et clair présenté à la divination. . . . Abolie, la prétention, esthétiquement une erreur, quoiqu'elle régît les chefs-d'oeuvre, d'inclure au papier subtil du volume autre chose que par exemple l'horreur de la forêt, ou le tonnerre muet épars au feuillage; non le bois intrinsèque et dense des arbres. Quelques jets de l'intime orgueil véridiquement trompetés éveillent l'architecture du palais, le seul habitable; hors de toute pierre, sur quoi les pages se refermeraient mal.[5]

Mallarmé calls for a kind of poetry that achieves the condition of absolute music, for he wishes to purge poetry of the clumsy responsibility of mimesis and to reduce it to a refined, dynamic framework of interacting essences. The "tiers aspect fusible et clair" will be the result of the relationship between exact images. The communication of information in poetry, then, will be much like the communication of information—the result of relationships between pure tones—in a sonata of Beethoven or Mozart.

Mallarmé is calling for a purity achieved by negation here. He wishes to deny the world of objects ("refuse les matériaux naturels") in order to achieve the purity, the "idealism" of fugues and sonatas just as Alberti wanted to shun the glitter of gold to reach a noble, dignified, and purified style of art. Monuments, the sea, the human face, Mallarmé says, should not be described but evoked: "Les monuments, la mer, la face humaine, dans leur plénitude, natifs, conservant une vertu autrement attrayante que ne les voilera une description, évocation dites, allusion je sais, suggestion."[6] Like music, poetry should be able to resist the temptation of explication ("suspendre . . . la tentation de s'expliquer").[7] But even music should not begin with direct elemental correspondences between instruments and sounds ("sonorités élémentaires par les cuivres, les cordes, les bois") but with the idea of music.[8] Thus, the word, expressing the idea, is supreme, and poets may take back what rightfully belongs to them ("reprendre notre bien").[9]

The structure of poetry must be generated from within the poem itself, Mallarmé teaches. Thus, the author's presence, the *je*, is unnecessary and can be removed. Poetry is then depersonalized and made abstract, thus differing greatly from the highly personal poetry of Baudelaire. The irregular jolts of emotion in Baudelaire were housed within periodic structures. In Mallarmé, an antiperiodic sensibility becomes a norm. The irregularity of each structure will house a unique idea that will resound with other abstractions. Together they combine to form the "tiers aspect"—the true subject of poetic contemplation. The poem originates in a concept of denial, of what poetry should not be. A poem should not be a recitation of the expected; it should be a series of suspenseful events created by the denial of sections, with variations and oppositions. "Tout devient suspens, disposition fragmentaire avec alternance et vis-à-vis concourant au rythme total, lequel serait le poème tu, aux blancs."[10] The poem will originate in the white spaces around it, in the "blancs."

All of this culminates in Mallarmé's final development of his notion of music as an idea within the realm of poetry: "Un Coup de dés."[11] In the preface to this most modern of poems, Mallarmé again refers to the interweaving "blancs" which define the prismatic subdivisions of "l'idée." The text asserts itself by taking a unique momentary shape. The shapes speed up and slow down the movement of the poem through the white spaces. Here, too, Mallarmé adds that narrative is avoided ("on évite le récit"). Between the white spaces, the poem is foreshortened and augmented to fit the exact requirements of the momentary form of the idea. Principal, secondary, and adjacent motives are delineated in specific printed shapes.[12] These shapes indicate, like symbols in a system of musical notation, their importance in an oral recitation of the poem. "La différence des caractères d'imprimerie entre le motif prépondérant, un secondaire et d'adjacents, dicte son importance à l'émission orale et la portée, moyenne, en haut, en bas de page, notera que monte ou descend l'intonation."[13] The reuniting of *vers libre* and the *poème en prose* took place, Mallarmé says, under the influence of music—not music as an idea, but music as heard in a concert.[14] Once again Mallarmé asserts that he has recaptured music in the idea. By the act of "transposition," Mallarmé argues that poetry can be purified into a music of essences.[15] The process of substitution for poetry is now as complete and immediate as it is for music. The idea of poetry for Mallarmé equals and even surpasses the idea of music for Schopenhauer. Undoubtedly, Mallarmé learned from Schopenhauer's idea of music, because for Mallarmé, the movement of poetic images is like the movement of musical tones.

The relations between the words may seem to make no didactic sense, but Mallarmé intends to create, in poetry, a fluid movement of the soul and nothing more. Mallarmé's poetry is meant to follow or correspond to the movements of the will or the soul just as closely as the theoretical idea of music described by Schopenhauer and Wagner. Mallarmé does this, though, by bypassing the tendency of Wagner and Baudelaire to exploit the emotions. Both Wagner and Baudelaire exploited the emotions to make direct, arresting correspondences between the emotions and the narrative and descriptive elements in poetry. Because they did this, they belong to the earlier movement of Romanticism; because Mallarmé chose not to use the emotions for dramatic ends, but to savor them for themselves, he belongs, along with his musical counterpart, Claude Debussy, at the forefront of the ensuing Symbolist movement.

In the stage directions for act 1 of *Parsifal,* Wagner calls for "blue light."[16] Out of this smoky blue light of late Romanticism, which is certainly a crepuscular light, a light blurred by the shadows, Mallarmé's pure, rarefied azure emerges. Nevertheless, the interrelationship between Wagner and Mallarmé amounts to an intriguing paradox. One can easily trace, for example, the signifier of the swan from Wagner's music dramas to Mallarmé's dramatic poetry, yet in each case the same sign works in a markedly different system and encompasses a different radius of meanings.

> Gurnemanz: Was gibt's?
> Erster Knappe: Dort!
> Zweiter Knappe: Hier! Ein Schwan.
> Dritter Knappe: Ein wilder Schwan!
> Vierter Knappe: Er ist verwundet.
> Andere Knappen (vom See her stürmend): Ha! Wehe! Weh!
> Gurnemanz: Wer schoss den Schwan?[17]

Parsifal, of course, shot the swan and its death is a happy omen that indicates the arrival of the Christian innocent who will solve the basic crisis of the music drama. Lohengrin, "knight of the swan," appears in an earlier opera in a boat that is hauled down the river by another more potent swan. This swan, in fact, happens to be enormous in size and, fittingly, its symbolic presence in the opera is overbearing and unmistakable, for it signifies the arrival of the supernatural, the divine, the true, the good, and the omnipotent in the sphere of the merely human. This is a simple act of correspondence making that suits Wagner's needs as a composer of operas and as an artist of the theater.

The swan in Mallarmé's "Le Vierge, le vivace, et le bel aujourd'hui" appears in a rather different context:

> Un cygne d'autrefois se souvient que c'est lui
> Magnifique mais qui sans espoir se délivre
> Pour n'avoir pas chanté la région où vivre
> Quand du stérile hiver a resplendi l'ennui.[18]

Here, the swan is of "another time" and "without hope of gaining freedom." He is "magnificent" but pointless because of his inability to "sing" himself to a warmer region where he could live comfortably at this time when "sterile winter" dazzles with resplendent ennui.

The swan is a sign of noble disorientation in Mallarmé. Certainly this is the case with Hérodiade, who, as R. G. Cohn has noted, is the "swan princess."[19] Mallarmé's swan is in "useless exile," isolated in an environment of hostile, indifferent whiteness made up of ice and snow.

> Fantôme qu'à ce lieu son pur éclat assigne,
> Il s'immobilise au songe froid de mépris
> Que vêt parmi l'exil inutile le Cygne.[20]

The swan of Mallarmé is disoriented, as is man in the modern world, and, in fact, a thorough reading of Mallarmé's complete poem allows one to see how the former—the disoriented swan—suggests and evokes the condition of the latter—the disoriented man. Mallarmé's poem marks a shift in meaning that developed as the swan travels from the works of Wagner to Hugo to Baudelaire ("Le Cygne") to Gautier ("Symphonie en blanc majeur") and finally to Mallarmé himself.

Parsifal, "der reine Tor" (the pure fool), is the hero of everyone, the hero of the *Volk*. He has, in fact, the allegorical universality of the medieval Everyman. Mallarmé wanted to create the hero who was no one ("La Figure que nul n'est").[21] He set about doing this while fully aware that music was an abstract art which renders the emotions in sound without the specificity of narrative description. Music was an ideally ambiguous art for Mallarmé.

Although, as Calvin Brown has noted, Mallarmé the poet would have despised Mallarmé the musician, the poet, along with de Wyzewa and Dujardin, and perhaps because of them, did understand certain important things about music.[22] Mallarmé knew that the connotations of music are infinite but that the pattern of relationships between the tones, the structure of the music itself, gives shape to a wave of possible meanings. These possible meanings are endless but the fixed structure provides a definite shape to the meanings. Meaning is at once open-ended and preconstructed, bounded and boundless. The relation between Mallarmé's notion of "les images exactes," like interacting musical tones, sets off the reverberations of meaning, that "tiers aspect" which is open to the limitless potentiality of the human imagination. Forming the "tiers aspect" for Mallarmé is the same activity as rendering the "émotion produite" for de Wyzewa.

As one peruses the critical writings of Wagner and Mallarmé, it becomes increasingly clear that both artists were intrigued by the primal power of the word. Wagner's theories on the *Stabreim* and the vowel sounds expounded in *Opera and Drama* bear a resemblance to the careful study of word roots, vowel sounds, diphthongs, and consonants in Mallarmé's "Les mots Anglais." Cohn has shown the implications of the study of English words in relation to Mallarmé's use of the French language in his poetry.[23] Mallarmé sees the vowels and diphthongs as the "flesh" and the consonants as the "skeleton" of the WORD.[24] Similarly, Wagner calls open vowels "man's first emotional language."[25] The *Stabreim* forms the "composing" elements of speech, drawing upon the power of consonants to create the phenomenon of alliteration.[26] Mallarmé and Wagner, moreover, both express deep respect for the potency of myth. Both artists turn to the dream as a way of revivifying the banal state of the arts. But it is the way in which Wagner and Mallarmé apply these rudimentary ideas, ideas they mutually value so highly, that makes them supremely different.

What binds the poetics of Mallarmé and Wagner together is a hatred of banal symmetry and a tendency to replace the expected with the unexpected. As we have seen, Wagner goes against the standard pattern of musical composition by chopping apart the basic syntactical unit of European music in the first half of the nineteenth century—the *musical period.* In pre-Symbolist poetry, the constricted interaction of contiguous line and lexicon dominates the music of verse and generates a frigid periodic sensibility. Mallarmé's poetic breaks up the function of this traditional music by loosening the customary links between the axis of selection and the axis of combination. The old means of differentiating sections is subverted. Mallarmé provides a fresh, asymmetrical rhythm of poetic thought.

Mallarmé's poetry, like the music of Wagner, enhances the possibilities of verse by challenging the commonplaces of poetic tradition. Here the parallel between the two artists ends, however. Whereas Wagner uses his musical ambiguities to heighten dramatic specificity of meaning, Mallarmé intentionally decreases the specificity of meaning in his verse. Thus, Mallarmé's poetry is not at all inherently Wagnerian. Instead, Mallarmé's aesthetic closely resembles that of Claude Debussy, who also intentionally reduced the specificity of meaning in his art. Both Mallarmé and Debussy became aware of the possibilities of the detached signifier by way of the late Romanticism of Wagner's *Gesamtkunstwerk,* yet both French artists used the detached signifier to forge the subsequent *écriture* of Symbolism.

In traditional poetry and music, we have seen how semantic possibilities are carefully controlled and carefully reduced. Stanzaic forms (periods) contribute to the tabular nature of both poetry and music and provide a sense of comprehensibility and unity. In addition, the sequential unity of literature, as Barthes has shown, is preserved by the ordering effects of hermeneutic sequences and the coordination of actions within a work.[27] There are the same kinds of limitations, Barthes says, in the careful ordering of traditional music and in the narrative process.[28] In Symbolist poetry— the threshold of modern literature—and in the music of Claude Debussy, expressive freedom is gained at the expense of the comprehensibility afforded by the old periodic systems.

It is this new and challenging expressive freedom that binds the great *églogue* of Mallarmé, *"L'Après-midi d'un faune,"* to Claude

Debussy's *Prélude à l'après-midi d'un faune.* Mallarmé's poem possesses a rich bouquet of sensuousness, but this sensuousness, this fecund glorification of human sexuality, is fertilized by a well-known source in Western literary tradition. Mallarmé finds his seed in Ovid. Although the Ovidian raw material had been rendered banal by the foppishness of French painting, the original myth still retains its vigor:

> And Mercury broke off the story
> And then went on to tell what Pan had told her,
>   her,
> How she said *No,* and fled, through pathless
>   places,
> Until she came to Ladon's river, flowing
> Peaceful along the sandy banks, whose water
> Halted her flight, and she implored her
>   sisters
> To change her form, and so, when Pan had
>   caught her
> And thought he held a nymph, it was only
>   reeds
> That yielded in his arms, and while he
>   sighed,
> The soft air stirring in the reeds made also
> The echo of a sigh. Touched by this marvel
> Charmed by the sweetness of the tone, he
>   murmured
> *This much I have!* and took the reeds, and
>   bound them
> With wax, a tall and shorter one together,
> And called them Syrinx, still.[29]

The uncertainty of the "faune" and the unreality of the real, themes Mallarmé exploits so exquisitely in his poem, have roots in the original Pan, who thought he held a nymph but merely possessed the natural tools with which he structured his own music—the sighing reed. Even the ancient precursor of the French "faune," victimized by the magical universe of mythology, creates his own solace through the sensuousness of music. He made the reeds of the Syrinx into his pipe. Music and eroticism intermingle in Ovid as well as in Mallarmé.

The transition from narration to evocation in Mallarmé is recorded in the three versions of the "faune" poem. In the "Monologue d'un faune," Mallarmé includes rather didactic stage directions which describe the faun holding two nymphs: "Un Faune assis laisse de l'un et de l'autre de ses bras s'enfuir deux nymphes. Il se lève."[30] Everything about the beginning of the poem is both declamatory and exclamatory in nature, and the description of "the clear rubies" of the raised breasts is of a quasi-pornographic style reminiscent of Baudelaire's worst poetry.

> J'avais des Nymphes!
> Est-ce un songe?
> Non: le clair
> Rubis des seins levés embrase encore l'air
> Immobile.
> (Respirant:)
> et je bois les soupirs.
> (Frappant du pied:)
> Où sont-elles?[31]

The second version, "Improvisation d'un faune," begins to resemble its final condition. The banal description is gone.

> Ces Nymphes, je les veux émerveiller!
> ! Si clair,
> Leur naïf incarnat qu'il flotte dans tout l'air
> Encombré de sommeil touffu.
> Baisais-je un songe?[32]

In the final "Après-midi d'un faune," "émerveiller," which means "to astonish" or "to amaze," becomes "perpétuer." "Leur naïf incarnat" becomes "leur incarnat léger." "Qu'il flotte dans tout l'air" becomes "qu'il voltige dans l'air," "encombré" becomes "assoupi," and "baisais-je un songe?" becomes "aimai-je un rêve?" All the changes make the language more abstract and less direct, less clearly descriptive. For example, "encombré," which means "encumbered with," is more picturesque than "assoupi de" ("heavy with"), which is a comparatively abstract notion of a feeling, and "baisais-je un songe?" is far more actively erotic than "aimai-je un rêve?"

Mallarmé, in the final version of the poem, which is far tighter than the other two, still does everything he can to pull against the traditional imposition of external equivalences that goes into the making of couplets. Periodic differentiation is no longer accepted passively. Now the poet pulls against the standard, organized movement of symmetrical verse and tries to replace the old monotonous flow with a new rhythm. The visual placement of the words represents the asymmetrical phrases of the new rhythm.

> Ces nymphes, je les veux perpétuer.
> > Si clair,
> Leur incarnat léger, qu'il voltige dans l'air
> Assoupi de sommeils touffus.
> > Aimai-je un rêve?[33]

In the final version, Mallarmé begins at the ambiguous multivalent instant of doubt, expectation, and creation. The nymphs have disappeared and the faun would keep them ("je les veux perpétuer"). Only the "souffle artificiel" of "l'inspiration," the musician's breath, can create the art that will preserve the grove with magical harmonies and create the illusion, but the passion of the flautist is first needed to blow the music of imagination into being.

Debussy only intended to write a prelude to Mallarmé's poem, he did not intend to set it to music. Nevertheless, the literary inspiration of the *Prélude à l'après-midi d'un faune* is clear (this is a tone poem in the tradition of late musical Romanticism) and the common debt Debussy and Mallarmé owe to Wagner is undeniable. Both cut away at the old molds to achieve free expression. Both the poem and the music attempt to defy the rigidities of formal structures. The irregular flute motive is carefully designed so that it can appear in innumerable contexts throughout Debussy's prelude. Debussy never escapes from it, just as the enactment of the imagination to fulfill desire ("je les veux perpétuer") is the central idea of the entire poem. The "souffle artificiel" of the flute is present throughout both poem and prelude (figure 3-1).

The theme, which is outlined by the ambiguous C-sharp–G tritone, is an act of metonymy. It is a musical fragment that will bind with continuously different musical associations throughout the prelude. The flute theme, embodying in music Pan's act of "perpetuation," expands, contracts, transforms into an enharmonic cloak of D-flat rather than C-sharp, and becomes couched in varying degrees of harmonic stability or instability. Each note of the theme is subject to alteration, but the overall outline is always there. Major transformations of the theme of Pan's flute continuously appear as it passes to different voices throughout the prelude. The lack of externally imposed couplings allows Debussy to expand and contract the theme with uncanny mobility. Almost every measure, in some way, can be accounted for in terms of the single originating theme, and the few measures that cannot are the measures of the harp arpeggio and the lengthy pauses (measures four through ten). Even these passages, however, can be linked to the long line of the theme.

3-1. Debussy, *Prélude à l'après-midi d'un faune*, measures 1–4

⊀Debussy developed this metonymic technique—of transforming fragmentary ideas into the varying contexts of different textures—as a method of composition contradistinct from the sonata form used by Beethoven⊀ The older method is metaphorical in nature, for in the sonata form, clearly differentiated periodic ideas are juxtaposed. We are forced to consider distinct ideas in the same context in the sonata form. They are yoked together in the flow of the music.

Debussy not only used his new method in another important work, but he also recycled the harmonic outline of the flute theme. Consider the metonymic development of the thematic material in *L'Isle joyeuse* (1904). Once again, the flute of Pan is heard, as it slides provocatively back and forth between the shadowy harmonic outline of exactly the same tritone—C-sharp and G. The initiating C-sharp of *L'Isle joyeuse* slides effortlessly in and out of the stable context of A major, even after the great splashing of harmonic color, the great *jaillissement* of sonorities outlined by the theme (see figure 3-2). Finally, the entire theme is viewed as a metonymic part associated with the overall context of an A tonality (see figure 3-3). Thus, Debussy achieves his tremendous climax by unifying the theme with the variation of the context. At the start of the *Prélude* as well, the flute of Pan is a part without a whole, an idea without a context. The external couplings of the old period, the traditional points of articulation and orientation have been removed. In the fourth bar, the flute is interrupted by a great wash of sound in the harp, which plays the same kind of mystifying chord (the half-diminished seventh) that opens the *Tristan* prelude (see figure 3-4).

For the sake of clarity, let us designate Debussy's chord as the "faun" chord and Wagner's as the "Tristan" chord. The two chords are the same, that is, coloristically and stylistically. Both are multi-valent in that they are available for tonal modulation into a great number of keys and, more important, both destroy the standard expectations of the periodic sensibility. They negate the expectation of the dominant response to the tonic, the dialectical complement of the tonic. They provide, literally, a great bath of free sound. Actually, Wagner's chord was far more disconcerting to nineteenth-century theoreticians than Debussy's because it cannot be arranged in a standard notation of the root position in which the intervals are spelled in thirds. The spelling of the chord in thirds does not correspond to the enharmonic root position (see figure 3-

3-2. Debussy, *L'Isle joyeuse*, measures 1–9.
Used by special arrangement with G. Schirmer, Inc.

5). With the change of one pitch—D-sharp to D-natural—one can
describe the "Tristan" chord as a dominant ninth chord of A minor, yet the chord as a whole provides an aural veil that would have
hidden any aural expectation of A minor from the cultured European ear of the nineteenth century. In fact, the "Tristan" chord is
as distant from the dominant of A minor as it is close, for by slipping two pitches chromatically downward—D-sharp to D-natural
and B to B-flat—we have, enharmonically, the foreign chord of
a dominant seventh built on the pitch of B-flat.

3-3. *L'Isle joyeuse*, measures 238–55. Used by special arrangement with G. Schirmer, Inc.

3-4. *Prélude à l'après-midi d'un faune*, measure 4

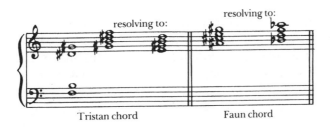

3-5

This is precisely the chord Debussy uses to disorient the ear in relation to E major in the *Prélude*. Spelled enharmonically—that is, so that the two chords should take the same enharmonic shape when played on the piano—the "Tristan" chord and the "faun" chord are both easily seen as a sonority made up of two minor thirds that are top-heavy with a major third—the standard "half-diminished seventh chord" (see figure 3-6). Debussy's "faun" chord also is available for either the dissonant sonority of a dominant seventh on B-flat (by changing C-sharp to D-natural and E-natural to F) or, for a facile transformation into E major, which is the overall tonality of the *Prélude*. This is accomplished by merely omitting the C-sharp and slipping chromatically upward from A-sharp to B. Debussy transforms his harmonically ambiguous themes as deftly as if he were in possession of the magical *Tarnhelm* from Wagner's ring and with it could alter the shape of musical ideas as simply as Alberich changes into a toad or dragon.

In both the "Tristan" chord and the "faun" chord, the most significant feature is that their standardized function within the system of the old harmonic code is less important than their coloristic value. In fact, within the context of standardized harmonic functions, their purpose is not clear. Like Mallarmé's signifiers, they, too, suggest and evoke in a newly free and open-ended way.

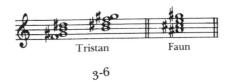

3-6

In Debussy's prelude, too, the chord is not especially mysterious in itself. What makes it mysterious is the context or lack of context in which it is placed. Debussy, like Wagner, has cracked open the customary musical period to expose his glittering, ambiguous signifier. All possible expectations of periodization are thwarted by the *frisson* of the harp, followed by the murmuring of the horns, and then by the mysterious silence. This pause, Suzanne Bernard has suggested, echoes Mallarmé's use of the "white space."[34] In terms of musical syntax, though, it served to disorient the European sensibility of the time, which demanded symmetry in phrase structure. The repetition of the "faun" chord and horn motive creates further fragmentation and distortion of the periodic sensibility. In fact, in the opening of the prelude, Debussy treats small and remotely connected fragments in a developmental fashion, just as Wagner does in his *Tristan* prelude. Debussy has placed blocks of tonally ambiguous chords in front of his resolution in E major. Each new bit of musical information breaks apart the logic that will lead us to a tonality. This is precisely the same process that Mallarmé practices. Huge chunks of metonymy fill up the line of French verse and slow us down.

Both the poem "L'Après-midi d'un faune" and Debussy's prelude to it are divided into 110 units. In the case of the poem, Mallarmé used 110 alexandrines. In Debussy's work, there are 110 measures. Each bar in the *Prélude,* however, is not of equal length. Debussy, starting a trend that will be continued throughout most of the twentieth century, freely changes meter when he needs to do so. Vacillating relationships between $\frac{9}{8}, \frac{6}{8}, \frac{12}{8}, \frac{3}{4}$ and $\frac{4}{4}$ time signatures make up the complex pattern of meters.

Arthur Wenk has tried to show a binding structural parallel between the *Prélude* of Debussy and "L'Après-midi" of Mallarmé.[35] Wenk's discussion, I believe, ultimately falls short of the mark despite his thorough scholarship. This is because what Debussy wrote was a work that is well within the tradition of the nineteenth-century symphonic poem. Like most composers who wrote symphonic poems, Debussy did not wish to create a literal rendering of his literary source in a musical form. Wenk himself quotes Debussy's views on exactly what he intended by writing a *prélude* to "L'Après-midi d'un faune":

C'est aussi le dédain de cette "science de castors" qui alourdit nos plus fiers cerveaux, puis, c'est sans respect pour le ton! et plutôt dans un mode qui essaye de contenir toutes les nuances, ce qui est très logiquement démontrable. Maintenant, cela suit tout de même le mouvement ascendant du poème, et c'est le décor merveilleusement décrit au texte, avec, en plus, l'humanité qu'apportent trente-deux violonistes levés de trop bonne heure! La fin, c'est le dernier vers prolongé: "Couple, adieu! Je vais voir l'ombre que tu devins." . . . La musique de ce Prélude est une illustration très libre du beau poème de Mallarmé. Elle ne prétend nulle-ment à une synthèse de celui-ci. Ce sont plutôt les décors successifs à travers lesquels se meuvent les désirs et les rêves du faune dans la chaleur de cet après-midi. Puis, las de poursuivre la fuite peureuse des nymphes et des naïades il se laisse aller au sommeil enivrant, rempli de songes enfin réalisés, de possession totale dans l'universelle nature.[36]

Thus, any attempt to show an identical formal scheme Debussy used to imitate the structure of the poem would be unsatisfactory. Nevertheless, it is tempting for any scholar or lover of either the poem or the music (or both) to see exactly where the 110 measures fall in relation to the 110 alexandrines, and this chore ought to be a part of any serious study of the interrelations between the two works.

It is also tempting to practice the nineteenth-century custom of correspondence making and try to uncover likely substitutions in the music for the words in the poem. Does not "mon doute, amas de nuit ancienne" seem to be rendered in the "faun" chord of the harp (in bar four)? The "doubt" that is a "mass of ancient night" is also acceptable, through an act of metaphor, as the mass of har-monic ambiguity manifested in the chord played by the harp. Simi-larly, the seventh alexandrine, "pour triomphe la faute idéale de roses," goes with the repetition of the harp chord. Both signify the self-induced illusion of eroticism that the faun "offers himself," for the music in bar seven, too, contributes to the harmonic veil of de-ception that hides E major. Or, later in the piece, in measure seventy-five, after the great climax in which the strings play their own "sonore, vaine et monotone ligne" (measures 67–74), the great ocean of orchestral sound subsides, leaving a single violin and a sin-gle clarinet exposed in an exquisite duet passage. It is a moment of transparent, translucent clarity that highlights only two instru-ments, allowing for a tremendous contrast of orchestral coloring.

In the poetry, the transition from line seventy-four to line seventy-five is marked by a change from italics to standard type, which indicates the transition from the full heat of the dream state to a state of comparative soberness. Is this a direct structural corre-spondence between text and music? Perhaps there is a relationship here, but we cannot say exactly what it is. Is Mallarmé's pun "he who seeks the LA" made into a triple pun by Debussy? "LA" means the scale pitch A and the *la* of feminity symbolized in the French article ("trop d'hymen souhaité de qui cherche le LA"). The meandering chromatic passage of the clarinet in measure thirty-four (corresponding to line thirty-four) also is seeking the pitch LA. The scale pitch A is the tone to which all instruments tune; it thus stands for the unity afforded by tonality. All sense of tonality has been obfuscated by the revolutionary whole-tone scales in the preceding bars (see figure 3-7) and the ensuing bars (see figure 3-8). Bar thirty-four itself contains music that literally does flirt with the pitch LA, but without ever finding it or settling upon it. In fact, all of these parallels between poem and music—starting with the 110 bars for the 110 lines—are nothing more or less than the tip of the hat and the knowing wink of Debussy, the musical dandy. He teases us with these intimations, but he has not written anything as stolid and prosaic as a note-to-word imitation.

Actually, by bar eleven any line-for-bar correspondence begins to break down. Bar eleven, which is characterized by a meter change from $\frac{6}{8}$ to the original $\frac{9}{8}$ is a point of structural significance in the dramatic flow of the music. Although Debussy hides all the skeletal outlines of his work with the ease of a master of musical disguise, undoubtedly bar eleven is one of recurrence and variation, for the original flute theme now has its first accompaniment, its first context. The metonymy now has a definite textural point of reference (see figure 3-9). Mallarmé, in line ten of the poem, has already embarked on his practice of playing against the alexandrine by using enjambment to such an extent that the semantic flow of the poetry begins, with the syntactic flow, at the end of the line and not at the beginning. Moreover, in the poem, line ten, not line eleven, is the beginning of a new thought and a new sentence. Debussy needed an extra measure.

> ou si les femmes dont tu gloses
> Figurent un souhait de tes sens fabuleux!
> Faune, l'illusion s'échappe des yeux bleus   10
> Et froids, comme une source en pleurs, de la plus
>   chaste:
> Mais, l'autre tout soupirs, dis-tu qu'elle contraste.[37]

Mallarmé's rhythmic irregularities have a distinctly different shape than Debussy's in spite of the deep affinity between the two works.

3-7. *Prélude à l'après-midi d'un faune*, measures 32–35

3-8. *Prélude à l'après-midi d'un faune*, measures 35–37

3-9. Prélude à l'après-midi d'un faune, measures 11–15

Mallarmé challenges the alexandrine with enjambment. By continually using enjambment, Mallarmé thought he had created a kind of musical accompaniment, a kind of counterrhythm to the traditional meter of the poem.

Plus tard, vers 1875, mon "Après-midi d'un Faune," à part quelques amis, . . . fit hurler le Parnasse tout entier, et le morceau fut refusé avec un grand ensemble. J'y essayais, en effet, de mettre, à côte de l'alexandrin dans toute sa tenue, une sorte de jeu courant pianoté autour, comme qui dirait d'un accompagnement musical fait par le poète lui-même et ne permettant au vers officiel de sortir que dans les grandes occasions.[38]

Nevertheless, Mallarmé does adhere to the norm of the alexandrine throughout the poem.

Debussy is a revolutionary in that he has fashioned the lengths of his measures to fit his musical ideas, instead of the older method of forming ideas to fit the standards of conventional musical measures. In this, he has carried the revolutionary practices of Wagner even farther. The extreme irregularity of the measure lengths, which are always tailored to fit the flow of the phrases, could never be manipulated into an exegesis that would correspond exactly with the 110 alexandrines in Mallarmé's poem.

The real links between the two works of art are those of idea and technique, and these relationships are not results of literal structural mimicry. Musical ideas permeate the imagery of Mallarmé's poetry, which was, of course, the initial work of the two. Music as an idea inspired Mallarmé. The literary rendition of music, in turn, inspired Debussy. In terms of technique, both poem and music are characterized by the concatenation of asymmetrical syntactical clusters of signifiers that move semantically in metonymic combinations. In Mallarmé's final vision, which is far removed from its Ovidian source and the poet's own "first" monologue, the imagination creates the nymphs and the imagination is embodied in the music of the flute. Mallarmé thus alters the myth to fit his purposes. This kind of liberty is an act of modernity, an act that characterizes the entire poem.

Barthes's style of analysis tells us a great deal about the modernity of Mallarmé's poem. Barthes, for one thing, has sharpened our awareness of the keen distinction between the standard code of cultural references and their actual function in a literary work. In "L'Après-midi d'un faune," the flow of semantic movement in the poetry and the cultural reference code are at odds. The clearest example of this is the negating of the importance of the myth and the increased significance of the faun's creativity. Mallarmé purposely blocks our expectations of the mythic development—part of the cultural baggage embodied in a knowledge of Ovid—and presents the faun, standing alone, as the source of his illusion.

j'élève au ciel d'été la grappe vide
Et, soufflant dans ses peaux lumineuses,
   avide
D'ivresses, jusqu'au soir je regarde au
   travers.[39]

Barthes has told us that the codes of actions and questions combine to form a tonal text just as harmony and melody are loyal to a tonic in tonal music. By enlarging upon this notion, we have seen how the periodic nature of traditional poetic forms (built up by externally imposed couplings) functions like the periodic nature of traditional musical forms. Tonal music and "tonal" poetry are both shaped by the tendency of the mind to organize in periodic groups. Traditional tonality works within a system of simple repetitions. Barthes would certainly have to agree that that system has been thoroughly challenged here:

CONTEZ

Que je coupais ici les creux roseaux domptés
Par le talent; quand, sur l'or glauque de
   lointaines
Verdures dédiant leur vigne à des fontaines,
Ondoie une blancheur animale au repos.[40]

"Contez" can mean to relate events in a detailed way, to confide, to present an imaginary story with cleverness, to tell a false story in order to trick someone.[41] Which one does Mallarmé mean? All of them. They are part of the interweaving themes of self-induced illusion and dream that permeate the music of the whole. "Contez" is an action. The faun says to himself, "You will tell." It is an enigma—what will he relate? This tonally open-ended beginning to Mallarmé's phrase is as exposed to developmental possibilities as the tiny, unstable motive that begins Debussy's prelude.

Whereas a traditional poet would complement the idea by satisfying the demands of "Contez," it is followed here by a dense cluster of Symbolist jewels. The faun was cutting (the imperfect tense combines with the italics to indicate the remoteness of the dream state) the hollow, profound reeds (both senses are justified) and thus subduing nature with his talent. As he does this, he discovers the objects of his desire. On "the clear gold" of "distant green freshness" that dedicates its "vines" to "springs," an animal whiteness in a state of repose happens to be undulating. Mallarmé has presented us with a semantic impossibility. There can be no such thing. The circuits of Barthes's five codes have overloaded. According to Ovid, the nymphs turn into reeds; the faun does not need to cut reeds to fashion his instrument. The action code has revolted against the code of cultural references. Next, we have a wealth of glittering signifiers placed side by side. Mallarmé's row of signifiers resound as if they were individual members of a musical system, as if they were interacting sonorities vibrating on the page.

Our senses experience synesthesia as we read. Clear bluish goldness signifies beauty, richness. Perhaps it is the ground upon which the "blancheur animale" stands. But Mallarmé does not want us to see that ground. He wants us to feel the music of "glaucous goldness," a single, vibrating sonority of gorgeousness. We are then treated to another signifier—"lointaines verdures"—which might be translated as the "distant fresh greenness of greenery." Why does the poet write "lointaines"? Perhaps only to enhance the exotic ambience necessary for a dream state. "Verdure" signifies the freshness of greenery as well as the greenery. Again, Mallarmé wishes us to feel the music of essences, not to view a mere forest or, in this case, a mere "bosquet."

This second signifier resounds with the first to create a sensuous series of ambiguities. How can the gold belong to the verdure? What, then, is the gold? Mallarmé will not explain this. He will leave his colors shimmering in the air like the mysterious chord in the prelude to *Tristan*. The gold brings to mind the senses of touch and sight, the verdures, the senses of sight and smell. The verdures, moreover, dedicate their vine to the springs. This is another use of the action code—the act of dedication. Now we have more signifieds—of wine, food, intoxication (from the "vigne")—which make us remember our abilities to taste and see; and water, drink, fertility (from "fontaines")—which makes us hear and see. All of this is going on and we have not yet reached the nymphs! We must see, hear, touch, taste, and smell goldness with greenness with vines of dedication that are inclined to dedicate to springs.

But where are we? How can these things be together? Are we near the "calme marécage"? Or are we in the dream state? Mallarmé has negated the importance of the action code and the hermeneutic code and filled up his poetic line with signifiers that cannot help to clarify these two aspects of the semantic process. Thus, the importance of the two most vital codes of the "tonal text" is

·threatened. If these signifiers have aesthetic value and they do not help us to understand the tonal unity (Barthes's phrase) but instead create tonal disunity, then they represent a new style. Mallarmé has enhanced the "plural" of his "text" or, since we are dealing with poetry, we may say he has enhanced the "plural" of his verse. The signifiers have been freed. Mallarmé has opened the gateway to modern poetry.

Of course, Mallarmé's singing signifiers never quite reach a state of cacophony. They are still bound just within the borders of French syntax and even within the confines of the alexandrine and the traditional rule of rhyme. Here is where Mallarmé's relationship with his musical *confrère*, Claude Debussy, is so helpful. Debussy manages to house his *Prélude à l'après-midi d'un faune* within the embrace of E major, although we do not know that E major is to assume tonal importance until the twenty-first bar of the work. Mallarmé and Debussy share an aesthetic principle. They delay the sense of their line of syntax. They squeeze every possible ounce of sensuous ambiguity out of their syntactical systems, systems that were understood within their cultural milieu to create certain resultant meanings. Then, at the last possible moment, they allow the demands of contiguity to take over.

Mallarmé does all he can to submerge the usual symmetries of poetry in "L'Après-midi." The entire breaking of the line characterizes the style of the entire work and rivals the revolutionary fracturing of periodic movement in Debussy's *Prélude*. Bernard has identified the analogous silence in Debussy's music and Mallarmé's poem.[42] The two great pauses that follow the horns in the *Prélude* destroy the orderly progression of rhythm that was so vital to Western music. Mallarmé, as Bernard points out, does the same thing with his white spaces.[43]

More significant, however, is Mallarmé's purposeful negation of just the kind of linguistic anchor identified by Nicholas Ruwet in *Langue, musique, poésie*.[44] Traditional poetic development, like traditional musical development in Debussy's work, becomes impossible. The phantasmagorias of signifiers are therefore free to flash out at us from the page and create their own music of vibrations. Note how much extensive damage has been done to the caesura. The flow of the line is chopped up time after time. The syntactical importance of a beginning of a phrase is immediately negated by a cluster of signifiers. The alexandrine cannot flow, and the great deal of time that is required for the digestion of these clusters obscures the aural unity that is normally furnished by rhyme. Let us consider only a few examples:

1. Mon doute, amas de nuit ancienne, s'achève
2. Réfléchissons . . .
3. Faune, l'illusion s'échappe des yeux bleus
4. Que non! par l'immobile et lasse pâmoison
5. Mais bast! arcane tel élut pour confident
6. Rêve, dans un solo long, que nous amusions
7. Tâche donc, instrument des fuites, ô maligne
8. Ainsi, quand des raisins, j'ai sucé la clarté
9. D'ivresse, jusqu'au soir je regarde au travers.
10. Tant pis! vers le bonheur d'autres m'entraîneront
11. Couple, adieu; je vais voir l'ombre que tu devins.[45]

We have nothing to hold on to as we read. The rhythmic displacement here is the rhythmic ambiguity of Wagner and Debussy. There is no obvious function of equivalence to hypnotize us with the primitive chant of verse. The repetitiveness of rhythm does not underscore the meaning as it does in this excerpt from Baudelaire:

Je suis la plaie et le couteau!
Je suis le soufflet et la joue!
Je suis les membres et la roue,
Et la victime et le bourreau![46]

Ruwet notes that the equivalence principle cannot explain the slight changes in the relationship between syntax and sense. We must remember, however, that a poet like Baudelaire was intuitively aware of the power of coupling in language and knew how to play *against* it in order to avoid banal repetition. Mozart, a composer who wrote in a period when musical style was highly symmetrical, also knew this intuitively.

Mallarmé, on the other hand, does not merely play against the alexandrine. He thwarts its authority; he makes it a fossil. He sews his chunks of irregular rhythmic groups together, weaving a long line of twisting, sinuous patterns. The thread of syntax grows in an irregular, through-composed style that resembles the musical phrases in a music drama of Wagner:

Mais, bast! arcane tel élut pour confident
Le jonc vaste et jumeau dont sous l'azur on
    joue:
Qui, détournant à soi le trouble de la joue,
Rêve, dans un solo long, que nous amusions
La beauté d'alentour par des confusions
Fausses entre elle-même et notre chant
    crédule;
Et de faire aussi haut que l'amour se module
Évanouir du songe ordinaire de dos
Ou de flanc pur suivis avec mes regards clos,
Une sonore, vaine et monotone ligne.[47]

Azure, fantasy, and reality intermingle through the power of music. We follow the shades of thought: "such a secret chose a confidant"; "the confidants" are the vast twin reeds played under the azure; "they relieve the trouble of the cheek" (a bewildering metonymy for the faun himself); "dream" is in a long solo so that we amuse the surrounding beauty with false confusion; the "confusion is false between the beauty and our real song"; and "to make as high as love modulates" (both *high* and *modulates* are here used as musical terms); "modulation" distilled above "the mundane dream of a back or flank" (more chunks of metonymy). Finally, Mallarmé grants us the relief of a cadence, just as Debussy finally grants us E major in the *Prélude*. All of this music resounds in a "vast, sonorous, monotonous line." Mallarmé has created that vast, sonorous music in the poem itself.

Note how Mallarmé surrounds "rêve," a word of only two syllables, with commas. He breaks up the alexandrine and underscores the importance of dream. The notion of dreaming therefore reverberates like a disturbing harmony throughout the entire sentence. We have taken a long path to relate a simple thought: a mystery of great import has found music as a source of relief and expression, and the sonorous line of music is the result. This is not important, however. The real music of Mallarmé lies in his shimmering chain of images and in the intricate tapestry of syntax in which they are encased.

Baudelaire, who introduced an entire vocabulary into literature, did little to rebel against the usual practices of structuring poetry. For Baudelaire, as well as for Beethoven, conventional forms provided the linguistic anchors upon which the line of syntactic tensions secured the dramatic sense of the work of art. Mallarmé, drawing upon his uniquely personal ideas of music, created a far more complex kind of poetry, a poetry that loosens the conventional line of connection between syntax and sense. Mallarmé's obfuscation of the syntactic movement of a poetic line rivals the revolutionary fracturing of the musical period in Debussy and Wagner.

The real aesthetic *confrère* of Mallarmé, however, is not Wagner but Debussy. In the most intrinsic way, Mallarmé's small body of dense, elegant poetry is far closer to Debussy's music, although the French composer had a difficult and tumultous love-hate relationship with Wagner's art. Debussy, speaking about Wagner's *Ring* cycle, could mock it with his acerb, urbane wit:

Que ces gens à casques et à peaux de bêtes deviennent insupportables à la quatrième soirée. . . . Songez qu'ils n'apparaissent jamais sans être accompagnés de leur damné "Leitmotiv"; il y en a même qui le chantent! Ce qui ressemble à la douce folie de quelqu'un qui, vous remettant sa carte de visite, en déclamerait lyriquement le contenu![48]

The titan of the *Gesamtkunstwerk* was too loud and brassy for Debussy. The French composer preferred a poet "who only hints at what is to be said" and who creates poetry with "no place or time," and "no big scene."[49] Debussy, most of all, was not an Impressionist so much as he was a Symbolist. Certainly, he was not an "Impressionist" in the pejorative sense of a composer who gathers together a loosely bound collection of attractive sounds that appeals to the senses but lacks structural coherence. Like Mallarmé, Debussy was a craftsman, and every syntactic and semantic ambiguity in his music is carefully created and can be explained, after careful study, within the larger context of the whole. Finally, Debussy's own interests beyond the sphere of the purely musical do not lead us, in any substantial way, to the Impressionist painters. Instead, the composer shows a sustained interest in the leading poets of Symbolism and a lifelong interest in Mallarmé, which begins at the conservatoire, comes to fruition in the *Prélude à l'après midi d'un faune* (1892), and culminates, at the end of his life, in the setting of three Mallarmé poems, the hermetic, secretive *Trois poèmes de Stéphane Mallarmé.*

4. The Song Form and the Symbolist Aesthetic

The amalgam of literary texts that prompted Debussy either to write works he completed or to attempt others he did not manage to finish is a microcosm which shows the path taken by literary Symbolism as it emerges from late Romanticism. Debussy's interest in literature as a source intended for use in his musical activities began in the 1870s with Musset, Leconte de Lisle, and Banville. In the 1880s he found Verlaine, continued with Banville, and briefly turned to Bourget and Mallarmé. In 1889, the *Cinq poèmes de Charles Baudelaire* were completed, and Debussy also started a symphony on Poe's *Fall of the House of Usher* (which he himself eventually turned into an opera libretto). Debussy's father led him into collaboration with the important Wagnerian Catulle Mendès on an aborted opera project, *Rodrique et Chimène* (1892). The 1890s were distinguished by Debussy's interest in Mallarmé and *Amphion*, a project he planned with the young Paul Valéry, but never carried out. Other poets whose works furnished texts for Debussy's projects in the nineties are Louÿs, Rossetti, and Henri de Régnier. The turn of the century marked the emergence of Debussy's work with Maeterlinck, continued settings of Verlaine, and a projected collaboration with Victor Segalen. Finally, at the end of his life Debussy turned once again to Mallarmé, when he set the *Trois Poèmes*. These last songs represent the culmination of Debussy's lifelong practice of intermingling his interest in literary affairs with his own creative life.[1]

Debussy's involvement with literature goes far deeper than most musicians would suspect. It is common knowledge that Mallarmé's "Après-midi d'un faune" was originally conceived as a theater piece. So, too, was Debussy's *prélude* to the poem. This is largely because both composer and poet shared a mutual source of inspiration—Théodore de Banville's *Diane au bois*.[2] Banville's use of a seductive flute solo prefigures Pan's flute in the efforts of both

Mallarmé and Debussy. Debussy, moreover, wrote a whole score in which he attempted to set Banville's small play. Villiers de l'Isle Adam's *Axel* also furnished material for a Debussy project. Unfortunately, Debussy only set one scene of the play and that fragment has been lost. Debussy also wished to set *Pelléas et Mélisande* to music, as well as another Maeterlinck play, *La Princesse Maleine.* If the playwright had allowed Debussy to do so, we might have yet another Maeterlinck-Debussy opera today.

However, the best document we do have that shows in a detailed way the interaction between Debussy the aspiring poet and Debussy the master musician is the *Proses lyriques* (1893). For this work, Debussy first wrote his poems and then set them to music. There are four poems in the *Proses lyriques*: "De rêve," "De grève," "De fleurs," and "De soir." The poems are unquestionably of the Symbolist vintage that ripened in Paris in the 1880s and 1890s, and, as a whole, they are filled with Wagnerian symbols that have been sifted through a Symbolist strainer. They are also filled with Symbolist clichés. Most of all, they pay homage to the "Art poétique" of Verlaine (1882), for both the music and the poetry follow the credo of Verlaine's famous quatrain:

> De la musique avant toute chose,
> Et pour cela préfère l'Impair
> Plus vague et plus soluble dans l'air,
> Sans rien en lui qui pèse ou qui pose.[3]

Debussy's poetry is uneven, unmeasured, and without the standard practices of rhyme. Nevertheless, internal couplings abound in the poetry. He shows, like Whitman in *Leaves of Grass*, the tendency to bind his words together with assonance, with alliteration, with word repetitions emphasizing parallel grammatical patterns, with simple anaphora, and even with internal rhymes. The new music of free verse is preserved by internal couplings which occur at irregular points in the overall flow of the poetry:

DE RÊVE

> La nuit a des douceurs de femmes!
> Et les vieux arbres sous la lune d'or,
> Songent à celle qui vient de passer,
> La tête emperlée,
> Maintenant navrée!

A jamais navrée
Ils n'ont pas su lui faire signe. . . .
Toutes! Elles ont passé
Les Frêles, les Folles,
Semant leur rire au gazon grêle,
Aux brises frôleuses
La caresse charmeuse des hanches fleurissantes!
Hélas! de tout ceci, plus rien qu'un blanc frisson. . . .
   Les vieux arbres sous la lune d'or,
Pleurent leurs belles feuilles d'or
Nul ne leur dédiera
Plus la fierté des casques d'or
Maintenant ternis!
A jamais ternis!
Les chevaliers sont morts sur le chemin du Grâal!
La nuit a des douceurs de femmes!
Des mains semblent frôler les âmes
Mains si folles! Mains si frêles!
Au temps où les épées chantaient pour Elles! . . .
D'étranges soupirs s'élèvent sous les arbres
Mon âme! c'est du rêve ancien qui t'étreint![4]

The poetry is laden with clichés of Symbolist imagery. "The night has the sweetness of women and the old trees under the golden moon dream," Debussy writes in the first line. A post-Baudelairean preoccupation with synesthetic patterns of metaphor abounds in Debussy's poetry. Sweetness ("douceur"), light ("lune d'or") and fine stones ("emperlée") intermingle to create an atmosphere.

Debussy attaches thematically unrelated symbolic strands. The "empearled" figure who passes is never identified. Why is she grieving? Debussy does not bother to explain. Why, too, does Debussy slip from the singular unnamed woman to the plural? "They did not know the sign," he writes; then he adds, "they have passed, the fragile ones, the mad ones, sowing their laughter in the slender grass." There is a general aura of anxiety, but no clearly worked out thematic development of actions and questions. Like Mallarmé, he is not clear here, and this helps to evoke the atmosphere of "De rêve." We may once again witness an example of how a French writer rarified and purified the old Wagnerian symbols, leaving them cloaked in the uniquely French environment of *mystère*. In Wagner or Baudelaire, we would know who the suffering, bejeweled woman is and we would know her relation to those who are "fragile' or "mad." In Debussy, as in all Symbolist poets, we are not given such specific information.

Debussy, like Mallarmé, develops his imagery metonymically. First the "pride of helmets of gold" evokes the chivalric overtones. Then the knights as a whole appear: "The knights are dead on the road to the Grail." Are the Wagnerian knights chasing the Wagnerian grail? Certainly, the ubiquitous Wagnerism in French culture of the nineties claims some responsibility for them. The helmets are tarnished and the knights are dead in Debussy's poem, though. Moreover, Debussy leaves the "chemin du Grâal" and repeats the first words of the poem in the ensuing line: "the night has the sweetness of women." Then he writes "of hands seeming to brush the souls." This is Symbolist evocation. The incantatory atmosphere created by repeating the first line is followed by a contrasting line of "hands" and "souls." There is no narrative logic, but only the power of poetry to suggest with images. Mallarmé would not need the cumbersome "semblant" in this phrase. Mallarmé also would never write the simple couplings that characterize the poem: "maintenant ternis! A jamais ternis." Neither would he indulge in the charming little internal rhyme "brises frôleuses" and "caresse charmeuse" (also a coupling). This is the easy, free-flowing sound of Verlaine's verse, not the lush density of Mallarmé's.

As for Debussy's music for his own poem, one instantly notices a marked difference between the score for *De rêve* and his later songs. This early music is at once filled with residues of old conventions and a new assertion of freedom of sound. The music is lush and harmonically dense. The ambiguous chain of augmented chords that wanders downward in a tritone relationship settles, finally, on a dominant pedal in measures four and five (see figure 4-1). The sound is uniquely Debussy's, but the technique was not unknown to either Wagner or Liszt. Liszt's use of the augmented chord in the *Faust* symphony is probably even more revolutionary than its use in *De rêve*.

Most important in these songs is Debussy's manner of writing melodic lines without the old periodic couplings, a technique he later mastered in his opera *Pelléas et Mélisande*. In the *Figaro* of 16 May 1903, Debussy articulates his view of "melody" as "antilyrical": "La mélodie, si je puis dire, est presque anti-lyrique. Elle est impuissante à traduire la mobilité des âmes et de la vie. Elle convient essentiellement à la chanson qui confirme un sentiment fixe."[5] Mu-

4-1. Debussy, *Proses lyriques,* No. 1, *De rêve,* measures 1–4

sic, for Debussy, had to be taken apart, so that it would tune in to the complexities of words. The old square melodic lines, the worst of the old conventions, simply got in the way. The accompaniment of the text of "De rêve," starting with the words "nul ne leur dé-diera plus," is made up of fragmentary ideas that underscore the psychological implications of the words in a manner reminiscent of a Wagnerian opera. However, Debussy's writing here clearly pre-figures his later music for *Pelléas.* Consider the remarkable similarity between measures fifty-three to fifty-four of *De rêve* (figure 4-2) and the "fate" motive in *Pelléas* (figure 4-3). The pitches, the register of the pitches, and the rhythms in the song excerpt clearly resemble the vitally important passage from act 1 of the opera.

4-2. *De rêve*, measures 53–54

4-3. Debussy, *Pélleas et Mélisande*, act 1, scene 1, measures 5–6. Copyright ©
1907, Durand S. A. Editions Musicales (and/or United Music Publishers).
Used by permission of the publisher. Theodore Presser Company,
sole representative U.S.A.

Debussy allowed Wagnerian overtones to creep into the passages in the text dealing with helmets, knights, and the Grail. Rich seventh and ninth chords provide a support for the small motive, which resembles the sound of a far-off hunting horn or distant military trumpets (see figure 4-4). The call of the horn appears in various keys throughout the rest of the song. It is a distant view of Wagnerism as seen through a filigree of Symbolist lace, the once powerful horn of Siegfried recalled by a modern and a dandy in a fin-de-siècle salon. Siegfried's call was loud and vigorous, however, and Debussy's knight calls in a whisper from the shadows of the past and from the secret personal world of the dream.

4-4. *De rêve,* measure 56

The four independent works that together make up *Proses lyriques* are homogenous in nature. Together they represent a distinct moment in Debussy's evolution away from Wagnerism. Wagner's presence is most heavily displayed in the *Cinq poèmes de Charles Baudelaire* (settings of "Le Balcon," "Harmonie du soir," "Le Jet d'eau," "Recueillement," "La Mort des amants"). Robin Holloway, in his very recent study *Debussy and Wagner,* has collected a few of the striking parallels between musical passages in *Tristan* and *Recueillement,* although he has neglected to mention some even more obvious similarities between the passages of "douleur" in the poem and the more dolorous moments of Brünnhilde in the *Ring.*

Holloway has pointed out the difference between the "elliptical" form of the Mallarmé songs and the comparatively massive Baudelaire songs. The importance of this distinction cannot be overemphasized, for Debussy's songs mark his evolution as a composer, just as Mozart's piano concerti show a lifelong process of continual refinement and development. The late Mallarmé pieces show a final movement toward music of intimated complexity, a music that is sophisticated in what it does not say as well as in what it does say. Referring to the Baudelaire songs, Holloway argues that "the complexity . . . is that of many notes, a density of working-out. In this sense only they are the most complex music Debussy ever wrote, and it is here that he comes nearest to a traditionally Wagnerian fullness of motivic development."[6]

The *Proses lyriques,* and the nineteen songs composed on texts by Paul Verlaine, lie midway between the two extremes of the Baudelaire *Cinq poèmes* and the later Mallarmé *Trois poèmes.* By tracing the evolution of Debussy's compositional style from the Baudelaire songs through both the *Proses lyriques* and the Verlaine songs to the culminating Mallarmé songs, one witnesses the gradual purging of Wagnerism from Debussy's music. In the turgid introduction of the piano and the wide intervallic skips on "mère des souvenirs, maîtresse des maîtresses," Debussy is writing in the shadow of the *Ring* (see figure 4-5). The exclamations of Brünnhilde, who cries "Hojotoho! Heiaha!" in act 2 of *Die Walküre* (see figure 4–6), bear the familial marks of musical ancestry in relation to Debussy's music. Elsewhere in *Le Balcon,* the full-fledged climax of the piano before the words "je sais l'art d'évoquer" (see figure 4-7) is a worthy descendant of the most emotive orchestral interlude in *Tristan.* When considered next to Baudelaire, the texts for the four *Proses lyriques* are comparatively secretive, inward, and filled with subtle self-mockery. Moreover, Baudelaire's poetry, as we have already noted, is highly structured in the traditional sense. Debussy allows himself far greater freedom with his own verse.

Figure 4–5 *(continued)*

4-5. Debussy. *Cinq poèmes de Charles Baudelaire*, No. 1, *Le Balcon*, measures 1–6

4-6. Wagner, *Die Walküre*, act 2, scene 1, measures 94–97.
Used by special arrangement with G. Schirmer, Inc.

4-7. *Le Balcon*, measures 86–89

Later in his life, Debussy remarked, in a small article in *Musica,* that Henri de Régnier, a writer of "pure, classic poetry," "cannot be put to music." The article had a provocative title: "Sous la musique que faut-il mettre? De beaux vers, de mauvais, des vers libres, de la prose?"[7] In the same article, Debussy points out the difficulty of setting poetry and the wisdom of creating one's own text for a musical work:

> Les vrais vers ont un rythme propre qui est plutôt gênant pour nous. Tenez, dernièrement, j'ai mis en musique, je ne sais pas pourquoi, trois ballades de Villon. . . . Si, je sais pourquoi: parce que j'en avais envie depuis longtemps. Eh bien, c'est très difficile de suivre bien, de "plaquer" les rythmes tout en gardant une inspiration. Si on fait de la fabrication, si on se contente d'un travail de juxtaposition, évidemment ce n'est pas difficile, mais alors ce n'est pas la peine. Les vers classiques ont une vie propre, un "dynamisme intérieur," pour parler comme les Allemands, qui n'est pas du tout notre affaire.
>
> Avec la prose rythmée on est plus à son aise, on peut mieux se retourner dans tous les sens. Si le musicien devrait faire lui-même sa prose rythmée? Pourquoi pas? Qu'est-ce qu'il attend? Wagner faisait ainsi; mais les poèmes de Wagner, c'est comme sa musique, ça n'est pas un exemple à suivre. Ses livrets ne valent pas mieux que d'autres. C'est pour lui qu'ils valaient mieux. Et c'est le principal.[8]

Embodied in free-flowing lyricism of the *Proses lyriques* is Debussy's creation of a kind of verse that ideally offers itself to the inflections of musical tones without the obtrusive counter rhythms inherent in metrical poetry. "De grève" is bounded by the irregularly recurring lines on "silk": "soie blanche effilée" (white, unweaving silk), "soie verte irrisée" (green, iridescent silk), "soie verte affolée" (green, bewitched silk), and "soie blanche appaisée" (calmed, white silk).

DE GRÊVE

Sur la mer les crépuscules tombent
Soie blanche effilée!
Les vagues comme de petites folles
Jasent, petites filles sortant de l'école,
Parmi les frousfrous de leur robe
Soie verte irrisée!
Les nuages, graves voyageurs
Se concertent sur le prochain orage

Et, c'est un fond vraiment trop grave
A cette anglaise aquarelle. . . .
Les vagues, les petites vagues
Ne savent plus où se mettre
Car voici la méchante averse
Froufrous de jupes envolées
Soie verte affolée!
Mais la lune, compatissante à tous!
Vient apaiser ce gris conflit
Et caresse lentement ses petites amies
Qui s'offrent comme lèvres aimantes
A ce tiède et blanc baiser. . . .
Puis plus rien!
Plus que les cloches attardées
Des flottantes églises
Angelus des vagues! . . .
Soie blanche apaisée! . . .[9]

The shadows, the waves, the clouds are intermingled in the poet's mind. The moon is "compatible to all" or "pitying all." The moon is the great reconciler that calms the "gris conflit." After the kiss of the moon, more than "tardy clocks," than "floating churches" that are the "angelus, of waves," the "shore" scene is, finally, "white, calmed silk."

The four poems of *Proses lyriques*—"De rêve," "De grève," "De fleurs," "De soir"—are linked in sound by a unique kind of phonological modulation. *Rêve*, phonologically, is completely contained within *grève* (g[rêve]), and, perhaps, one might argue that there is a semantic connection as well, for "De grève" is a dream vision of a seashore. In *fleurs*, the vowel sound changes only slightly, still retaining the overall *e* sound, as the vowel shifts from the *ê* or /ɛ:/ of *rêve* to the *eu* or /œ:/ of *fleurs*.[10] The *r* sound, forming an /œ:r/ sound, is present in one way or another in all four titles. Debussy certainly may have intended to modulate away from the original sound of *rêve*, while retaining some of its original qualities, just as he retains one pitch of an original chord as he deftly modulates into a foreign key in his musical works. Finally, the *e* vowels are completely dropped for the last poem as the mouth is forced to open up to form the *oir* sound of *soir*: /a:r/. The *r* consonant, however, remains. Thus, we may argue that some part of the initial *rêve* remains throughout, and subsequently, the notion of "dreaming" is infused in all four poems. Although Debussy is a master of subtle transformations of sonorities in music, the real master of subtle transformation of sounds in words is Paul Verlaine. Verlaine, as we shall see, is the inspiring force behind the four poems.

The third poem, "De fleurs," is the Baudelairean exception in Debussy's Verlainean quartet. Its emotive expression of "douleur" and its preoccupation with "evil flowers" are obviously derivative of Baudelaire. Nevertheless, the first line of "De fleurs,"—"In the ennui so disconsolately green of the hothouse of anguish,"— recalls the title of Maeterlinck's important book of verse, *Serres chaudes*. The second line, "The flowers enlace my heart with their evil stems," immediately brings to mind Baudelaire's *Fleurs du mal*. Although Debussy is certainly talented as a poet, he exposes his amateurish grasp of verse with the rather obvious play of words upon "violets" that "violate." The violet irises "were the water of dreams where my dreams plunged." Debussy, using the clumsy French past definite tense here, does preserve the thematic unit by openly referring to the notion of "rêve," which was so thematically important in the first poem. With his exclamation ("My soul dies of too much sun", Debussy is using the natural world to find images that express his "spleen," his internal disorientation. In this he joins Baudelaire and not Verlaine. In order to see this distinction, one has only to read along with "De fleurs," first, Baudelaire's "Spleen," a poem in which the sky, the earth, and the rain all reflect the individual anguish of the poet, and second, any other poem from Verlaine's *Paysage triste*. Debussy's "De fleurs" falls clearly between the lyrical sadness of Verlaine's Symbolism and the Romantic agony of Baudelaire.

"De soir" is filled with echoes of Verlaine's most famous poems. "Dimanche sur les villes" and "Dimanche dans les coeurs" present an analogical pact between poet and environment almost identical to that of "Il pleure dans mon coeur." Even two of the most important images, "coeur" and "ville," are repeated.

> Il pleure dans mon coeur
> Comme il pleut sur la ville,
> Quelle est cette langueur
> Qui pénètre mon coeur?[11]

Debussy's "chantante d'une voix informée," too, is suspiciulsy reminiscent of Verlaine's "pour un coeur qui s'ennuie, / o le chant de la pluie"; and the first lines of "De soir" have a rhythmic flow reminiscent of Verlaine's "Chanson d'automne." The rather crude use of anaphora in Debussy's poem pales before the subtle assonance of Verlaine's. In both of the following excerpts, rhyme is used freely to make couplings only when they are desired, but in Verlaine the results are far more hypnotic:

> Dimanche sur les villes,
> Dimanche dans les coeurs!
> Dimanche chez les petites filles
> Chantant d'une voix informée
> Des rondes obstinées
> Où de bonnes Tours
> N'en ont plus que pour quelques jours![12]
>
> —Debussy, "De soir"

> Les sanglots longs
> Des violons
>   De l'automne
> Blessent mon coeur
> D'une langueur
>   Monotone.[13]
>
> —Verlaine, "Chanson d'automne"

Debussy explores the theme of "dimanche" just as he would a musical idea. In line eight, he changes the tone of the poem and retains "dimanche" just as if he were restating a musical theme while simultaneously modulating to a new key and providing a brassy, bustling orchestral accompaniment for it. The throbbing urban scene he describes is worthy of the fresh imagery that will be injected into French poetry, shortly after the turn of the century, by Guillaume Apollinaire.

> Dimanche, les gares sont folles!
> Tout le monde appareille pour des banlieues d'aventure.
> En se disant adieu avec des gestes éperdus!
> Dimanches, les trains vont vite,
> Dévorés par d'insatiables tunnels:
> Et les bons signaux des routes
> Echangent d'un oeil unique
> Des impressions toutes mécaniques.[14]

The busy train station, the Sunday excursion into the suburbs so typical of urban life, the modern tunnels and signals (which exchange mechanical messages)—all are aspects of "dimanche." Here Debussy is not evoking essences with the Symbolist *écriture*, but describing reality with the detailed eye of a Realist.

This interlude ends with the next line; Debussy plunges back into the more familiar language of his literary *confrères*.

> Dimanche, dans le bleu de mes rêves,
> Où mes pensées tristes de feux d'artifice manqués
> Ne veulent plus quitter le deuil
> De vieux Dimanches trépassés.
> Et la nuit, à pas de velours,
> Vient endormir le beau ciel fatigué,
> Et c'est Dimanche dans les avenues d'étoiles.[15]

Sunday now takes the poet into the "blue" of his "dreams," where his "sad thoughts" of "spoiled fireworks" will "not stop mourning the old past Sundays." To show the interior activity of the contemplative mind, Debussy instantly turns back to the ambiguous language of Symbolism. In the mind, "dreams" can be "blue," they can evoke thoughts of "ruined fireworks," and they can become a metonymy that leads to the passage of forgotten time, to Sundays which have long sinced passed. Verlaine, too, writes of the "douleur" of memory in "Chanson d'automne."

> Tout suffocant
> Et blême, quand
> Sonne l'heure,
> Je me souviens
> Des jours anciens
> Et je pleure.[16]

Exactly what aspect of the "old Sundays" is worthy of "le deuil" is not explained by Debussy. Actually, Debussy's "deuil" is reminiscent of Verlaine's, which also exists without explanation, "sans raison":

> Il pleure sans raison
> Dans ce coeur qui s'écoeure.
> Quoi! nulle trahison?
> Ce deuil est sans raison.[17]

In the last seven lines of "De soir," Debussy combines his Verlainean rhythm and imagery with a dose of Mallarmé's ambiguity. "The gold on silver Virgin lets fall the flowers of sleep!" Debussy exclaims:

> La Vierge or sur argent
> Laisse tomber les fleurs de sommeil!
> Vite, les petites anges, dépassez les hirondelles
> Afin de vous coucher, torts d'absolution!
> Prenez pitié des villes,
> Prenez pitié des coeurs,
> Vous, la Vierge or sur argent![18]

Debussy slips abruptly and subtly into church here. A Romantic should have found a much more didactic way to describe the religious significance of Sunday. Debussy leaves the powerful Christian image hovering in the line, without a specific place in space or time. The final aspect of Sunday, the spiritual one, has been accounted for, and thus the last of the *Proses lyriques* ends.

The setting of *De grève*, like that of *De rêve*, has a free, asymmetrical flow that is facilitated by the unmeasured verse. Ostinato figures, similar to those in the *Doctor Gradus ad parnassum*, or *The Snow Is Dancing* of the *Children's Corner Suite*, or the piano toccata, abound in *De grève*. The repeated note patterns here suggest the maritime setting of the poem. The piano parts, in the tradition of the German art song, have the role of generating the psychological and physical background of the melody. If anything, in Debussy's art songs, the piano part has more importance, not less. Indeed the piano part for *De grève* is more like a miniature toccata than an accompaniment.

The song is *durchkomponiert* in that Debussy never returns to his figurations once he has ceased to need them. The four states of the silk ("soie") show this clearly (see figure 4-8). The third aspect of silk, the "soie verte affolée," is the most distinctive of the four because of the octave declamation in the melody, the tritone in the accompaniment, and the great wash of harmonic ambiguity (and freedom) furnished by the whole-tone scale. Otherwise, the melodic line of *De grève* seems almost inert. It does little more than move about in small chromatic steps, meandering, finally, back to a D major tonality. The vocal line here supplies a context for the harmonic subtleties in the piano part, where most of the musical activity lies hidden. Debussy later uses this kind of minimalist melodic writing on a larger scale when he sets *Pelléas et Mélisande*.

The setting of *De fleurs* features the same kind of organum sound that Debussy uses in the *Cathédrale engloutie* prelude and the *Placet futile* song. Long pedals are used to suggest the illusion that the piano can sustain tones indefinitely as can an organ. On the whole, the work is not markedly different from the kind of stylistic and technical approaches to composition used in the first two works in *Proses lyriques*. *De soir* has a more interesting setting. Particularly important in this song is the way in which Debussy creates the musical counterpoint for the anaphora used in his poem. "Dimanche," almost always distinguished by a strong interval—a perfect fifth or fourth in the vocal line—marks the beginning of a new musical phrase. Here the musical signifiers combine with the linguistic signifier to give unity to the work of art in spite of its irregular phrase structure (see figure 4-9).

Figure 4–8 *(continued)*

4-8. Debussy, *Proses lyriques*, No. 2, *De grève*, measures 8–9, 16–17, 32–33, 56–57

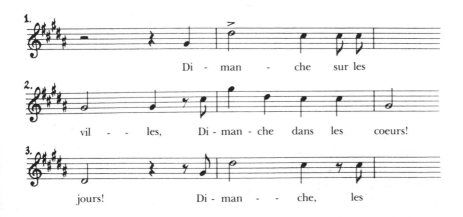

Figure 4–9 *(continued)*

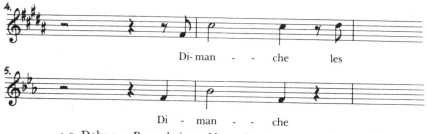

4-9. Debussy, *Proses lyriques*, No. 4, *De soir*, measures 2–3, 4–6, 14–15, 26–27, 42–43

Another unusual feature of the song becomes quite clear after our literary discussion of the poem. When Debussy moves in the poem from the modern, real world of the railroad and station back to the internal world of the dream, he feels a necessity to compose a modulation from the key of B major to the distant key of E-flat major (see figure 4-10). This is another great *frisson* of ambiguity that is as disorienting to conventionally disposed ears as any modulation in the *Prélude à l'après midi d'un faune*.

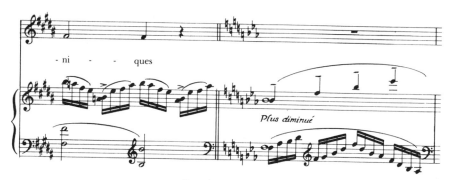

4-10. *De soir*, measures 40–41

Finally, Debussy shows his intimate knowledge of Symbolist *écriture* in his setting of the phrase "la vierge or sur argent." The first time the phrase occurs, Debussy writes music that links the "virgin" to the "gold on silver" (see figure 4-11). But the last time we hear these words, Debussy breaks them apart. "Virgin" is now separated in time (one whole beat) from "gold on silver." The division gives both images importance as separate symbols and heightens the ambiguity of the phrase (see figure 4-12). The piano, moreover, continues by echoing the pitches denoted for "gold on silver":

4-11. *De soir,* measures 75–79

4-12. *De soir,* 98–108

G-sharp–B. The two pitches rock gently back and forth until they are absorbed by the long pianissimo pedal on G-sharp that marks the end of the work. Even here there is no resolution, for Debussy slips the B into an impish A-sharp, which hovers above G-sharp until the sound dies away. As Debussy himself observed, harmony does not exist merely to be resolved.[19] Harmonic sounds can remain suspended in the air until they are no longer audible.

Debussy continues to develop his technique of setting the prose poem to music with Pierre Louÿs's *Chansons de Bilitis* (1897). Louÿs's *chansons* display the customary Symbolist predilection for erotic themes in a pastoral setting. His poems, which were banned and branded as obscene in the United States until the 1930s, are simple and obvious when compared to the virtuousity of Mallarmé. Nevertheless, the old images caught the eye and ear of Debussy once again: "the flute of Pan," the erotic metonymy of "la chevelure," and "the nymphs." No more evidence of this is necessary than the titles of the three Louÿs poems used by Debussy: "La Flûte de Pan," "La Chevelure," "Le Tombeau de naïades."

Debussy's relationship with Verlaine is more complicated and thus deserves far more attention than his relationship with Louÿs. Debussy's link begins with Madame Antoinette-Flore Mauté de Fleurville, Verlaine's mother-in-law, who was Debussy's piano teacher during his formative years. Wenk recounts that "it was she who urged that Debussy pursue a career in music and she who trained the ten-year-old boy for his entrance examinations to the *conservatoire*."[20] Two of Verlaine's poems, "Clair de lune" and "En sourdine," were set to music by Debussy not one time but twice each.

Verlaine's "En sourdine" might be described as a poem in the key of *ond,* just as Mallarmé's sonnet "Ses purs ongles très haut dèdiant leur onyx" is often called the "sonnet in -yx." Verlaines's ear clearly gravitates towards internal rhyme and assonance. In "En sourdine," the *ond* sound, which we might notate more accurately as / $\tilde{\mathfrak{z}}$:d/, dominates the aural patterns of the words. Aside from the subtle articulation of the *d* consonant, this is chiefly a nasal vowel, which in itself is already a sound that is muted ("en sourdine"). The muted vowel sound appears as a recurring tonal center in the poem.

> Calmes dans le demi-jour
> Que les branches hautes font,
> Pénétrons bien notre amour
> De ce silence profond.
>
> Fondons nos âmes, nos coeurs
> Et nos sens extasiés,
> Parmi les vagues langueurs
> Des pins et des arbousiers.

Ferme tes yeux à demi,
Croise tes bras sur ton sein,
Et de ton coeur endormi
Chasse à jamais tout dessein.

Laissons-nous persuader
Au souffle berceur et doux
Qui vient à tes pieds rider
Les ondes de gazon roux.

Et quand, solennel, le soir
Des chênes noirs tombera,
Voix de notre désespoir,
Le rossignol chantera.[21]

"Font," "pénétrons," "profond," "fondons," "nos," "laissons," "ondes," "gazon" all contain the on or / $\tilde{5}$:/ sound. The third stanza, one of contrast, moves from *on* to the comparatively bright *i* or /i/ vowel of "demi" and "endormi." To alter an *on* and *i* sound in poetry with the idea of changing timbre as a primary objective is to perform, within the realm of language, an act of music. René Ghil, author of the Symbolist tract on synesthesia, *Traité du verbe,* would have argued that Verlaine changes from "the brass" to "violins" as he writes *on* and then *i*.[22] Certainly, within the spirit of the nineteenth century, we might observe the similarity between Verlaine's vowel change and the transition between the "dark sound" of the French horns and the "bright sound" of the woodwinds, and as Gombrich has argued so convincingly, such metaphorical descriptions of sound are entirely justifiable and are, in fact, unavoidable.[23]

Most important, however, is the question we must ask ourselves upon confronting the first stanza: are we aware first of the sheer sounds of the words or of the construction of a clear semantic picture? The activity of the components of actions and questions is minimal in the first stanza and throughout: "calm in the half-light that the high branches make" and "penetrate well our love with this profound silence" are related not thematically but atmospherically. To understand the atmospheric relationship of the ideas and to understand that the atmosphere is more important than the simple explication of the theme is to comprehend Verlaine and the basic aesthetic principle of Symbolism.

Evoking the "profound silence" are the "crepuscular light"

and the "high branches." Without "seeing" those images, we would not be able to "hear" the silence. "Pénétrons," "fondons," "ferme," "laissons nous persuader" embody the activity of the lovers. Finally, in the last stanza they are one with the voice of the nightingale. It has become the voice of their despair. The poem, in terms of thematic content, is no different really from Keats's "Ode to the Nightingale." The English poet, too, hears the nightingale as the voice of his despair:

> Darkling I listen; and for many a time
> I have been half in love with easeful Death,
> Called him soft names in many a mused rhyme,
> To take into the air my quiet breath;
> Now more than ever seems it rich to die,
> To cease upon the midnight with no pain,
> While thou art pouring forth thy soul abroad.
> In such an ecstasy!
> Still wouldst thou sing, and I have ears in vain—
> To thy high requiem become a sod.[24]

Keats's poem, although it is a great one, seems noisy, fussy by comparison. Verlaine dwells on one singular idea, nothing else. He renders the forming of the analogical pact between the human mind and nature. The poem is simply and only about this. There is no elaboration as there is in Keats's ode. "Pénétrons" is "let us penetrate." "Fondons" is the imperative of *fondre,* "to melt," not fonder, "to establish." The lovers are to mingle or mix their "souls," "hearts," and "senses" amidst the tenebrous languidness of nature. They, thus, are to smell, hear, see, and touch the pines and strawberry trees. This is, once again, the nineteenth century call of synesthesia. But Verlaine's call is subdued, subtle, and ingeniously direct.

Debussy's music for "En sourdine" is marked by a masterful exploitation of harmonic ambiguity. It is, nevertheless, a music of litotes rather than Wagnerian hyperbole, although Debussy uses precisely the same pitches of the *Tristan* half-diminished seventh chord in the first, third, fourth, and fifth measures of *En sourdine.* In Debussy's song, the suspended, offbeat ostinato patterns on G-sharp and C-sharp blur rhythmic differentiation between the phrases. The tiny motive that follows the ostinato is only a fragment the size of a full period, and since it lacks the defined breadth of the period, it too adds to the rhythmic ambiguity. Tonality is hidden by chords of the seventh and the ninth which occur at the beginnings, and not in the middle, of phrases. The old dominant function of the seventh chords, moreover, is undermined. Thus, they have value in a coloristic sense. This outweighs their significance in relation to the overall tonal center of the piece—B major. Finally, the texture of the music is thin and streamlined. Thus, Debussy expunges much of the earlier Wagnerism in the Baudelaire songs in his setting for "En sourdine."

C'est l'extase typifies the kind of masterful use of anaphora Debussy intended for his own poetry in *Proses lyriques*. "C'est l'extase langoureuse," "c'est la fatigue amoureuse," and "c'est tous les frissons des bois" are each prepared by a descending motive in the piano part. These motives are built on chords with a strong dominant sensibility that is furnished with a feeling of weightlessness by the addition of coloristic pitches. The dominant of E, built on B, prepares the ear for resolution. Debussy does not provide that resolution, though, until the ninth bar. The descending motive provides the equivalent for the "languorous ecstasy," the "amorous fatigue," "the frissons of the woods." It is a kind of musical "soupir."

For an academician of the nineteenth century, Debussy's song must have had a strikingly irregular sound. It would have sounded, literally, as if the composer had started in the middle of the phrase and not at the beginning. The melodic line of "c'est l'extase" imitates the piano motive in that it, also, starts in the middle of the bar and descends. Throughout the setting, Debussy overlaps the piano part with the vocal line, wedding the two parts with musical counterparts for enjambment and ellipsis. Once again, Debussy hides the seams between the different sections of his music, but it is the way in which he starts on the dominant that brings him so close to the *poésie* of Verlaine (see figure 4-13). For an earlier composer, the movement to the dominant took place in the heart of the periodic phrase. Debussy had no need for such a long and rigid structure. He had to fit the short lines of Verlaine, lines rich in internal assonance and rhyme, into a musical form.

C'est l'extase langoureuse,
C'est la fatigue amoureuse,
C'est tous les frissons des bois
Parmi l'étreinte des brises,
C'est, vers les ramures grises,
Le choeur des petites voix.

4-13. Debussy, *Ariettes oubliées*, No. 1, *C'est l'extase*, measures 1–15

O le frêle et frais murmure,
Cela gazouille et susurre,
Cela ressemble au cri doux
Que l'herbe agitée expire. . . .
Tu dirais, sous l'eau qui vire,
Le roulis sourd des cailloux.

Cette âme qui se lamente
En cette plainte dormante
C'est la nôtre, n'est-ce pas?
La mienne, dis, et la tienne,
Dont s'exhale l'humble antienne
Par ce tiède soir, tout bas?[25]

In his setting of "Il pleure dans mon coeur," Debussy provides the "rain" of the poem in musical sound with an ostinato pattern that is present in almost every beat of the music (see figure 4-14). It is coupled with a little figure in the left hand which appears every time the "rain" image occurs (see figure 4-15). Debussy's free-flowing style of writing enables him to juxtapose the G-sharp minor tonality with the foreign A major tonality within the first four lines of the poem. On "ville," he slips from the D-sharp to a chromatically related D natural, which is supported by a luxuriant dominant ninth of A major. Thus, the new tonality on "Quelle est cette langueur / Qui pénètre mon coeur" is easily established. This enables the composer to write within a huge melodic range within the first sixteen bars of the piece.

If "En sourdine" is written in the key of *ond*, the "Il pleure dans mon coeur" is written in the key of *eur*:

Il pleure dans mon coeur
Comme il pleut sur la ville,
Quelle est cette langueur
Qui pénètre mon coeur?
O bruit doux de la pluie
Par terre et sur les toits!
Pour un coeur qui s'ennuie,
O le chant de la pluie!
Il pleure sans raison
Dans ce coeur qui s'écoeure.
Quoi! nulle trahison?
Ce deuil est sans raison.

C'est bien la pire peine
De ne savoir pourquoi,
Sans amour et sans haine,
Mon cœur a tant de peine.[26]

4-14. Debussy, *Ariettes oubliées*, No. 2, *Il pleure dans mon coeur*, measures 1–2

4-15. *Il pleure dans mon coeur*, measures 1–6

"Pleure," "coeur," "langueur," of the first stanza contrast with "bruit," "pluie," "ennuie" of the second stanza. In the third stanza, *eur* returns with "pleure" and "s'écoeure," which are combined with "raison" and "trahison." Also, "coeur" appears in both stanzas two and four. Thus, even in the contrasting stanza of the "pluie" rhyme, the *eur* sound echoes, and it appears in the concluding stanza alongside "peine" and "haine." The sound of "il pleure" therefore resonates throughout the entire poem.

It is the sheer binding power of the internal rhymes that keeps Debussy from performing the kinds of adventurous harmonic experiments of his Mallarmé works. This work is clearly written in G-sharp minor, and G-sharp throbs in the music as ubiquitously as does the *eur* sound in the poem. The only cessation of the "pleure" ostinato in the music is in those moments in the text that deal with suffering. On the words "Quoi! nulle trahison? / Ce deuil est sans raison" and "Mon coeur a tant de peine," Debussy lapses into momentary indulgences of Wagnerism. The accompaniment before "nulle trahison" (see figure 4-16) sounds suspiciously like the first bars of Tristan (see figure 1-11). Unlike Debussy's oft quoted satire of the *Tristan* motive in *Golliwog's Cakewalk*, here he is serious. And housed within the ninth chord on "peine" is the sound of the old *Tristan* half-diminished seventh.

4-16. *Il pleure dans mon coeur,* measures 47–48

Ironically, it is precisely Verlaine's interest in making his verse a verse "de la musique avant toute chose" that seemed to attract Debussy on the one hand, and, on the other, kept him in a relatively conservative frame of mind when setting Verlaine's texts. We can explain Debussy's harmony in the Verlaine songs quite conveniently within the old descriptive system. Nevertheless, Debussy does not write periodic phrase structures for Verlaine. Wenk has shown how Verlaine's verse differs from the symmetrical verse of de Vigny, but he might have mentioned the conservative organization of Baudelaire's verse as well.[27]

Verlaine was the poet who freed verse from the heavy-handedness of the alexandrine, and he was given full credit for this by Mallarmé himself. When asked to evaluate Verlaine's place in the history of poetry, Mallarmé replied:

C'est lui qui a le premier réagi contre l'impeccabilité et l'impassibilité parnassiennes; il a apporté, dans *Sagesse,* son vers fluide, avec, déjà, des dissonances voulues. . . . Mais le père, le vrai père de tous les jeunes, c'est Verlaine, le magnifique Verlaine dont je trouve l'attitude comme homme aussi belle vraiment que comme écrivain, parce que c'est la seule, dans une époque où le poète est hors la loi: que de faire accepter toutes les douleurs avec une telle hauteur et une aussi superbe crânerie.[28]

Verlaine prepared the way for Mallarmé by overcoming the dryness of the Parnassian aesthetic. Nevertheless, Debussy and Mallarmé, in their respective fields, were both quiet revolutionaries. In spite of his controversial life, Verlaine was a far less controversial poet than Mallarmé, and his kind of poetry is far less difficult. Wenk sums up the difference between Debussy and Verlaine admirably when he says that Debussy's music aspires to the state of poetry just as Verlaine's poetry aspires to the state of music.[29] We might add to this distinction by noting the difference between the "music" of Mallarmé and that of Verlaine. Mallarmé's music was intended to exist on the page. Like Debussy, Mallarmé wrote music that aspires to the condition of poetry, but Mallarmé needed music only as a theoretical idea. Verlaine, though, wrote poetry that yearns to leave the realm of language and enter a universe of pure sounds.

We have seen earlier how Debussy realized Mallarmé's aesthetic in musical form in the *Prélude à l'après-midi d'un faune.* The case for kinship between Mallarmé and Debussy becomes even more obvious if one considers the other major Debussy work that was sparked by Mallarmé's texts: the *Trois poèmes de Stéphane Mallarmé* (1913). The only other work by Debussy to use a Mallarmé text is the *Apparition* song, which was written during Mallarmé's student days at the conservatory. The *Trois poèmes* are the last three songs Debussy wrote. The composer died just five years after completing them. Thus, Debussy's interest in Mallarmé spans the length of his musical lifetime. Obviously, the poet was a major interest for Debussy, perhaps even rivaling the passion of Schumann for his favorite writer, Jean-Paul.

This late work is made up of settings of three of Mallarmé's poems—"Soupir," "Placet futile," "Autre Éventail"—for voice and piano. Once again, Mallarmé neutralizes rather conventional verse forms with his dense *écriture* in the *Trois poèmes.* In these poems, as in "L'Après-midi d'un faune," the true pattern of the poetic thought pulls against the periodicity of the stanza forms. Nevertheless, Debussy's treatment of these difficult poems is most significant here, for the *Trois poèmes* show his development toward a music antithetical to convention, highly personalized, and abstract. The *Trois poèmes* are works of expressive freedom and revolutionary modernity, yet they are written in a hushed, elliptical style. In these final songs, Debussy completely sheds the nineteenth-century conventions and the languid Wagnerism that characterize his Baudelaire songs of the 1860s.[30]

The first of the songs, *Soupir* ("sigh"), is framed by a motive the composer has marked in the score as "doux et soutenu." No attempts at writing within the old functional chord system are evident here. Sound is free and open-ended, and the listener is treated to the uncluttered vibrations of intervals of the fifth and fourth (see figure 4-17). By the fifth bar, a low A-flat indicates that the five tones—A-flat–B-flat–C–E-flat–F—make up a pentatonic scale built on A-flat. A-flat, though, is not a "key" in the old sense. It is simply a point of tonal orientation. Debussy, in introducing the song with these sparse pitches, devoid of the thickening thirds of traditional harmony, indulges in old fashioned tone painting. He depicts in sound the movement of the "soul" as it "mounts" toward the "brow." This is an obvious correspondence between sound and text, as indisputably fitting as, for example, the motive of Melot's anger in *Tristan*. But what exactly is the thing that is going up? It is an abstract essence: a "soupir." The soul that mounts toward the dream is as the "soupir" of a white gush of fountain water climbing towards the azure.

Wenk, who has read Mallarmé closely, identifies "soupirer" as "an ambiguous word that includes both sighs of aspiration and sighs of resignation."[31] He might have mentioned, also, that both "soupirer" and "soupir" in Littré's *Dictionnaire,* Mallarmé's etymological source, have a distinctly musical connotation as well. Littré quotes Lamartine: "La flûte dans les bois et les chants sur les mers arrivaient jusqu'à nous sur les soupirs d'air."[32] "Soupir" in this sense means "des sons vagues qui se font entendre."[33] "Soupir" also is a "terme de musique," indicating a "silence qui équivaut à une noire" or a "signe ayant à peu près la forme d'une virgule et qui indique le silence."[34] And "soupirer," "dans le style poétique et élevé," means "dire," "chanter avec tendresse et mélancolie."[35] "Soupir," then, denotes a kind of musical silence as well as "sighs" of either expectation or disappointment. The poem itself is about an intangible, abstract subject that Mallarmé, with his particular genius, evokes but does not describe. "Soupirer," the central symbol of the poem, is elusive, whereas the anger of Wagner's Melot is not:

> Mon âme vers ton front où rêve, ô calme soeur,
> Un automne jonché de taches de rousseur,
> Et vers le ciel errant de ton oeil angélique
> Monte, comme dans un jardin mélancolique
> Fidèle, un blanc jet d'eau soupire vers l'Azur!
> —Vers l'Azur attendri d'Octobre pâle et pur
> Qui mire aux grands bassins sa langueur infinie
> Et laisse, sur l'eau morte où la fauve agonie
> Des feuilles erre au vent et creuse un froid sillon,
> Se traîner le soleil jaune d'un long rayon.[36]

4-17. Debussy, *Trois poèmes de Stéphane Mallarmé*, No. 1, *Soupir*, measures 1–4. Copyright © 1913, Durand S. A. Editions Musicales (and/or United Music Publishers). Used by permission of the publisher. Theodore Presser Company, sole representative U.S.A.

Traditional poetry is based on closed codes of actions and questions (common to all literature) that are heightened by the imposition of external and internal couplings. Mallarmé, as we have seen, pulls this system apart with his aesthetic ambiguities. Wenk has uncovered both the poem's central question—what is the "soupir"?—and the central action of the poem ("My soul climbs towards your brow like white fountain water sighing towards the sky").[37] But in parsing the poem into a diagram modeled on Chomskian transformational grammar, Wenk has neglected to point out sufficiently how the poem works when it is put back together.

The ornamentation of the action is the source of the beauty. By hiding the action, by delaying the verb "monte," until the fourth line, Mallarmé creates his "tiers aspect," his music of essences. "My soul towards your brow where dreams, O calm sister" is severed from "mounts" by an "autumn scattered with russet freckles" and "and toward the sky wandering in your angelic eye." Moreover, Wenk ought to have paid more attention to "rêve," which is a verb. The "brow" *dreams* "the autumn scattered with russet freckles." This action—as impossible as "verdures dedicating their vines to springs"—delineates a baffling countermovement to "mon âme monte." And who is the "calm sister" with the "angelic eye"? In Baudelaire, we would know; in Mallarmé, we do not. After "monte," a word communicating the movement upward toward the azure, a word heightened by its asymmetrical status in the fifth alexandrine of the poem, Mallarmé begins his simile with "comme." He does not begin simply with "comme," though, but with "as in a melancholy garden." The melancholy garden with the "blanc jet d'eau" is the equivalent for "mon âme." The soul is the melancholy garden to which the white "jet d'eau" is "fidèle." In the garden the faithful "jet d'eau" sighs towards the sky, but not only as in breathing but also as in breathing music. (See Littré's "soupirait sous les doigts l'hymne de tes douleurs."[38])

The second half of "soupire" deals with the reflection of "l'azur" in the garden. "Azure" made "pale and pure" and "softened" by October, reflects in "the basins" on the "dead water," and on the dead water, the leaves "wander" and hollow out a "cold furrow," where a light also trails in a "long ray." All of this takes place in the "jardin mélancolique," the key image with which Mallarmé suggests the setting. Without the garden, we miss half the poem; we have no tension between the "soupir" and the autumnal evocation.

Debussy shows great tact in his setting of the rhythm of Mallarmé's words to the rhythm of his own music. Following Mallarmé's example, Debussy pays less attention to the patterns of the couplets than to the actual flow of the words. "Monte" and "fidèle," two vitally important words in the poem, are thoughts that are carried beyond the end of one line and isolated at the beginning of another. Rather than forcing the enjambed words into the square mold of a $\frac{4}{4}$ meter, a musical equivalent for the drone of the alexandrine, Debussy creates a special shape for them. He adds an extra beat for "monte," while "fidèle" is given its own measure.

In general, Debussy follows the irregular contour of the poetry and thus allows the shape of the words to shape the melodic line. In this, Debussy is still following Wagner and echoing his hatred of artificial symmetry. Note how "monte" is connected in the melody to "de ton oeil angélique." Debussy does not expose the rhymes as in the older style of periodic differentiation. In Schubert songs, for example, rhymes signify the ends of musical phrases. Debussy, following the poetics of Mallarmé, hides the rhyme. He makes it hard for the ear to catch the sonic equivalences of rhyme in the poem. "Monte" as an idea is more important than the rhyme, so Debussy gives it special attention in the setting. In general there is no poetic formality in the setting. Parallel points in the poetry end on weaker or stronger beats, depending upon the rhythmic value Debussy finds appropriate for a particular word.

Wenk has observed that Debussy, in his use of Mallarmé texts, connects "reality" to "tonality" and the world of imagination to "tonal ambiguity." In his discussion of "L'Après-midi d'un faune," he refers to the "association of tonality and reality."[39] In light of Barthes's observations on the true condition of literature and of the critical arguments proposed above, we might rephrase Wenk's views. Traditional uses of tonality in Debussy are analogous not to reality, but to the literary conventions that give the illusion of reality. Conventional tonality is an aural scheme that orients the ear, just as linear perspective is a system of organizing forms on a two-dimensional plane that gives the illusion of three dimensions. "Reality" exists to the same extent in literature or music as "depth" exists in a flat painting.

Music, as Delacroix wrote in his journal, is unique in that it is an art form which consists almost entirely of conventions. Debussy's contribution to the history of music is his role as a great negator of conventions. His raison d'être as a composer was the avoidance of clichés. When one considers the way harmonic tonality framed the periodic boxes of older music, one sees why Debussy was a revolutionary who allowed music to become more, and not less, realistic. As he says in the voice of Monsieur Croche (the model for Valéry's "Monsieur Teste"), his critical persona, "musical sound should be free like the open air."[40] In *Soupir*, the melody freely illustrates the ideas of the text. "Et vers le ciel errant de ton oeil angélique / Monte" is marked by an unfettered wandering into E major, which, in terms of the older musical style, is extremely foreign to the original tonal orientation of A-flat and also illustrates in sound the "errant wandering" of the "eye" in the text. The garden is always signified with low, chromatic, closed, comparatively inactive melodic material. "Comme dans un jardin mélancolique" is made up of just two pitches—D and E-flat. By comparison, "fidèle" and "un blanc jet d'eau soupire vers l'azur," are given many pitches and large intervallic jumps (outlined by the leap from E-natural to C). The pattern of fitting narrow melodic movement to the imagery of the melancholy garden and wider melodic movement to imagery describing the upward thrust toward light and sky is continued throughout.

Debussy's melodic ideas are not contingent upon a rigid tonal scheme, just as Mallarmé's imagery is not contingent upon a rigid narrative structure. Both artists use a syntax of parataxis and not hypotaxis, a syntax of juxtaposition rather than hierarchy. Thus they both achieve a subtle yet extraordinarily wide range of coloristic shifts. Although Wenk has correctly identified the various tonal orientations of the harmonies and has divided the poem and the music into corresponding sections, the structural relations and harmonic movement of *Soupir* are essentially nondevelopmental. One section follows the other but there is never a reconsideration of a whole section. In fact, the whole idea of an art made up of sections is contrary to the nature of the piece. Once an idea is structured in the music, it is dropped and it gives way to another. Only minutiae, like the "soupir" motive of measures one and two, are repeated, and chordal combinations cannot be fitted into a rigid harmonic system because Debussy used them for their rich coloristic quality, not their logical relation to a functional tonality. The piling of thirds upon simpler chords obscures tonality. Rewriting the sonorities in the accompaniment of measures nine to ten makes this quite clear (see figure 4-18). Here Debussy evokes the blue-note quarter tone by sounding both the major and minor third of the chord. This is a practice common to American jazz musicians but certainly is not intrinsic to European harmonic codes.

In general, as much as there is continued change in *Soupir*, the recurrence of minutiae preserves a kind of static unity. Actually, *Soupir* is characterized not by harmonic movement, but by harmonic stasis. A-flat (or its enharmonic equivalent G-sharp) is either present or implied in some way in every bar of the piece. A-flat is absorbed by the changing contexts of the other pitches, but it al-

4-18

ways hovers, a continuous droning pedal tone, just as the idea of the "soupir" permeates the poem. Even in the momentary flirtation with E major (discussed above) on "et vers le ciel errant," A-flat is veiled but present as the third of an E-major chord—G-sharp. A-flat is a metonymy available for absorption in the whole. It even lurks behind the passage identified by Wenk as "Section C," and it provides a counter pedal to the figure that Wenk calls an "E pedal" (see figure 4-19). With the words "sur l'eau morte où la fauve agonie," Debussy exposes the pedal with the triplet figure in the bass. The A-flat now flirts between the tritone relation with D-natural and the stabler perfect fifth with D-flat, which forms something like a IV chord in A-flat major, but certainly not a pure subdominant chord (see figure 4-20). Debussy would not want a subdominant chord, an old banal abstraction; he preferred a sonority that is more organic and closer to the quality of pure, natural sound.

Only with "creuse un froid sillon" does Debussy seem to escape from A-flat by sliding down a half step to the C pedal. But even the C, since it is in the strong relation of a major third with A-flat, recalls the early dominating pitch (see figure 4-21). With "d'un long rayon," the harmonically rich sonorities built on B-flat and E-flat function like the old dominant chords and prepare for the subtle reiteration of A-flat in the penultimate bar. But A-flat is only understated softly in the bass. The last sound heard in the piece is the wisp of the "soupir" motive (see figure 4-22).

"Placet futile," like "L'Après-midi d'un faune," is an incantation of desire, but an incantation that celebrates an act of poetry rather than an act of eroticism. "Nommez-nous," the poet intones, not once but three times, as though the capacity to name a thing is equal to the privilege of having it.

4-19. *Soupir,* measures 12–16. Copyright © 1913, Durand S. A. Editions Musicales (and/or United Music Publishers). Used by permission of the publisher. Theodore Presser Company, sole representative U.S.A.

4-20. *Soupir,* measures 23–24. Copyright © 1913, Durand S. A. Editions Musicales (and/or Untied Music Publishers). Used by permission of the publisher. Theodore Presser Company, sole representative U.S.A.

4-21. *Soupir,* measures 25–27. Copyright © 1913, Durand S. A. Editions Musicales (and/or United Music Publishers). Used by permission of the publisher. Theodore Presser Company, sole representative U.S.A.

4-22. *Soupir,* measures 28–31. Copyright © 1913, Durand S. A. Editions Musicales (and/or United Music Publishers). Used by permission of the publisher. Theodore Presser Company, sole representative U.S.A.

"I expend my passion but have only the modest rank of abbé," admits the poet. By contemplating the touch of the lips of the "princesse" upon a cup, the frustrated lover's desire has been inflamed, even to the point where he envies the role of Hébé, the mythological figure, who poured wine into the cups of the gods. But this is not the original mythic Hébé, in all of her primitive vitality, not an Hébé who is equal in value to a Wagnerian god. Mallarmé has a different use for the old classical myths. She is not *the* Hébé, but one of the many Hébés ("an Hébé") on the dinnerware made by the house of Sèvres, a firm that made porcelain goods near Paris from the 1750s on and was thus a French institution.[41] In fact, Sèvres was to French porcelain as Murphy was to Murphy-bed. No, this Hébé is emptied of meaning. She is, indeed, inert, lifeless on the porcelaine "tasse." Yet because the "princesse" touches the lip of the cup and therefore the Hébé, the poet is jealous of her. The poet is not even as well off as the Hébé jutting forth ("poind") on the edge of the cup and does not even count as much as a nude figure elsewhere on the Sèvres.

When the poetic voice says "nommez-nous," whom is he addressing? Certainly, the beloved, the "princesse." The princess, addressed with the "vous" imperative, must name the "nous" as "shepherd of her smiles." According to Littré, *berger* means both "garden" and "dans la poésie pastorale, amant, amante." Also, *nommer,* a word rich with shades of meaning, signifies not only "to name," but "to appoint" ("nommer quelqu'un à un emploi, à une charge"). Thus, the line may be translated as "name us [both senses of appointing and naming] lover of your smiles." In Littré, *placet* is a plea (even in the legal sense) and a "kind of small poem in the form of a plea."[42] Mallarmé was also aware that the verb *placer* touches upon exactly the same notion as *nommer*: to give or assign order or rank ("rang, donner un rang, une position"), and it also means "placer un mot, un propos, etc., le dire dans un moment où il peut produire un effet."[43] Both *nommer* and *placet,* then, mean to perform an act of language and to give an order of rank. Therefore, both are "futile," for the poet has only the "rang discret" of an "abbé." Finally, the poem is built around a single "futile" act, for "to name" is "to place in words," which is ultimately "to appoint."

The poet practices disparate acts of naming in "Placet futile." He attempts to capture his desire in synesthetic waves. First, we learn what the poet is not: an "Hébé" or a "nude figure" on "Sèvres's porcelaine," a "hairy dog," "candy," "rouge," or "dainty games." The lover "knows" the princess as a series of various synesthetic qualities: her "glance" that falls on him, "blondeness" of which divine "coiffeurs" were the "goldsmiths," her "strawberry laughter." All of these "ranks," these acts of "placer" are not the desired ones. They make up the manifestations of the action code of "Placet futile": to name and appoint. But what is the problem of the poem (hermeneutic code)? Simply put, the poet has one rank, a rank of sterility—the chaste role of the abbé—and he wants another—the position of the shepherd/lover; but the poem as a whole is about the complex interplay between the giving and taking of names. Once again, Mallarmé takes ordinary, even banal symbols and makes them evoke complex, philosophical, and vital subjects.

A comparison between the earlier version of the poem, published in 1862 with the title "Placet," and the later version (1887) shows how Mallarmé refined the poem from its comparatively straightforward original form, into its final elliptical, ambiguous shape:

Placet

J'ai longtemps rêvé d'être, ô duchesse, l'Hébé
Qui rit sur votre tasse au baiser de tes lèvres;
Mais je suis un poète, un peu moins qu'un abbé,
Et n'ai point, jusqu'ici, figuré sur le Sèvres.

Puisque je ne suis pas ton bichon embarbé,
Ni ton bonbon, ni ton carmin, ni tes jeux mièvres,
Et qu'avec moi pourtant vous avez succombé,
Blonde dont les coiffeurs divins sont les orfèvres,

Nommez-nous . . .—vous de qui les souris framboisés
Sont un troupeau poudré d'agneaux apprivoisés
Qui vont, broutant les coeurs et bêlant aux délires,

Nommez-nous . . .—et Boucher sur un rose éventail
Me peindra, flûte aux mains, endormant ce bercail,
Duchesse nommez-nous berger de vos sourires.[44]

Placet futile

Princesse! à jalouser le destin d'une Hébé
Qui poind sur cette tasse au baiser de vos lèvres,
J'use mes feux mais n'ai rang discret que d'abbé
Et ne figurerai même nu sur le Sèvres.

Comme je ne suis pas ton bichon embarbé,
Ni la pastille ni du rouge, ni jeux mièvres
Et que sur moi je sais ton regard clos tombé,
Blonde dont les coiffeurs divins sont des orfèvres!

Nommez-nous . . . toi de qui tant de ris framboisés
Se joignent en troupeau d'agneaux apprivoisés
Chez tous broutant les voeux et bêlant aux délires,

Nommez-nous . . . pour qu'Amour ailé d'un éventail
M'y peigne flûte aux doigts endormant ce bercail,
Princesse, nommez-nous berger de vos sourires.[45]

Debussy's setting for *Placet futile* is built around the tonal orientation of G, but any attempt to argue that the piece is in G minor, in spite of the importance of G as a central pitch and the two flats (E-flat and B-flat) in the key signature, could easily be refuted. The pentatonic and whole-tone scales replace the customary pitches of G minor, as Wenk has noted. Once again, asymmetry is the rule. Periodic couplings are flirtatiously shifted in the music and the periodic form of the poem (that of the sonnet), too, is obscured.

Chords built on parallel fifths were taboo in formal musical style before Debussy. The French composer loved the sound of chords written in parallel motion and could not see why they should not be allowed. He used them frequently in his music and in *Placet futile* he employs them to good advantage. The precedent for parallel chord movement is not to be found in standard nineteenth-century harmonic practice. Debussy finds the proper sound for Mallarmé's "Placet futile" by going back much farther into the past. He resurrects the sounds of the parallel organum common in European music until the year 1200 (see figures 4-23 and 4-24).

Sit glo - ri - a   Do - mi - ni,   in sae - cu - la   lae - ta - bi - tur Do - mi - nus in   o - pe - ri - bus   su - is.

4-23. Parallel Organum, *Musica enchiriadis* (c. 850)

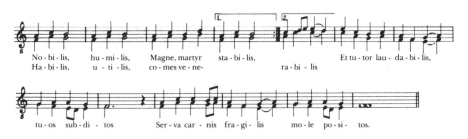

No - bi - lis,   hu - mi - lis,   Magne, martyr   sta - bi - lis,   Et tu - tor lau - da - bi - lis,
Ha - bi - lis,   u - ti - lis,   co - mes ve - ne-   ra - bi - lis

tu - os   sub - di - tos   Ser - va car - nis fra - gi - lis   mo - le po - si - tos.

4-24. Parallel Organum, *Hymn to St. Magnus* (twelfth century)

The parallel movement of pitches, used in the setting of a text, always with the third of the chord present for the filling out of the harmonic texture, is present in both the *Hymn to Saint Magnus* and in Debussy's score. It appears, in *Placet futile,* in the falling theme of the opening piano measures and in the setting for the first four lines of the text. Even when Debussy modulates to an E-flattish type of pitch orientation on "comme je ne suis pas ton bichon em-barbé," the organum sound is still present (see figure 4-25).

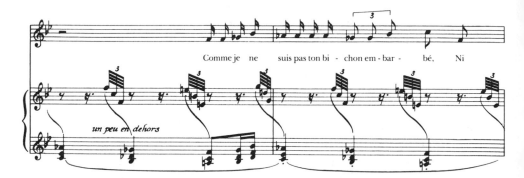

4-25. Debussy, *Trois poèmes de Stéphane Mallarmé, No. 2, Placet futile*, measures 11–12. Copyright © 1913, Durand S. A. Editions Musicales (and/or United Music Publishers). Used by permission of the publisher. Theodore Presser Company, sole representative U.S.A.

Debussy, however, peppers his organum sound with the ironies of a fin-de-siècle dandy (although the piece was written in 1913). A standard E-flat major cadence surfaces, for example, on the words "ni de rouge." This old cliché is only a feint, though. In earlier nineteenth-century music, such a strong cadence marked the end of a musical thought. Here it sits right in the middle of one. "Rouge" is just one more thing that is named in the poem. Mallarmé's phrase continues and so does Debussy's. The composer dissolves the music into a cloud of whole-tone harmonic ambiguities on "ni jeux mièvres." The three chords on "moi je sais ton regard clos tombé" are perfect examples of a pattern of chords worthy in their complexity of the most Wagnerian lushness while, at the same time, recalling in their parallelism the sounds of organum.

Debussy impishly employs, then, sound patterns much older than those of common nineteenth-century musical practice, yet he fills out his medieval harmonization with the assurance of a great master of nineteenth-century harmony. In this way, he finds the ideal music for Mallarmé, who empties his old symbols of meaning in order to give them new meaning.

The last bars of *Placet futile* and the last song of *Trois poèmes, Éventail*, are linked by the twin images of the fan and the wing.

Once we hear the words "pour qu'amour ailé d'un éventail" in the *Placet futile* song, we know that Debussy has constructed a correspondence between the wings of the fan and all the grace note figures in the piece. And when the lover is finally labeled as shepherd and sings "m'y peigne flûte aux doigts endormant ce bercail," he is accompanied by the musical realization of the fluttering of the fan in the piano trills. The final wisps of sound that accompany the word "sourires" simultaneously evoke the flutters of the shepherd's flutes, the fan, and the wings of love (see figure 4-26). Moreover, they provide a structural bond with *Éventail* (the poem is entitled "Autre éventail" in Mallarmé's *poésies*), for the last of the songs begins with the same flutter of the fan (see figure 4-27). The pentatonic scale on G-flat falls onto a C by the second measure. Then the music descends downwards with the familiar kind of parallelism of *Placet futile*. Here, Debussy, too, enriches the parallel harmonies by piling third upon third with the harmonic sophistication of a post-Wagnerian. When spelled in their root positions, the complexity of the chords becomes quite obvious (see figure 4-28). But the very lushness of the chords keeps them suspended above and away from a clear tonality. The sonorities seem to resist descent, just as an "éventail" would be held up by the air as it moves downward or sideways.

4-26. *Placet futile*, measures 32–34. Copyright © 1913, Durand S. A. Editions Musicales (and/or United Music Publishers). Used by permission of the publisher. Theodore Presser Company, sole representative U.S.A.

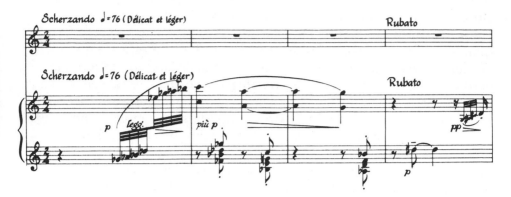

4-27. Debussy, *Trois poèmes de Stéphane Mallarmé, No. 3, Eventail*, measures 1–4. Copyright © 1913, Durand S. A. Editions Musicales (and/or United Music Publishers). Used by permission of the publisher. Theodore Presser Company, sole representative U.S.A.

4-28

The poem "Autre éventail" centers around the fan of Mallarmé's young daughter Geneviève, who, besides her immortalization in this poem and Debussy's song, also had the honor of sitting for a portrait by the American painter James McNeill Whistler. She is the "rêveuse" who moves the fan in the twilight air:

O rêveuse, pour que je plonge
Au pur délice sans chemin,
Sache, par un subtil mensonge,
Garder mon aile dans ta main.

Une fraîcheur de crépuscule
Te vient à chaque battement
Dont le coup prisonnier recule
L'horizon délicatement.

Vertige! voici que frissone
L'espace comme un grand baiser
Qui, fou de naître pour personne,
Ne peut jaillir ni s'apaiser.

Sens-tu le paradis farouche
Ainsi qu'un rire enseveli
Se couler du coin de ta bouche
Au fond de l'unanime pli!

Le sceptre des rivages roses
Stagnants sur les soirs d'or, ce l'est,
Ce blanc vol fermé que tu poses
Contre le feu d'un bracelet.[46]

Here "oh dreamer" and "(you) know" are isolated, in unique Mallarméan fashion, by commas, and the two phrases form the basic action of the poem: "Dreamer know." What should the dreamer know? With a subtle twisting of words, with a "subtil mensonge," the fan is able to turn the universe upside down and place itself at the center. As Littré tells us, a *mensonge* is not only a "lie" but also a literary term meaning "a fiction."[47] The fan argues a "subtle fiction" in "Autre éventail" and this is what the "rêveuse" must know. Both *battement* and *coup* have musical connotations in Littré. Thus, we might translate the second stanza as: "A freshness of twilight comes to you with each pulse [of the fan] in which the imprisoned beat holds back the horizon delicately." The "mensonge" has begun. The horizon is now manipulated by the fan. The presence and absence of space are subject to the beat of Geneviève's "éventail."

"Vertige!" exclaims the fan. *Vertige* is figuratively an "égarrement des sens" (a bewilderment of the senses) in Littré.[48] It is the sensation of randomness, pointlessness, the "pur delice" of existing "sans chemin." It is the "shiver of space" which is like a "grand kiss that, mad to be born for no one, cannot spout forth or subside." The fan's movement is born without destiny, empty of meaning, yet it holds the horizon in its "wing" and it makes "space" for no reason. The "fold" ("pli") of the fan is "unanimous" in that its presence is ubiquitous, even to the point where the youthful energy of the young Geneviève runs from the end of her mouth to its base ("au fond de l'unanime pli"). In "Un Coup de dés," which is filled with linguistic echoes of the shorter "Autre éventail," the dice of "le maître" take the place of the fan, and at the feet of the dice-thrower, the horizon is "unanime" ("à ses pieds / de l'horizon unanime").

The last stanza recalls the dense imagery of "L'Après-midi d'un faune." Impossible images create an atmosphere that evokes the interplay of light and air around the fan and the girl. "The scepter of roseated shores stagnant on the gold evenings" is contingent upon the fan. In fact, this scepter is the fan ("ce l'est"). The fan, even more than the "roseated shores stagnant on the golden evenings," is a scepter because it functions as a kind of baton (Littré uses the phrase "bâton du commandement" in the beginning of the entry for *sceptre*).[49] The "bâton" leads the distribution of space with its "closed, white light" that Geneviève "places against the fire of a bracelet."

Debussy hides, once again, the metric conventions in his setting of the words and tries to do justice to their more intrinsic flow. "Sache," for example, is given its own major third, way from the rest of the text. However, "sache" and "songe" of "mensonge" have exactly the same notes—the B-sharp to G-sharp major third. Debussy, then, agrees with my interpretation, for he has clearly connected the thought "know the lie/fiction" in his music. Did the composer also make a pun or "songe" (dream) within "mensonge" and suggesting, then, "Dreamer, know the lie/dream"? Above all, Debussy does not bind Mallarmé's quatrain with external couplings. Each expression of each line is free and independent.

The tonal and harmonic ambiguity in Debussy's music for "Autre éventail" is so extensive that it rivals the preserialistic writings of Schoenberg's *Buch der hängenden Gärten.* The old harmonies resound in individual instances like isolated artifacts, but they no longer have a unifying function. Debussy picks up a sound of the

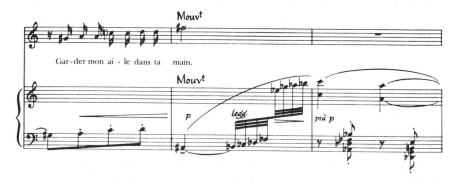

4-29. *Eventail*, measures 11–13. Copyright © 1913, Durand S. A. Editions Musicales and/or United Music Publishers). Used by permission of the publisher. Theodore Presser Company, sole representative U.S.A.

older harmony as he needs it, as he travels along his meandering way, much as Picasso or Duchamp pick up artifacts to make a "ready-made." Unity is preserved, not by harmony but by the recurrence of small ideas. Before the second quatrain is heard, the fan motive is sounded once again (see figure 4-29). And Debussy will need the figure one more time, before "le sceptre des rivages roses," the last quatrain of the poem.

Played without accompaniment, the melodic setting for the second stanza is as atonal as anything found in the *Pierrot lunaire* of Schoenberg. However, Debussy, with the mastery of a magician of harmony, slyly turns an A-flat into a G-sharp, the third of an E-major chord. Thus, he prepares the ear for a long series of E pedals over a span of six measures (see figure 4-30). Debussy's harmonic inversion, moving from the foreign A-flat to the E-majorish sounds, is an act of compositional virtuosity. Moreover, it expresses

4-30. *Eventail*, measures 18–24. Copyright © 1913, Durand S. A. Editions Musicales (and/or United Music Publishers). Used by permission of the publisher. Theodore Presser Company, sole representative U.S.A.

the inverted logic of the fan, which is now the center of the universe and holds back the horizon ("recule l'horizon délicatement").

"Vertige!" is distinguished in Debussy's music by a splash of chromatic color reminiscent of his piano prelude of 1912, *Feux d'artifice*. In both cases, chromaticism expresses the dazzling of the senses, the disorienting of the mind. The rapid movements of the notes now express the "frisson" of "space," just as they render the "frisson" of the fireworks in *Feux d'artifice*. The total harmonic ambiguity perfectly fits the emptiness of the space that is "mad at being born for no one."

The stifled laugh, which ripples from the corner of Geneviève's mouth to the "unanimous fold," is accompanied by pedals on F and E-flat, and, most importantly, the fluttering effect of the long four-bar trill on G and A (see figure 4-31). The trill unfolds into a reiteration of the fan motive, which is now heard for the last time.

4-31. *Eventail*, measures 40–42. Copyright © 1913, Durand S. A. Editions Musicales (and/or United Music Publishers). Used by permission of the publisher. Theodore Presser Company, sole representative U.S.A.

The coloristic harmonies that accompany "le sceptre des rivages roses / stagnants sur les soirs d'or" prefigure the free sketching of natural sounds in Olivier Messiaen's *Catalogue d'oiseaux*, yet their parallelism, once again, is characteristic of medieval organum, part of the prehistory of nineteenth-century European music. To free sound from convention, Debussy went both forward and backward in time. On top of all this, he also managed to write these unusual sonorities in a periodic form (see figure 4-32). The rhythmical symmetry and harmonic equivalence between the fourth and eighth bars of the passage (in spite of the enharmonic spellings) make these final chords into a hypotactic phrase. But it is alien here. It is to be played "doux et lointain," and it, too, evokes. It provides the moody vision of "rivages stagnants" ("stagnant shores") on the "evenings of gold." The melodic line for the passage, moreover, does not correspond at all to the period, but resembles the freedom of Schoenbergian *Sprechstimme*.

4-32. *Eventail,* measures 50–57. Copyright © 1913, Durand S. A. Editions Musicales (and/or United Music Publishers). Used by permission of the publisher. Theodore Presser Company, sole representative U.S.A.

The E pedal surfaces in the last bars of *Éventail* once again. Debussy, like Mallarmé, is always just as much a craftsman who has mastered a tradition as he is a revolutionary. Just as Mallarmé disguises his freedom within the dictates of rhyme and meter, Debussy allows an E tonality to glow softly in our ears in the final seconds of the piece. The B pedal in the final measure of the preceding period is transformed into a dominant pitch. Using a technique that would suit an old conservative like Mozart's rival Salieri, Debussy falls into the key of E minor. There are even two bars of introduction, making the music sound as if it were about to slip into a rendition of a French folk song (see figure 4-33).

4-33. *Eventail*, measures 59–60. Copyright © 1913, Durand S. A. Editions Musicales (and/or United Music Publishers). Used by permission of the publisher. Theodore Presser Company, sole representative U.S.A.

Actually, the E pedal here is no surprise. It is either present or implied throughout the entire composition. In the same way, Debussy juxtaposes a D-flat pedal against the strains of the *Marseilleise* in the last measures of *Feux d'artifice*. D-flat, which has been making a latent bid as a tonal center throughout the entire composition, wins in the end (see figure 4-34). But the flirtation with a tonality, in both cases, can only be clearly identified during the final bars of music. These are instances, once again, of the master tipping his hat and winking his eye at the arbiters of convention. For only a musician who has years of experience and pours over the scores of *Éventail* and *Feux d'artifice* can uncover their hidden tonalities, and the listener who can hear the importance of D-flat in the prelude or E in the song on the first hearing in the concert hall is probably, even today, nonexistent. Tonality is to Debussy as rhyme is to Mallarmé, and meter, which is flouted by both artists, is also preserved by both artists. The secret pleasure, moreover, of uncovering the real tensions between tradition and innovation is accessible only to the initiated.

In spite of Wagner's enormous importance, his high Romanticism should never be confused with the Symbolist aesthetic of Mallarmé and Debussy. The surfaces of Wagner's art are carefully designed to take in a mass audience, while in Mallarmé and Debussy, the refinement of their elliptical styles seals the work of art in a private zone, where it is chaste, untouched by the knowing hands of decorum, or the innocent hands of the naïve, waiting for an interpreter who can unravel its secret meanings and savor its delicious ambiguities.

4-34. *Preludes* for piano, Book 2, No. 12, *Feux d'artifice*. Copyright © 1913, Durand S. A. Editions Musicales (and/or United Music Publishers). Used by permission of the publisher. Theodore Presser Company, sole representative U.S.A.

5. The Book of the Hanging Gardens

Is *Das Buch der hängenden Gärten* (The Book of the Hanging Gardens), Schoenberg's settings of fifteen poems by Stephan George, a work of crisis? Carl Schorske, in *Fin-de-Siècle Vienna,* includes a brief discussion of the *Georgelieder,* Opus 15, in his chapter entitled "Explosion in the Garden: Kokoschka and Schoenberg."[1] Because of the massive scope of his historical study, Schorske does not attend to the interrelations of poetry and music in the *Georgelieder* in a detailed fashion, but only makes some important general remarks about the cycle, placing the cycle properly in its cultural milieu:

> Older by twelve years than Kokoschka, Schoenberg had been more deeply involved than the painter with the aesthetic movement of the fin de siècle. He shared with his older contemporaries, intellectual pioneers of Vienna's elite—Hofmannsthal, Freud, Klimt, and Ernst Mach—a diffuse sense that all is flux, that the boundary between ego and world is permeable. For him as for them, the firm traditional coordinates of ordered time and space were losing their reliability, perhaps even their truth.[2]

Schoenberg's music for the cycle is an art of the subjective, an art that is the antithesis of the kind of objective music of the old "hierarchical tonal order," a music built out of an ordered system of interdependent "triads."[3] We have already traced in detail the origins of the subversion of this old "order," which Schorske describes perhaps too briefly, but quite eloquently. As Schorske sums it up, the "old hierarchical tonal order" of "Western music" was built on the "authority," "stability," and "repose" of the tonal triad.[4] Schorske is referring to the rationalized system of describing musical sound that we have called functional tonal harmony. Working against the ordering, authoritative principle of the triad in the tonal system was the concept of modulation, Schorske adds. Modulation amounted to "a heightened state of ambiguity."[5] Wagner began to break this dialectic apart with his notion of continuous melody. Schoenberg continued the deconstruction of the old dialectic in the *Georgelieder* by writing music that seemed to be continuously modulating, music that lacked clearly defined cadential punctuation and tonal resolution.[6]

If Schoenberg wrote a completely subjective kind of music, then the music of Rameau was completely objective. "Not for nothing," Schorske writes, "was Rameau the court musician of Louis XV, the clearest and most uncompromising theorist of the 'laws of harmony.' "[7] It is these so-called "laws," "laws" that had been so profoundly challenged by Wagner and Debussy, which Schoenberg finally overthrows in *The Book of the Hanging Gardens*. Sound no longer is functional at all in this work; it is free.

In George's poems, as in the poems of Mallarmé, one finds the dissolution of the old narrative and ratiocinative backbone of the lyric. Like "L'Après-midi d'un faune," George's *Book of the Hanging Gardens* is a complex exploration of eroticism in verse, and this exploration, like the faun's, takes place inside the mind. The poetics of ambiguity serves admirably as a means of rendering eroticism as viewed from an orientation of almost total subjectivity. When Schorske writes that George's poems are "sturdy in meter and sound" and thus provide a "firm poetic frame" for Schoenberg, he is certainly right, but only in the sense that rhythmically and prosodically the poems are quite traditional and, in fact, almost stolidly conservative.[8] However, George also employs the semantic innovations of Symbolism, and, actually, the lyrics are quite advanced and modern in that sense. The poems display a Symbolist voice in their command of ambiguity, in their systematized negation of direct discourse, in their consistent negation of expected combinations of signifiers, and in their creation of the interacting vibrations of semantically ambiguous symbols.

George's garden is not described as a refined, ordered place of repose, but the garden—a fantastic, exotic paradise—is evoked gradually, with suggestive details added one by one. Each signifier that evokes the garden contributes to the overall suggestion of a wild, uncontrolled locale where fantastic things may occur. George avoids a clear and logical description of the garden in the first poem; the "leafy thickets," the "snow-yielding stars," the "spitting mythical beasts," the marble basins do not fit together to form a cogent whole.

Unterm schutz von dichten blättergründen
Wo von sternen feine flocken schneien
Sachte stimmen ihre leiden künden
Fabeltiere aus den braunen schlünden
Strahlen in die marmorbecken speien

Draus die kleinen bäche klagend eilen;
Kamen kerzen das gesträuch entzünden
Weisse formen das gewässer teilen.[9]

Furthermore, like Mallarmé, George evokes the inhabitants of his topos metonymically. We see parts of the whole first. Later, we will see more, but here the inhabitants of the garden, or perhaps they are habitués or one-time visitors (we cannot be sure at this time), are only evoked by the "candles" that "come" and the "white forms" that "divide" the "water."

The trochaic pentameter of the lyric is, as Schorske would agree, highly regular. It is so regular, in fact, that it creates a kind of monotonous, prosaic quality. No words are heightened or underscored in an obvious way and the droning of the *en* sound and the *m* and *n* consonants creates a kind of hum that approximates the nasality of French verse. George, too, does not capitalize the German nouns, a stylistic trait that can be construed as a tribute to the French Symbolist poets he admired. But the best and most comprehensive proof of the presence of French poetry in the mind of George is the translation, by Jean Cassou and Max Deutsch, of the poetry from German into French. Here we see and hear the old symbols dressed in French garb once again:

Sous la touffe épaisse des feuillages
Où filtre une neige fine d'étoiles
Douces voix, racontez vos souffrances,
Dans les vasques des monstres fantasques
Ouvrent de sombres gorges rayonnantes
Et la plainte des ruisseaux s'écoule:
Etincelles, embrasez les ombres,
Blanches formes, divisez les ondes.[10]

The *Georgelieder* and "L'Après-midi d'un faunc" have similar loci: a lush grove bordering on a body of water. But what a great contrast there is between the music that comes out of those two groves! The sounds of the faun's flute watering the thickets with chords is clearly expressed in the fluid, seamless music of Debussy.

George's topos, if anything, is even more ambiguous than Mallarmé's, for it is evoked in the title of the collection of verse in a baffling way. "Hanging gardens" are, after all, carefully controlled and nurtured by the hand of man, and yet these particular gardens are also a wild and dangerous place. They become increasingly dangerous, in fact, as they take on the role of reflecting the psychological trauma of the lover who narrates the poems.

. This ambiguous topos generates an entirely new kind of music. Here Schoenberg achieves what Adorno has referred to in his *Philosophy of Modern Music* as a "transcendent negation" of tonality, a kind of enforced yet noble suffering that demands continuous attention and is meant to disturb and unsettle us as we listen. For Adorno, Wagner's art practiced a comparatively shallow method of "representing the passions."[11] This concept, as Adorno clearly knows, has its origins in the seventeenth-century *Affektenlehre*.[12] Schoenberg merely carries the development along from the shallower *espressivo* style to a deeper, more subjective expression:

> Passions are no longer simulated, but rather genuine emotions of the unconscious—of shock, of trauma—are registered without disguise through the medium of music. These emotions attack the taboos of form because these taboos subject such emotions to their own censure, rationalizing them and transforming them into images.[13]

Whether Adorno's excessively ornamented yet insightful observations on Schoenberg can be proved is an important question. However, the answer to that question does not affect the ability of Adorno's words to create the milieu out of which Schoenberg's art emerged. Adorno, as a student of Schoenberg, as a philosopher, composer, and pianist, as a native of Frankfurt, had a unique vantage point from which he viewed historical conditions in the late nineteenth century, the century that generated the modern sensibility. That sensibility, as both Schorske and Adorno concur, was born out of a sense of crisis.

What sounds at first like a D pedal in the opening bars of the music for this first poem turns out to be a nebulous flirtation with a number of tonalities. Which will dominate? D? F-sharp? F-natural? E? Each irregular phrase is characterized, too, by huge intervallic leaps at the end, which disorient the ear. Schoenberg thus prepares for the "thick leafy thickets" with a cloudy, dissonant introduction in the piano (see figure 5-1). The major and minor seconds that had been used to create such revolutionary coloristic effects in

Debussy usually could be explained in terms of inversions of seventh chords. Here, however, they are free, independent sounds, well outside the descriptive rules of the old music. In general, Schoenberg's music for Opus 15, like music before the Baroque, is a music of intervals. Here, the intervals are completely free. The sounds of the second, the major and minor third, echoing in different positions, transposed in recurring thematic patterns, resound in our ears. Schoenberg does not use a fixed tonal orientation of any kind. Nothing is absolute. All is relative.

5-1. Schoenberg, *Das Buch der hängenden Gärten (Georgelieder)*, No. 1, measures 1–8

As the garden fills with forms and objects the music becomes more animated. On "sachte stimmen," for example, the piano contributes an arresting interjection on D-sharp which grows into a long and fluid atonal line. The arabesques become more animated as the "spitting *Fabeltiere*" appear in the garden as well. The piece as a whole reaches a climax on "kamen Kerzen" when the soprano sings a high G-sharp and the earlier filigree consolidates into thick chordlike clusters in the accompaniment (see figure 5-2).

5-2. *Georgelieder,* No. 1, measure 17

Chords resembling the sounds of the earlier music fall under the hand in the piano part of the *Georgelieder.* Although they look, sound, and feel like the old sonorities, they are forms without function (see figure 5-3). We cannot help but associate them with diminished chords or the minor chords of the past. This certainly is part of the crisis of the *Georgelieder,* a crisis that drove Schoenberg toward his theory of twelve-tone music, which he formulated a little over a decade later. The piece ends with echoing minor thirds—G-sharp to E-sharp—which are dissonant and disturbing enough. Schoenberg negates even these repetitions and equivalences, though, with the two chords in the right hand (see figure 5-4).

In the first song, Schoenberg does not bother to emphasize the trochaic pentameter of the poetry in any way, and, in fact, he does everything he can to avoid its metrical impositions as he constructs his own rhythms. The *en* sound, at the end of each line in the poem, forms a weak, feminine ending. Schoenberg allows this to carry over into his setting and he writes descending patterns of pitches on "gründen," "schneien," "künden," "schlünden," "speien,"

5-3. *Georgelieder*, No. 1, measures 14–15

5-4. *Georgelieder*, No. 1, measures 20–24

"eilen," "entzünden," and "teilen." The accented syllable is always given a strong part of a beat, while the weak syllable always comes after the beat. If anything, this reinforces the sound of the free, descending interval as the thematic kernel of the piece. This pattern first appears in the piano in bars two and four and evolves from the G-sharp to G-natural (minor second) to C-sharp to A-sharp (minor third). There is no trace of the old periodicity in Schoenberg's melodic line in spite of these unifying elements.

In the second poem, we learn that the hanging gardens are made up of varying sections of groves and flowery meadows. One also finds porticos with many-colored tiles, slender storks with rustling beaks, ponds teeming with fish, rows of gently gleaming birds "trilling," and golden reeds that murmur.

Hain in diesen paradiesen
Wechselt ab mit blütenwiesen
Hallen buntbemalten fliesen.
Schlanker störche schnäbel kräuseln
Teiche die von fischen schillern
Vögel-reihen matten scheines
Auf den schiefen firsten trillern
Und die goldnen binsen säuseln—
Doch mein traum verfolgt nur eines.[14]

Once again, the echoes of Mallarmé's "bosquet" are clearly discernable if one peers for a moment at the Deutsch-Cassou translation.

Dans ces limbes les bocages
Succèdent aux galeries claires,
Les gazons aux dalles.
Le bec des cigognes frise l'onde,
le poisson scintille. L'ombre
d'une bande d'ailes sur le toit
dessine un trille,
et les joncs dorés murmurent.
Je ne rêve qu'à mon rêve.[15]

In Mallarmé, too, the reeds ("joncs, roseaux") surround the faun and furnish sound and music and the branches of the grove are "many" and "subtle" ("en maint rameau subtil"). George goes out of his way, though, to create an aura of wild lushness and fertility in his hanging gardens, perhaps on an even grander scale than Mallarmé's topos. The lushness of the hanging gardens evokes the thematic eroticism of the poems. In the second poem, though, they only serve as a foil for the epigrammatic last line: "Yet my dream pursues only one thing." What might that one thing be? George, invoking the hermeneutic code, will never tell us clearly in unadorned unambiguous language. Nevertheless, the "one goal" will be gradually evoked as we continue to explore the gardens in the succeeding poems.

Schoenberg continues to write free triadic structures to accompany his wandering, chromatic melodic line. These triads are old sounds, from the old functional system, but here they appear without function. Or do they have a function? The ghost of European tonality seems to haunt Schoenberg here. A glance at the setting of the text alone shows significant couplings built around the pitch of B (see figure 5-5). The B–A–B–A pattern occurs twice, on "this paradise" and "golden murmuring reeds." Furthermore, the pitches for "bunt bemalten fliesen" lead right to the B-major scale, from F-sharp to B. On "fliesen" too, Schoenberg writes what looks like a I $^6_3$ chord in B major (see figure 5-6). Finally, on the lyrical, haunting pianissimo for "goldnen binsen säuseln," Schoenberg seems to combine the old tonic and dominant functions, but he sounds the two chords at once and does not resolve them. The skeleton of the V chord in the right hand does not cede to the B–E–D-sharp resolution in the left. Nevertheless, all of the pitches necessary for a rich I$_9$ triad are sounded in this bar: B–D-sharp–F-sharp–A-sharp–C-sharp (see figure 5-7). Schoenberg's negation of tonality here, however, is ingenious and almost brutal, if we compare it to the impish flirtations of Debussy.

5-5. *Georgelieder*, No. 2, measures 1–14

5-6. *Georgelieder*, No. 2, measure 5

5-7. *Georgelieder*, No. 2, measures 9–10

The new chord of the fourth beat after "säuseln" destroys all hope of B major for the rest of the piece. This is an ideal preparation for George's disturbing epigram. The dream here is in opposition to the beauty of the gardens and is not yet one with the lushness of the gardens. Schoenberg's negation of B major renders this poetic idea in musical sound. Tonality, quite literally, has been deconstructed here, but the old music echoes within Schoenberg's revolutionary sounds. Does one not hear the rhythms of Beethoven's Opus 110 once again in the rhythms of Schoenberg's accompaniment (see figures 5-8 and 5-9)?

5-8. *Georgelieder*, No. 2, measures 5–8

5-9. Beethoven, Piano Sonata in A-Flat Major, Opus 110, Moderato cantabile, measures 100–104

In the third poem, the notion of the beloved appears. The gardens are her "preserve," we learn in the first line. Schoenberg's dense, volatile music here expresses the intense anxiety of the *ich* or "I." The poem and the music both now focus on the personal disquiet of the lover and not on the gardens.

> Als neuling trat ich ein in dein gehege
> Kein staunen war vorher in meinen mienen
> Kein wunsch in mir eh ich dich blickte rege.
> Der jungen hände faltung sieh mit huld
> Erwähle mich zu denen die dir dienen
> Und schone mit erbarmender geduld
> Den der noch strauchelt auf so fremdem stege.[16]

Both the music and the poetry build up to the plea for attention and patience: "Choose me to serve you, yet choose with pitying patience." The *ich* is an adolescent and begs for his naiveté to be overlooked.

Schoenberg makes the iambic rhythm of the poem a part of the music, for he captures the skip of the iamb in the dotted rhythm of the thematic material. The rhythm and the small motive distinguished by it (see figure 5-10) bind the piece together. The right hand repeats the motive literally at the end of the song (see figure 5-11). Schoenberg augments the idea and closes with what would have been described, within the old functional harmonic system, as a I $^6_4$ chord (see figure 5-12). Once again, though, Schoenberg gives the old triads new contexts, by avoiding all of the old periodic couplings and causing the old sounds to occur in new places. Periodicity is avoided in the treatment of the dotted motive, which is systematically augmented and spread across the bar lines in different ways. The harmonies, out of their rhythmic contexts, sound fresh.

The poetry and the lover move closer together in the fourth poem:

> Da meine lippen reglos sind und brennen
> Beacht ich erst wohin mein fuss geriet:
> In andrer herren prächtiges gebiet.
> Noch war vielleicht mir möglich mich zu trennen
> Da schien es dass durch hohe gitterstäbe
> Der blick vor dem ich ohne lass gekniet
> Mich fragend suchte oder zeichen gäbe.[17]

5-10. *Georgelieder*, No. 3, measures 1–2

5-11. *Georgelieder*, No. 3, measure 23

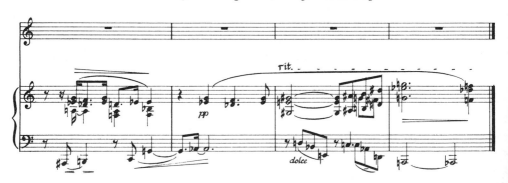

5-12. *Georgelieder*, No. 3, measures 23–26

The still lips of the *ich* burn with passion. He waits before the iron trellises of the gardens and muses over his trespassing in the magnificent terrain of other "herren." Who are these other "herren"? George never identifies them. Clearly, though, he wants us to associate the gardens, sealed by high trellises, with the beloved. They are both, in some way, officially or morally, forbidden to the poet. Both the beloved and the gardens are "terrain" or "property" on which the poet ought not to tread. He does, nevertheless. A glance that seemed to seek him out or give him a sign ("zeichen") was all the provocation he needed. In the forbidden paradise, the lover now waits.

In the fifth poem the lover still awaits the arrival of the mysterious "she" in the gardens. In Mallarmé, the cheek ("la joue") of the faun, through its labor ("trouble"), created the music of the nymphs. Here the cheek of the lover spreads out on the floor of the garden to make a stool for the pretty sole of the beloved. This is a metaphor of agony and desperation.

> Saget mir auf welchem pfade
> Heute sie vorüberschreite—
> Dass ich aus der reichsten lade
> Zarte seidenweben hole
> Rose pflücke und viole
> Dass ich meine wange breite
> Schemel unter ihrer sohle.[18]

Schoenberg chooses a particularly meandering melodic line with large contours to suit the tentative, unassured style of the lover.

Adorno refers to the "lyrical warmth" of the song. Yet the lyricism is qualified by the continual avoidance of tonal stability.[19] For example, the lovely passage "Rose pflücke und viole" seems to yearn for a cadence (see figure 5-13). The rhythm is repeated three times on the notes E and F, once in the piano and twice in the vocal phrase. These repetitions provide a temporary sense of orientation and stability. Will the music subside with a long expected resolution, perhaps to E-flat major, F minor, or D-flat major? After all, the sound of the old B-flat dominant seventh is heard—although it is misspelled in the Wagnerian fashion—when one accounts for all the pitches heard on the last syllable of "Rose."

Actually, Schoenberg is once again using the gambit of the old misplaced dominant chord first devised by Wagner in the *Tristan*

5-13. *Georgelieder*, No. 5, measures 10–12

prelude. Is this a hidden homage to Wagner? Even the first three pitches are the same, except for the fact that their order is reversed: A–F–E becomes E–F–A. The rhythm, too, becomes suspiciously similar if we take the trouble to look at the two excerpts side by side (see figures 5-14 and 5-15). In both cases, we have a long suspended appoggiatura, which seems to have no place to which it can resolve. The dominant seventh sound built on B-flat in the Schoenberg is only slightly more veiled than the unexpected dominant seventh on E in the Wagner. Furthermore, if the canonic imitation of the vocal line in the piano had been carried out into a full, literal repetition, Schoenberg might not have been able to avoid a tonal solution. Instead, he alters the melodic material and absorbs it into a new pattern of nonfunctional chords. The disturbing image of the cheek/stool is thus given a fittingly dissonant realization in music (see figure 5-16).

5-14. Wagner, *Tristan und Isolde,* Prelude, measures 1–3

In the sixth poem the lover is "dead" to all tasks except that of summoning the beloved with his senses, and his senses become dead to the gardens, too, at this point. The book undergoes an interlude of thematic transition that focuses on the turbulent adolescent emotions of the lover. The gardens, in fact, now disappear

5-15. *Georgelieder, No. 5, measures 10–11*

5-16. *Georgelieder, No. 5, measures 13–18*

from view for the next four poems (poems six through nine), which deal solely with the anxieties and anticipations of the lover. Schoenberg, for these four portions of his "book," writes an even more atonal, pointillistic kind of music which prefigures his serialist pieces of the 1920s (especially the *Piano Suite,* Opus 25). Paradoxically, the four poems offer the smallest amount of evidence of the French Symbolist *écriture* of all the fifteen lyrics set by Schoenberg in the *Book of the Hanging Gardens.*

> Jedem werke bin ich fürder tot.
> Dich mir nahzurufen mit den sinnen
> Neue reden mit dir auszuspinnen
> Dienst und lohn gewährung und verbot
> Von allen dingen ist nur dieses not.[20]

In fact, ten of the twelve pitch possibilities of traditional European music are sounded in the sixteenth bar of the sixth piece. Note the dodecaphonic sound, too, of the piano passage, which Schoenberg marks "etwas flüchtig," and which introduces the last line of the poem (see figure 5-17).

5-17. *Georgelieder,* No. 6, measure 16

Anaphora helps to express the almost Baudelairean agony of the seventh lyric. "Fear and hope" prevent "rest and sleep," as his words are "stretched" into "sighs." Schoenberg tends to avoid the standard clichés of "tone painting" here, except for the huge intervallic drop from G natural to F-sharp in "seufzer dehnen" (see figure 5-18). Composers tend to treat anaphora in poetry as anaphora in music. They do this by repeating the same pitch to emphasize the repetition of the same word. Schoenberg sets the last four lines—which begin, respectively, with "das ich," "das mein," "das ich," and "das ich"—by starting on four different metrical positions in the bar. Furthermore, he only repeats one pitch—D—but this coupling on "das" only introduces two highly disparate phrases. The integrity of his "musical prose" is thus preserved. Finally, note the ghost of Beethoven, who haunts all of Schoenberg, as it appears here once again in the rhythms of Beethoven's Opus 110 (see figure 5-19).

5-18. *Georgelieder*, No. 7, measure 4

5-19. *Georgelieder*, No. 7, measures 7–8

"If I do not touch your waist today, the thread of my soul will snap." Perhaps "waist" is a better choice for "leib" here than S. S. Prawer's "body" because "leib," which can function both in its metonymic sense as "waist" or "womb" and in its larger sense as "body," has more erotic suggestiveness when it is taken to signify the part and not the whole. Also, the suggestion of the part, not the whole, is more within the Symbolist mode, as we have seen.

> Wenn ich heut nicht deinen leib berühre
> Wird der faden meiner seele reissen
> Wie zu sehr gespannte sehne.
> Liebe zeichen seien trauerflöre
> Mir der leidet seit ich dir gehöre.
> Richte ob mir solche qual gebühre

Kühlung sprenge mir dem fieberheissen
Der ich wankend draussen lehne.[21]

Schoenberg's setting of this poem, with its *rasch* tempo, is the most frantic, aggressive, disjunct, and volatile of all the songs up until now.

The ninth poem is one of desperate supplication. The Beethoven Opus 110 still lurks behind the music in a tonally deconstructed form. The pleading of the lover is given a sizable six-bar prelude, which introduces the mood of the words. This, of course, is well within the tradition of the German *Lieder* cycle. Note, however, how the old rhythms of Beethoven have been given such an Expressionistic intensity in their new, dissonant suit of clothes (see figures 5-20 and 5-21). Not only the rhythms are similar here. Even the pitches are in the same general range of the piano. Furthermore, Schoenberg writes what sounds like a disguised four-bar periodic structure. Nevertheless, without the old external couplings of harmonic tonality, we cannot label Schoenberg's passage as a periodic structure, whereas Beethoven's, of course, clearly is one.

The gardens reappear in the tenth lyric. This lushness now combines with the expectant psyche of the lover, which has been evoked alone—without the topos of the gardens—in the final four poems. The two poles—garden and lover—merge to suggest a kind of aesthetic eroticism worthy of Mallarmé's best writing. Is this a lyric of consummation? The poet, waiting, becomes consumed by the beauty of the gardens. The flowers are a bed—both in the sense of the "flower bed" and the bed as a place of sexual activity. The purple black thorns that enclose the bed suggest the feelings of eroticism and danger in the mind of the lover through the images of the garden:

Das schöne beet betracht ich mir im harren
Es ist umzäunt mit purpurn-schwarzem dorne.
Drin ragen kelche mit geflecktem sporne
Und sammtgefiederte geneigte farren
Und flockenbüschel wassergrün und rund
Und in der mitte glocken weiss und mild—
Von einem odem ist ihr feuchter mund
Wie süsse frucht vom himmlischen gefild.[21]

The garden is now a cornucopia of fertility. Within it, towering

5-20. Beethoven, Opus 110, measures 1–4

5-21. *Georgelieder*, No. 9, measures 1–8

flower caps shoot up, sloping ferns glisten, white bellflowers tanta-
lize with aromatic fragrances. All of this is reminiscent of Mallarmé's "verdures dédiant leur vignes à des fontaines." Assonance
and both internal and external rhyme bind this lyric together in a
rather conventional way, but, once again, it is the content that
makes the poem a Symbolist one. The subtle, indirect yet undeniable association between garden and lover is a Symbolist technique.
The garden is not only a place in which the act of love occurs; it
actually becomes one with the act of love and is inextricably bound
to our understanding of this act of love.

If Beethoven's spirit leaves momentarily in this song,
Wagner's certainly takes its place. Schoenberg, first of all, avoids all

of the "square phrasing" inherent in the poem as he formulates his own rhythms for the words. Moreover, Wagner's great love scene from act 2, scene 2 of *Tristan und Isolde* also takes place in a flower bed. George may not have had this in mind when he wrote the poem, but Schoenberg certainly did when he wrote the music. The gently pulsating triplet groups, which create such likely substitutions for the sensual and dreamlike embrace of Tristan and Isolde, resurface here in a pantonal form (see figure 5-22). Also, the slowly rising chromatic line that permeates *Tristan und Isolde* appears once again in Schoenberg's song (see figure 5-23). In terms of pitch, rhythm, and texture the similarity is far too great to be dismissed as a mere coincidence. Schoenberg uses the Wagnerian passage in his bass line (figure 5-24), in the treble (figure 5-25), and as a contrapuntal figure (figure 5-26). If Schoenberg had resolved "süsse" (see figure 5-26) as if the D-sharp were an appoggiatura (see figure 5-27), we would be back in the world of *Tristan*.

5-22. *Georgelieder*, No. 10, measures 16–19.

5-23. Wagner, *Tristan und Isolde*, act 2, scene 3, measures 371–74

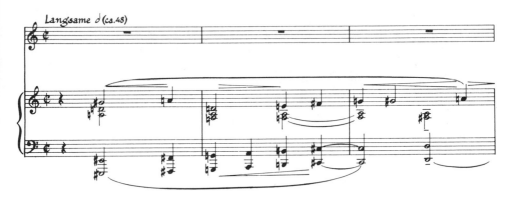

5-24. *Georgelieder*, No. 10, measures 1–3

5-25. *Georgelieder*, No. 10, measures 11–13

5-26. *Georgelieder*, No. 5, measures 23–28

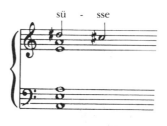

5-27

Schoenberg, of course, did not resolve that sonority or any other sonority in the piece with the old sense of coupling. An A-major chord on "süsse" would have constructed a much too obvious point of reference in relation to other sonorities in the tiny piece. It is this systematic negation of the old harmonic patterns that allowed Schoenberg to come so close, in his uniquely daring fashion, to composers like Beethoven and Wagner, and yet still remain original.

Writing on Schoenberg's music for the eleventh lyric, Adorno refers to the "pulsating pianissimo at the climax of the almost un-bearable expressive intensity" that comes with the words "als wir hinter dem beblümten tore."[23] Yet this is already a lyric of reminiscences, a lyric that is already recalling the intensity of the passion that has been spent. On the other hand, the previous lyric, the lyric of the fecund garden, was a lyric of the present. The passion of the lovers, then, is evoked through the imagery of the hanging gardens. There is no direct narration of an erotic act here. George leaves all that out and evokes it through his symbols. Only afterward were the lovers conscious of their "spurting breaths." After what? We must fill that in for ourselves:

> Als wir hinter dem beblümten tore
> Endlich nur das eigne hauchen spürten
> Warden uns erdachte seligkeiten?
>
> Ich erinnere dass wie schwache rohre
> Beide stumm zu beben wir begannen
> Wenn wir leis nur an uns rührten
> Und dass unsre augen rannen—
> So verbliebest du mir lang zu seiten.[24]

Perhaps Adorno is right about the "unbearable expressive intensity of the music." The piano introduction here is quite sizable and dramatic. Once again, sounds that in older contexts led to specific places now do not preshape the directions of musical events. A sonority—which sounds in measures two through four (see figure 5-28)—is just one half step away from an exact repetition of the familiar "Tristan" chord, although this bit of Wagnerian residue does not slip into a dominant on E as the original does (see figure 5-29).

5-28. Wagner, *Tristan und Isolde,* Prelude, measures 1–3.
Used by special arrangement with G. Schirmer, Inc.

5-29. *Georgelieder,* No. 11, measures 2–4

The chordal pattern of measures four and five, repeated toward the end of the piece in measure nineteen, seems to cry out for an F-sharp/G-flat minor resolution to the old-fashioned ear (see figure 5-30). Schoenberg does not write one, though. This anticadential treatment of sonorities that for decades in European music had always prepared the cadence gives Schoenberg's music the frightening "intensity" noted by Adorno. The C–D-flat–C-flat–D-flat pattern that follows the old precadential chord leaves us in a cloud of what Schorkse referred to as "heightened ambiguity." Finally, when Schoenberg adds the high E–F-sharp pianissimo, we are totally lost. Nevertheless, the effect is also completely hypnotic, and we have been prepared by the composer for the poet's soft words—"als wir hinter dem beblümten tore."

5-30. *Georgelieder,* No. 11, measures 4–7

The gardens, the topos of the erotic, are juxtaposed against the forboding condemnation of a disapproving society in the twelfth poem. "Shapeless shadows" move upon the wall that is the border between sensual paradise and society. The shadows signify the world outside in the largest sense. More specific are the watchmen who may come and find the lovers. Are the lovers in great danger? George distinctly raises this question but, as usual, does not answer it. The white sand before the town is suggested as a place of punishment for the lovers of the gardens. There their blood will be soaked up, quaffed by the barren ground.

> Wenn sich bei heilger ruh in tiefen matten
> Um unsre schläfen unsre hände schmiegen
> Verehrung lindert unsrer glieder brand:
> So denke nicht der ungestalten schatten
> Die an der wand sich auf und unter wiegen
> Der wächter nicht die rasch uns scheiden dürfen
> Und nicht dass vor der stadt der weisse sand
> Bereit ist unser warmes blut zu schlürfen.[25]

George sets the fertile gardens against the dry land before the community. The intimacy of the lovers is thus placed in the context of an overwhelming sense of disaster, as in many of Yeats's Symbolist lyrics of the 1890s and, for that matter, in much of the poetry of Maeterlinck as well.

The "éventail" of Mallarmé surfaces in the thirteenth lyric. This time, the beloved is holding it, as she leans against the silver willow. "Sparks" appear around her head, as they did around the nymphs ("fleurs des étincelles"). The bending willows and flowers strewn along the surface of the water create a first hint of the mutability of the gardens. The happiness of the stolen moments of love will be as fleeting as the flowers and vegetation of the hanging gardens, which eventually wither in the autumnal winds:

> Du lehnest wider eine silberweide
> Am ufer mit des fächers starren spitzen
> Umschirmest du das haupt dir wie mit blitzen
> Und rollst als ob du spieltest dein geschmeide.
> Ich bin im boot das laubegewölbe wahren
> In das ich dich vergeblich lud zu steigen
> Die weiden seh ich die sich tiefer neigen
> Und blumen die verstreut im wasser fahren.[26]

Note how Schoenberg follows George in weaving a long line of music out of the long line of verse. Neither composer nor poet is concerned with periodic differentiation here. Schoenberg catches the leaning of the woman, the motions of the fan, the sparks, the rocking boat, the rustling leaves in the wandering chromatic triplets of the melodic line.

In the fourteenth poem, George's lyricism approximates the sound of Verlaine. The notion of mutability, especially of the seasons, and the anxiety of the lovers combine here just as they do in Verlaine's "Chanson d'automne." If the tenth poem was one of consummation, this is an autumnal poem, one that expresses the dying splendor in the gardens after the ripening and fruition of passion. Dying garden and subsiding passion are one here. Using seasonal metaphors to describe the content of the poem in relation to the lovers is highly justified, of course, for George himself starts the correspondences between lovers and nature by embedding them so profoundly in the imagery of the gardens.

> Sprich nicht immer
> Von dem laub
> Windes raub
> Vom zerschellen
> Reifer quitten
> Von den tritten
> Der vernichter
> Spät im jahr
> Von dem zittern
> Der libellen
> In gewittern
> Und der lichter
> Deren flimmer
> Wandelbar.[27]

Whose are the "steps" of the "destroyers"? Are they watchmen coming to catch the lovers? Is it the sound of the wind? If it is the wind, it is not a "destroyer and preserver," as it is in Shelley's "Ode to the West Wind," but only a destroyer. Autumn brings only destruction here, not the hope of rebirth as well. In this, George shares the same fin-de-siècle sense of dread that we may discern in Maeterlinck. Also, the gardens project their imagery on the lovers. Lovers and gardens become intermingled in an ambiguous way in the discourse of the poem. This is a Symbolist approach to poetry. A Romantic would merely have projected the emotions of the lovers into the surrounding gardens, thereby establishing a typical analogical pact between man and nature. In this respect George's poem is even more truly Symbolist in nature than the very similar "Chanson d'automne" of Verlaine.

Schoenberg writes an elegant, understated setting for this

poem. Comparatively pointillistic and sparse, the accompaniment does not intrude upon the long, meandering melodic line here. This melodic line, in fact, forms an ingenious correspondence between text and music because it features a long descent from E-flat to F-sharp. This line dips, rises briefly, then continues its descent, and rises again just as dead leaves fall from trees. The irregular rhythms of the music preserve the gentle rocking motions of the lyric. Asymmetry serves to make the rhythmic flow natural and organic in a pattern that truly resembles leaves as they fall in the natural rhythm of the wind. The only pause is on the words "vernichter / spät im jahr," where the gentle patter rhythm is expanded into longer time values (quarter notes, and so forth) and where Schoenberg writes an old ninth chord built on A (but without a tonal function). With "von dem zittern," though, Schoenberg groups his text in four-note patterns, rather than the triplets of the $\frac{6}{8}$ meter. The piano has the triplets here. It is as if the pulse of the wind had changed slightly, jerking the leaves a little, up and down, until they finally fall still closer to the garden floor (see figure 5-31).

The lovers part in the last poem, and the gardens appear, in all their splendor, one more time in the first two lines. "She will leave forever," says the lover. That is all we know of the love affair. The rest of it is evoked through the breakup of the gardens. Tall flowers "turn pale" and "break" as do the "glassy ponds." The gardens become hostile to the stumbling lover, who pricks himself on some palm trees. The destroying winds are "unseeable hands" that chase the leaves around the gardens, thus making the "hissing" groan and "jerking" rattle of death. George's final line recalls Baudelaire's "quand le ciel bas et lourd pèse comme un couvercle." The night features a sky covered with clouds and air that is "schwül." *Schwül* is a particularly disturbing German word which suggests, among other things, the uneasy, the langorous, mugginess, being closed-in, and sweltering humidity. Nature, which houses the lover in a paradise throughout the *Book of the Hanging Gardens*, sweeps in upon the lover in the end and becomes an indifferent torturer.

The important piano introduction, which is twelve bars long, has the pained dignity of Beethoven's introduction for his last piano sonata, Opus 111. Is there not a remarkable similarity between the short-long rhythmic pattern of the two pieces (see figures 5-32 and 5-33)? One is reminded, too, of the recitative passage in Opus 110 (see figure 5-34). Beethoven's recitative precedes the *Arioso dolente* in A-flat minor, certainly one of the most tragic adagios in his

5-31. *Georgelieder*, No. 14, measures 1–11

5-32. Beethoven, Piano Sonata in C Minor, Opus 111, measures 1–2

5-33. Schoenberg, *Georgelieder*, No. 15, measures 1–6

5-34. Beethoven, Sonata in A-Flat Major, Opus 110, measures 1–4

oeuvre. Schoenberg's setting of the text of this final poem is no less tragic in mood. The pitches for "tempel pfad und beet" outline a dominant to tonic cadence, which ends on the beginning of the bar. This goes with the final evocation of the gardens in all of their beauty. Our ears, at this point, are so disoriented though, that it is difficult to recognize Schoenberg's subtle tribute to the old tonal convention (see figure 5-35). The piano, repeating its powerful introductory theme, interrupts this brief flirtation with the past. As the gardens break up, the music becomes denser, more dissonant, more rhythmically disjunct (see figure 5-36).

The piano introduction continuously takes on new importance as Schoenberg treats his atonal, asymmetrical theme with old variation techniques (see figure 5-37). And before the final words of the cycle—"die nacht ist überwölkt und schwül"—the theme surfaces in the piano yet again (see figure 5-38). Its distinctive dotted rhythms binds together the long eighteen-bar postlude which closes the song cycle and signifies the end of the gardens. In Schoenberg's *Book of the Hanging Gardens*, music alone, inspired by George's words, sounds the final notes of despair.

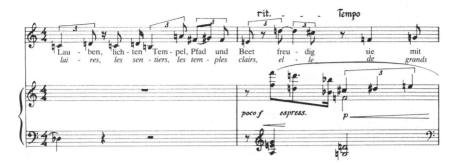

5-35. Schoenberg, *Georgelieder*, No. 15, measures 14–15

5-36. *Georgelieder*, No. 15, measures 19–22

5-37. *Georgelieder*, No. 15, measures 26–28

5-38. *Georgelieder*, No. 15, measures 29–31

6. The Lyric Play
and the Tone Poem

Great cultural movements that deeply affect developments in the arts do not simply disappear and give way to new
trends. Instead, their impact lingers and combines with new ideas.
This is certainly what happened in the late nineteenth century.
The cultural implications of Romanticism were on a larger scale,
perhaps, than any other period in the history of the West. Romanticism was a movement of the masses, and the growing network of
modern communication and transportation helped to spread its
ideas. Wagner, whose oeuvre makes up the high water mark of late
Romanticism came to symbolize the very idea of music towards the
end of the last century. Nevertheless, by the 1880s and 1890s, the
French, as we have seen, had instigated, in the fields of music and
literature, an important response to Romanticism, a response, indeed, that comprised the origins of modern art.

In Paris, in the nineties, late Romanticism and Symbolism
thrived together side by side. An account of the doings of Mallarmé and his friend and admirer Debussy during a week in May
1983 makes this quite clear. Debussy, an habitué of Mallarmé's salon on the Rue de Rome, accompanied Mallarmé to the Paris premiere of Wagner's *Walküre* on 13 May 1893.[1] Five days later, at the
Théâtre des Bouffes-Parisiens, they were together again. This time
they saw Lugné-Poe's production of Maeterlinck's Symbolist play
Pelléas et Mélisande.[2] Lugné-Poe—playwright, producer, director—
exposed the Parisian cultural world to the new plays of the Symbolists and Naturalists. He also distinguished himself in this particular
performance as the first to play Golaud in the city of Paris. An unusual feature of Lugné-Poe's production was a thin gauze curtain
which was placed before the audience, forming a border of ambiguity between audience and stage.[3] In the Metropolitan Opera's
1982–83 production of the opera *Pelléas et Mélisande,* a feeble imitation of this device was still employed. A thin layer of cloth resem-

bling the "dentelle" of Mallarmé's poetry was periodically lowered as part of the background scenery, sometimes to change the atmosphere and sometimes to signify the ends of scenes. The intention was clearly to create an ambiance reminiscent of the Symbolist theater. Far less courageous was this homage to the Symbolists than the original conception staged by Lugné-Poe in the nineties.

In terms of plot and even specific symbols, Maeterlinck's play is obviously indebted to Wagner's *Tristan und Isolde* and the *Ring* cycle, yet the temperament of Wagner's operas and Maeterlinck's plays are worlds apart. Debussy, the great composer of the Symbolist movement, eventually came to hate *Tristan und Isolde* and complained of "the debilitating breathlessness that pursues Tristan's sickly passion," "the enraged bestial cries" of Isolde, and, with respect to the *Ring*, the "pompous commentary on Wotan's inhumanity."[4] He saw Wagner's art as constructed from an aesthetic of overstatement. Maeterlinck's play was clearly formed out of a spirit of understatement. Nothing indicates the sensitivity of the best French minds of the time to that distinction more succinctly than that gauze curtain, which obscured the action, plot, characterization, and even dialogue at the first Paris performance of *Pelléas et Mélisande*. Yet *Die Walküre* had only reached Paris five days earlier!

The cultural overlap is recorded in a document left to us by Mallarmé—his review of Maeterlinck's *Pelléas*, which he published in two places (*Le Réveil mensuel de littérature* and the *National Observer*).[5] Mallarmé begins his essay by praising *Die Walküre* in a tone that recalls his *Revue Wagnérienne* essay; then he turns to Maeterlinck's play. Maeterlinck's theater of ambiguity, Mallarmé writes, had been unjustly abused by "les officiels juges de plusieurs grands journaux." Maeterlinck's poetic creates an art of the young, Mallarmé argues. The critics represent the old, and an aesthetic, that, if respectable, is also rather staid. The work that "ambushes" the stodgy old guard is *Pelléas et Mélisande*.

La pièce sauve du guet-apens, indiquait un choix sagace, *Pelléas et Mélisande,* de passion et d'inquiétude franchement. . . . Ambigu décor et forêt comme appartements. Le costume dans le ton, très bien, de l'esprit et des rôles; prêtant cette significative coloration au geste. Une matinée seule. Elite.[6]

The elliptical, brief scenes of Maeterlinck's play create the "tiers aspect" of ideal art. All that is "prepared" and "mechanical" is rejected. The old machinery of action and representation is disengaged. In this ideal music of Maeterlinck, a music forged out of silences and echoing phrases, real music would be inappropriate, even discordant.

Silencieusement presque, comme les traits partent épurés, en l'abstention du déchet qui suffit d'ordinaire! Silencieusement et abstraitement au point que dans cet art, lequel devient musique dans le sens propre, la partie d'un instrument même pensif, violon, détonnerait, par inutilité. Peut-être que si tacite atmosphère inspire . . . ce besoin souvent de proférer deux fois les choses, pour une certitude qu'elles l'aient été et leur assurer, à défaut de rien, la conscience de l'écho. Sortilège fréquent, autrement inexplicable, entre cent; qu'un nommerait à tort procédé.[7]

Maeterlinck's influence in the 1890s went far beyond Paris. As proof of this, one may consider, for example, the serious interest in Maeterlinck displayed in *Pan*, the fin-de-siècle Berlin journal. *Pan* features theoretical writing on the Belgian along with examples of his verse.[8] Above all, Maeterlinck's influence went beyond the purely literary sphere and stretched into the musical world. Maeterlinck became a source of literary inspiration for a large number of significant composers, and it is his rising prestige that signifies the waning of Wagner's influence as a literary source for nineteenth century composers. Of course, Debussy's opera *Pelléas et Mélisande* is the most important work that shows this shift.

Lesser composers also document the change. One of them is the quite capable Paul Dukas, who wrote a lengthy opera on a Maeterlinck play, *Ariane et Barbe-Bleu,* and a sizable piano sonata that was lauded by Debussy. Dukas is reviewed by Jean Marnold in the *Mercure de France.* Marnold refers to the "gamme par tons" played by Dukas with his "two chords" of the "augmented fifth."[9] Dukas's harmony is here dismissed as artificial, and the reviewer complains of the "slowness of movement" in the piece. Clearly we can see, though, that Dukas is caught up in the harmonic adventurousness of his time. Also mentioned along with Dukas in this review are Strauss, Wilde, Maeterlinck, and Debussy. As we can easily observe here once again, literature and music did not evolve in self-contained, mutually exclusive vacuums. The activities and ideas of one art form interpenetrated the activities and ideas of the other.

Maurice Ravel, like Debussy, set poems of Mallarmé in his *Trois poèmes de Stéphane Mallarmé.* Two of the poems, "Soupir" and

"Placet futile," were the same ones used by Debussy for his Mallarmé songs. Ravel, too, turned to Maeterlinck as a prospective literary source for an opera. He planned to set Maeterlinck's lyric play *Intérieur*. Unfortunately, the project was never carried out. Maeterlinck's *Pelléas et Mélisande* did inspire four musical projects that did come to fruition, however. The most important of them is Debussy's opera (1902). Fauré also wrote a four-part tone poem which he called *Pelléas et Mélisande* (1901). Schoenberg wrote a lengthy and lugubrious tone poem, heavily influenced by Wagnerian chromaticism, which also bears the title of Maeterlinck's play. Finally, Sibelius wrote yet another *Pelléas et Mélisande* in 1905.[10]

What are the differences between Maeterlinck's theater, a theater that so clearly inspired these musicians, and that of Wagner? To understand the distinction between the two theaters, we must first realize that Wagner's *Gesamtkunstwerk* was the source of the new theater, and, at the same time, diametrically opposed in its inherent nature to the nature of the new theater. Synesthesia was the first and most significant lesson the Symbolists learned from Wagner. In the Symbolist theater, dialogue gives way to natural sounds which take on just as much importance as the spoken word. The sound of a bell, the snapping of a string, the ringing of an ax, the rattling of cups, the hiss of the wind—all of these organic sounds are promoted from their place in the old Aristotelian hierarchy as part of the "spectacle" to a new level of thematic and symbolic importance. Wagner's luxuriant and overwhelming orchestration is the precedent for this, as are the natural noises such as Siegfried hammering *Nothung* into shape in the forge, or, as rendered in music, the water sounds of the Rhine, or the murmuring of the Teutonic forests. Visual symbols, too, are given new importance as lighting techniques are improved.

Even the sense of smell is invoked in the Symbolist theater. Chekhov, mocking these continental trends, has the tortured young Trepleff write and direct his own Symbolist play-within-the-play in the first act of *The Sea Gull*. Trepleff's actress, Nina, dressed in a white robe, begins with a verbose outburst. As she speaks, Trepleff has an odorous sulphur cloud released into the air. This scandalizes the insensitive and shallow audience:

> I am alone. Once in a hundred years I open my lips to speak, and in this void my sad echo is unheard. And you, pale fires, you do not hear me.... Before daybreak the putrid marsh begets you, and you wander until

sunrise, but without thought, without will, without the throb of life. For fear life should spring in you the father of Eternal Matter, the Devil, causes every instant in you, as in stones and in water, an interchange of the atoms, and you are changing endlessly. I, only, the world's soul, remain unchanged and am eternal.[11]

Chekhov is clearly poking fun at his play-within-the-play. Nevertheless, is Trepleff's idea really so different from the incense and perfume wafted into Lugné-Poe's theater during performances of Symbolist works?

Nina's monologue is reminiscent of another play, *Axel,* by Villiers de L'Isle Adam. Here, Wagnerian length is approximated in a purely dramatic work. Through Villiers, as well as through Wagner, Schopenhauerean pessimism made its way into the Symbolist theater. In the final portion of *Axel,* the section entitled "The Supreme Choice," the young nobles, Axel and Sara, decide to commit a joint suicide. Life is rejected as impure. The servants, Ukke and Luisa, are to be married into the vulgarities of life, while Axel and Sara are wedded in the purity of the void. Yeats was deeply moved by *Axel* and it is no accident that his lyric play *The Shadowy Waters* also ends in a suicide of the ideal that is committed by two noble lovers, King Forgael and Queen Dectora. Yeats's play, though, is a *lyric play,* which is a far different affair from the lengthy and verbose *Axel.*

What, then, is a Symbolist *lyric play*? Technically, the lyric play explores the possibilities of synesthesia. Metaphor is no longer ornamentation or decoration that embellishes the drama. Ornament and decoration become metaphors lodged in the core of the lyric play. Wagner, as we have seen, inspired this new approach. Thematically, the lyric play is generally concerned with the twin subjects of waiting and death. Modern man, devoid of the old notions of the Chain of Being and the correspondences between God's universe and man's world, stands alone in the Symbolist lyric theater.

More important than this, though, is the fact that the lyric play of the Symbolists systematically rejects the standard conventional codes of the European theater. Basically, this means a refutation of the old dramatic canon set up by Aristotle in the *Poetics.* Plot, first of all, is no longer important in the lyric play whereas it was the most significant thing for Aristotle. Thus, the lyric play is not concerned with a systematic development of a crisis, or with the purging of "pity and fear" that comes with catharsis, or with the standard Aristotelian devices of reversals and recognitions. The lyric play essentially is static and antidevelopmental. Characterization is next in line after the plot in Aristotle's hierarchy. The Symbolist play is not especially concerned with carefully developed characterization. The lyric play is more interested in *melos, opsis,* and *lexis,* that is, in the integration of sound, visual effects, and poetic diction.

Finally, the lyric play is not written in the symmetrical patterns of expression afforded by rhyme and meter. Without the old couplings, the lyric play explores asymmetrical rhythms that are far from the realistic flow of speech in the Naturalistic theater. Although the dialogue of the lyric play is unmeasured, it is highly poetic and is closely indebted to its source—the innovations of the Parisian Symbolists.

Maynard Solomon, in a recent book on Beethoven, points out that the old sonata form was much like the classical tragedy, which was divided into carefully differentiated acts.[12] The classical sonata was an essentially discursive form that allowed for the stringing of varied movements in a chain which provided exposition, development, conflict, and resolution. The lyric play turned against the old pattern of differentiated dramatic sections, against the partitioning of drama into acts and scenes, and turned toward a kind of seamless, through-composed form which was presented in one continuous movement. The lyric play, in its purest form, is a one-act play, although the notion of an "act" in the traditional sense is highly misleading here. Development of problems and crises as partitioned in the conventional unit of the act is less important than the repetition of significant recurring symbols within the shorter play. Dramatic direction, formerly housed within neatly partitioned acts, is now replaced by a continuous, nebulous sense of anxiety.

Aristotle's *Poetics* is a code book, in the Barthean sense, of cultural conventions. The lyric play, by definition, challenges this book of rules. Most important to the poetic of the lyric play, however, is the systematic negation of the action and question codes outlined by Barthes. Here, as in Symbolist poetry, modern literature is born. Interpretive questions that were formerly answered are here left completely unresolved. Actions are not carried out to their logical conclusion. Couplings are made by the repetition of phrases from the dialogue, by sounds that are promoted from the background into the heart of the play, or by recurrent visual symbols. The lyric play creates a theater of atmosphere, of *Stimmung*, and not a theater that expresses the logical resolution of problems. The lyric play explores the intrinsic power of the theater to generate subtle shifts in atmosphere. If "ripeness is all" for Shakespeare, then "mood is all" for the Symbolist playwright. "Ripeness" is no longer important.

The counterpart in music for these *Stimmung* plays explores the suggestive possibilities of harmony at the expense of other aspects of music, such as clear tonal and rhythmic form. New harmonic possibilities, which in turn led to rich orchestral experimentation, were worked out in novel ways to create a music of *Stimmung*, and not a music of the opera buffa or the dance. Rhythm oozed and flowed. It did not pulsate and articulate, on the whole, in late nineteenth-century music. This, too, is a result of Wagnerism. The German *Stimmung*, as Spitzer writes in *Classical and Christian Ideals of World Harmony*, is "untranslatable."[13] Actually, *Stimmung* encompasses, as Spitzer shows, a huge amount of semantic territory. It can function, in German, as a term for "atmosphere," "mood," or in a musical sense, "harmony." *Stimmung* also means "harmony" in the sense of pure concord or agreement and in the ancient sense of the "harmony of the spheres." Here the intrinsic, natural synesthesia in language has paved a way from the realm of literature to the realm of music.

Tonal harmony, the system codified by Rameau and explored to its fullest in the nineteenth century, is the component of the old European music that had the greatest power to evoke varied moods, to create subtle shifts in atmosphere. Before Wagner, clearly differentiated thematic ideas, usually housed within symmetrical periodic units, were given changing dramatic contexts by variations in tonal harmony. When thematic ideas became smaller and more flexible, the possibilities of tonal harmony were greatly enhanced. Clear structure gave way to a music of evocation.

European music, after Wagner and Berlioz, developed all of its resources to allow for the generating of the ever more impressive and varied evocations of *Stimmung*. It is here that the suggestive style of Symbolism overlaps with the music of the end of the century. The zenith of the *Stimmung* music was the *Tondichtung* or tone poem. The term *Tondichtung* was finally coined by Richard Strauss, who perhaps perfected the tone poem as a genre, but actually the tone poem had been in existence since Berlioz and Liszt.

Liszt himself used the term *Symphonische Dichtung* ("symphonic poem"). Furthermore, the roots of the tone poem are in the oeuvre of Beethoven.

Beethoven's music was the first music to be self-consciously "about something," a change in the history of music that Beethoven himself signified by his preference for the term *Tondichter* over *Tonkünstler*. The literary texts that were attached to musical works in the Romantic period continued this tradition of music that is "about something." The literary signifiers at the head of a Romantic work are generally short and epigrammatic and contribute mostly to the sense of mystery and self-importance that surrounds a piece and little to a logical or didactic explanation of what is actually in the piece. If music surfaces as an idea that generates aesthetic ambiguity in nineteenth-century poetry, then literature also surfaces as an idea that generates aesthetic ambiguity in nineteenth-century music.

In the narrowest sense, the tone poem is a through-composed piece which is built out of variations on small motivic ideas, is structured in one continuous movement, and in some way displays a debt to extramusical inspiration (most often a literary debt). Debussy's *Prélude à l'après-midi d'un faune* fits this definition perfectly, and, indeed, as Hugh MacDonald observes in the *New Grove Dictionary of Music and Musicians,* most tone poems are symphonic pieces. *Symphonic poem,* though, the term advocated by the *New Grove Dictionary,* does not convey the literary sensibility of the creators of the form as accurately as Strauss's term *tone poem.*[14] Like the lyric play, the tone poem was a relatively short-lived form, which reached its point of greatest importance in the last decade of the nineteenth century and the first decade of the twentieth. With the advent of modernism, the old tone poems and lyric plays disappeared, but their influence remains with us even today.

Richard Strauss wrote eight important tone poems: *Macbeth* (1888), *Don Juan* (1888–89), *Tod und Verklärung* (1888–89), *Till Eulenspiegel* (1894–95), *Also sprach Zarathustra* (1895–96), *Don Quixote* (1896–97), *Ein Heldenleben* (1897–98), *Sinfonia domestica* (1902–3).[15] Debussy thought highly of Strauss's tone poems, for the most part. Debussy, who did nothing in his life if not master the power of harmony to evoke moods, heard the same ability in Strauss. In a 1912 article, he likened Strauss to the Symbolist painter Böcklin. "Il y a de curieux rapports entre l'art de Böcklin et l'art de Richard

Strauss. . . . Même insouci d'un dessin préconçu, même goût pour chercher la forme directement dans la couleur, et tirer de cette même couleur des effets de pittoresque dramatique."[16] "Color" in music, for Debussy, means *Stimmung.* Harmonic subtlety, then, generates form in Strauss. Later, in the same article, Debussy turns to the subject of Strauss's tone poems:

> *Mort et Transfiguration,* sans avoir l'étincelante sûreté de *Till Eulenspiegel,* ou la grandiloquence passionnée du *Don Juan* contient néanmoins des formules restées chères à Richard Strauss, bien qu'il les ait améliorées dans la suite.
>
> Le commencement a des odeurs de sépulcre, dans lequel semblent se mouvoir d'inquiétantes larves; l'âme s'y livre à de durs combats, tendant de toutes ses forces à se libérer du corps misérable qui la retient encore à la terre. Mais, voici un hautbois qui chante une cantilène aux inflexions italiennes. On n'en saisit pas tout de suite le pourquoi, faute d'avoir pensé à temps à ces innomabrables migrations des âmes, restées si mystérieuses. D'ailleurs, si l'on se mêle de vouloir comprendre ce qui se passe dans un poème symphonique, il vaut mieux renoncer à en écrire.—Ce n'est certes pas la lecture de ces petits guides, où les lettres de l'alphabet représentent des membres de phrases-rébus, que l'on essaie de résoudre pendant l'exécution, qui fera cesser les fréquents malentendus entre l'auteur et l'auditeur.[17]

For Debussy, too, music is able to make one "sense" things extramusical. Actually, the singing melody of the oboe Debussy refers to here is the same kind of coloristic matching of solo instrument and harp he used himself in the *Prélude à l'après-midi d'un faune.* For Strauss, in this passage, uses not only the solo oboe, but also the solo flute and violin (see figures 6-1 and 6-2). Debussy does exactly the same thing in the tone poem of the faun. For Strauss, the ripe moment of death is rendered in music, but with compositional procedures undeniably similar to Debussy's. Thus, it is not surprising that Debussy praises Strauss so highly.

Both Strauss and Debussy turned away from the rigid architectural model of music to a more fluid and freely evolved style. Debussy states this quite explicitly on behalf of Strauss:

> A coup sûr l'art de M. R. Strauss n'est pas toujours aussi spécialement fantaisiste, mais il pense certainement par images colorées et il semble dessiner la ligne de ses idées avec l'orchestre. C'est un procédé peu banal et rarement employé; M. R. Strauss y trouve, au surplus, une façon de

6-1. Debussy, *Prélude à l'apres-midi d'un faune,* measures 79–81

6-2. Strauss, *Tod und Verklärung*, measures 20–22

177

pratiquer le développement tout à fait personnelle; ça n'est plus la ri-
goureuse et architecturale manière d'un Bach ou d'un Beethoven, mais
bien un développement de couleurs rythmiques: il superpose les tonali-
tés les plus éperdument éloignées avec un sang-froid absolu qui ne se
soucie nullement de ce qu'elles peuvent avoir de "déchirant" mais seulement, de ce qu'il leur demande de "vivant."[18]

Of the two composers, though, Strauss never escaped from his preoccupation with Wagnerism, whereas Debussy did absorb the
Wagnerian influence into his own unique voice. In the opening
bars of *Tod und Verklärung,* for example, Strauss's negation of the
bar line and the offbeat rhythms of the strings and tympani represent the faltering heartbeat of a dying man. This kind of thwarting
of the bar line, although used here with the inspiration of genius to
depict an extramusical idea, is prefigured in Wagner's *Vorspiel* to
Parsifal. Both the dense chromaticism of Strauss and the continuous evolution of short motives within that chromatic field, moreover, derive from the compositional innovations of Wagner.

Strauss, though, did not struggle with Wagnerism as desper-
ately as Schoenberg did. Whereas Strauss absorbed it happily,
Schoenberg's sense of individuality led him towards serialism. By
the time Schoenberg wrote the *Georgelieder,* which was still well before the twelve-tone music of the 1920s, he had found his path
away from Wagner. But his early tone poem *Verklärte Nacht* is a
child of the *Gesamtkunstwerk.* To understand this, one needs only to
note the shocking similarity between the final measures of *Die
Walküre* and the last bars of Schoenberg's tone poem (see figures 6-
3 and 6-4).

The tone poem, as we have said, was not an exclusively symphonic form, although it was predominantly written for a symphonic medium. One of the best tone poems of the first decade of
the twentieth century was certainly Ravel's trilogy *Gaspard de la
nuit: trois poèmes d'après Aloysius Bertrand.* Bertrand's sizable texts,
printed at the head of each of the three pieces, *Ondine, Le Gibet,* and
Scarbo, were written well before the Romanticism of Baudelaire.
Nevertheless, Ravel's music belongs in the milieu of symbolism; the
text, too, prefigures Symbolism, just as Büchner's *Woyzeck* prefigures the Expressionism of Berg's *Wozzeck.*

Le Gibet especially fits our definitions of both lyric play and
tone poem. It has virtually no development. It evokes a vision, an
atmosphere: "C'est la cloche qui tinte aux murs d'une ville sous

6-3. Richard Wagner, *Die Walküre*, act 3, scene 3 measures 712–18.
Used by special arrangement with G. Schirmer, Inc.

Figure 6–4 *(continued)*

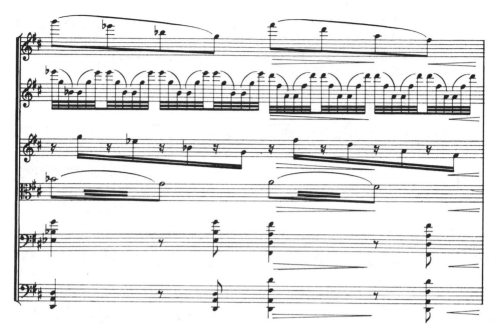

6-4. Schoenberg, *Verklärte Nacht* measures 419–21

l'horizon, et la carcasse d'un pendu que rougit le soleil couchant."[19]
The bell resounds throughout the entire piece, on B-flat/A-sharp,
in every single measure. Around the ostinato symbol for the bell,
Ravel weaves an intricate pattern of seventh and ninth chords.
Small and irregular thematic ideas continuously recur and echo
each other. There is no sharp delineation of contrasting sections.
The resounding bell preserves the static, hypnotic *Stimmung*
throughout (see figure 6-5) just as a recurring symbol does in a lyric
play. *Scarbo* is a marvel of musical structure. Its huge span is woven
out of only three notes (see figure 6-6). The motive appears in myriad contexts. It is an irregular motive, which is augmented and
shortened, given various time values and brilliantly contrasting
harmonic contexts. Like the flute theme in Debussy's *Prélude à
l'après-midi d'un faune,* it is punctuated with irregular "white spaces"
of silence, and its presence characterizes almost every measure of
the tone poem. Are we justified in constructing a correspondence
between the three words of Bertrand's prose poem that are treated
anaphoristically: "que de fois"? Perhaps, but the correspondence is
only made in Bertrand's poem by three repetitions and this does
not fit structurally with the countless transformations of the tiny,

antiperiodic theme in the music for *Scarbo.* Ravel, actually, used Bertrand's poem as a point of departure, just as Debussy used Mallarmé's poem as a point of departure in the *Prélude.*

6-5. Ravel, *Gaspard de la nuit,* No. 2, *Le Gibet,* measures 1–11. Copyright © 1908, Durand S. A. Editions Musicales, Editions Arima and Durand S. A. Editions Musicales Joint Publication. Used by permission of the publisher. Theodore Press Company, sole representative U.S.A.

6-6. Ravel, *Gaspard de la nuit,* No. 3, *Scarbo,* measure 1. Copyright © 1908, Durand S. A. Editions Musicales, Editions Arima and Durand S. A. Editions Musicales Joint Publication. Used by permission of the publisher. Theodore Presser Company, sole representative U.S.A.

If Ravel's *Gibet* is a classic example of a tone poem, then an ideal representative of the Symbolist lyric play is Rilke's *Weisse Fürstin* (1898). Actually, Rilke's small body of plays shows a transition from Naturalism to a distinct Symbolist poetic. *Ohne Gegenwart* (1897) and *Höhenluft* (1897) display a marked departure from the naturalistic *Jetzt und in der Stunde unseres Absterbens* (1896).[20] By the time Rilke wrote *Die weisse Fürstin*, he had steeped himself in the theories of Maeterlinck. *Die weisse Fürstin*, which appeared in an early version in *Pan* in 1899, takes place in the garden of a prince's villa by the sea. Visionary and disturbing pictures of women or monks waiting by the sea had been already painted by the Romantic artist Friedrich and the Symbolist Böcklin, but Rilke here takes the paintings and brings them to life in drama. The white princess is waiting in a lush garden for a lover who never comes. She is another Hérodiade, for she did not have relations with her dreamy husband. She is attended by a doting servant, Amadeo, and her sister, Mona Lara, who is dressed in faded blue. White and azure, two of the favorite colors of the Symbolists, are thus juxtaposed in the costumes of the sisters and set against the backdrop of a still sea.

Rilke presents us with a number of questions that he never answers: Who are the sisters? Where are they? Who is the lover? We are never told exactly, except for a few rather Italianate names that give us a sense of topos. Instead of the lover, death comes. What causes the death? A plague? This, too, Rilke does not specify. It seems that the monks are entering homes and bringing out the dead, but what, asks the messenger, do "they carry into every house?" The messenger begs the princess to "post guards" around the estate.[21] Why she should do this is never explained. Death, too, takes on larger significance for the princess than the danger from outside.

As the sun sets, the princess is still waiting. We hear the pulse of oars in the water first; then we see two monks in black masks. The monks stand motionless. The princess stands motionless. As the light dies, the tension mounts. Has death arrived? Rilke never resolves this question. A light in one of the windows high in the villa appears and in it a figure is seen waving steadily. With this puzzling, disturbing gesture, the play ends. *Die weisse Fürstin* has all of the hallmarks of the lyric play: the twin themes of waiting and death; the elliptical statements of the characters; the visual and aural importance of stage effects (that is, the sound of oars, the masks of monks, the lighted window) that stimulate the various senses beyond the level of the dialogue; no cogent formation of a plot; characters that do and say little to define their individual natures; notions of danger and death that are evoked but never shown; and finally, the twin codes of actions and questions that are left stranded and incomplete.

Although Hauptmann and Strindberg did not write lyric plays in the purest sense, important overtones of Symbolism are evident in their fin-de-siècle works. These writers are strongly nurtured by Naturalism, yet they turned to themes and techniques characteristic of the lyric theater of the Symbolists. Hauptmann shows, in *The Sunken Bell* (1897), a Wagnerian influence that is just as obvious as that in the early Schoenberg. Hauptmann's play has elves, dwarves, and trolls, who seem to be drawn from Teutonic myth, a familiar German forest and a rather obvious parallel with the symbol of the ring—the symbol of the bell itself. Why, exactly, does Heinrich allow Rautendelein to coerce him into building the giant bell and lugging it up the mountain? Both the ring and the bell end up out of the reach of humanity and submerged in a body of water. In Wagner we know exactly why this happens and what the ring stands for. In Hauptmann, we cannot say exactly what the bell signifies. We have to fill it in for ourselves. This denuding of symbol from the explanation of discourse alone places Hauptmann in the Symbolist theater.

Strindberg turns away from his Naturalistic plays and toward the spirit of music in two plays—*The Ghost Sonata* and *A Dream Play*. This is the same sort of evolution that is displayed in Rilke's plays. *The Ghost Sonata,* which is probably named after a piano trio by Beethoven, is a Symbolist play because of its debunking of standard plot development and characterization in favor of the free use of symbols. Strindberg distorts the old naturalistic themes in *The Ghost Sonata.* The play takes place in three loci: outside the house, in the "Round Room" and in the "Hyacinth Room." The bourgeois house is here transformed into a magical realm where anything can happen. Roaming through each of the settings are characters who used to be firmly fixed in social and political positions in the Naturalistic play: a company director, a student, a milkmaid, a caretaker, a colonel, an aristocrat, and so forth.

At the start of the play, sounds stimulate the senses. We hear church bells, a steamship bell, and the tones of an organ. At the end of *The Ghost Sonata,* the strains of a harp and the glow of a white light fill the hyacinth room in the true spirit of post-Wagnerian synesthesia. Then *The Island of the Dead,* by the Symbolist painter Böcklin, looms behind the death scene. At the same time, Strindberg calls for the sounds of quiet, mellifluous music. Death is resolution in *The Ghost Sonata,* as is the return to the tonic in music. Strindberg, by ending his work with the theme of death, has also returned, for he began his play with the same somber tonality.

When we first meet the student Arkenholtz in *The Ghost Sonata,* he has just achieved his newly heroic status in another house of death—a house destroyed by fire. Although this theme of death oppresses us from the beginning of the play, the student, in spite of his filthy hands, is a saver of lives. Life, then, is equated with filth and with the tension of exposition. The student becomes a murderer at the close of the play and transforms into another kind of savior. The student purifies the hyacinth girl. He removes the dross of life. Death, newly described in the context of murder, is equated with the act of liberation, of cleansing, of resolution. Thus, the termination of life is the overall *Stimmung* of this disturbing sonata, and the student Arkenholtz sends the girl he would have loved to join Villier's Axel and Sara in the void.

Strindberg denudes his old Naturalistic themes in *The Ghost Sonata.* He isolates them and thereby heightens their expressive power. Once isolated, these newly intensified themes interact as a chain of symbols much like the semantically impossible signifiers of Mallarmé. The chain of interacting symbols resembles the structure of music, and the audience that is assaulted with this antididactic progression of signs is supposed to encounter an experience similar to the listener's experience in the concert hall.

The heavy weight of the past, a Naturalistic theme of primary importance, presses upon our breasts in *The Ghost Sonata* even more intensely than it did in *Miss Julie.* The privileges and limitations of heredity, questions of inheritance and disinheritance, the paradoxes of familial legitimacy and illegitimacy still concern Strindberg as much as they did in his earlier work. Now, however, each formerly Naturalistic theme surfaces and sends forth its thematic information and then disappears from sight until it is needed again a few lines later. Is *The Ghost Sonata* an exact parallel to the musical sonata? This is far less important than the novel freedom from the old code book of conventions Strindberg gave to the new

theater. In Strindberg, drama, too, was now as free of the requirements of logical development and journalistic description as absolute music was.

Another writer of lyric plays who challenged European dramatic conventions was Hugo von Hofmannsthal, but the origins of
his plays are in the refined Symbolist verse he wrote as a young
man. It is possible to see Hofmannsthal's oeuvre as developing in
one continuous direction. Out of Hofmannsthal's Symbolist poetry
emerged his lyric plays, and out of his lyric plays grew his opera
libretti. As Hofmannsthal develops as a literary artist, the *ich* of his
lyric voice begins to take on the masks of characters. Nevertheless,
the tone of the verse remains the same. For example, "Zu einer To-
tenfeier für Arnold Böcklin," a tribute to a fellow artist that is just
as refined as Mallarmé's "Toast Funébre à Théophile Gautier" or
the various "Tombeaux," is recited through the persona of a youth
dressed in a Venetian costume.

It is a transitional work, for it is a poem written in the form of a
tiny theater piece, a tiny lyric play. The poem, too, begins out of the
spirit of music. Hofmannsthal provides a literary description of
musical sound. The young speaker advances, followed by "torch-
bearers" during the last "bar" of a symphony. Poetry, here, "takes
back its own" from music in the true Symbolist tradition. The new
music will be the lament of the mourner, who has seized center
stage.

> (In die letzten Takte der Symphonie tritt der
>   Prolog auf, seine Fackelträger hinter ihm.
> Der Prolog ist ein Jüngling; er ist venezianisch
>   gekleidet, ganz in Schwarz, als ein Trauernder.)
> Nun schweig, Musik! Nun ist die Szene mein,
>   Und ich will klagen, denn mir steht es zu![22]

The *écriture* of Symbolism pulsates throughout this hommage to
Böcklin. Hofmannsthal, speaking through the voice of the young
Venetian, claims that his soul fed on the dreams of Böcklin as the
swan "kissed" its "nourishment" out of the "white hands" of naiads.

> Und wie der Schwan, ein selig schwimmend Tier,
> Aus der Najade triefend weissen Händen
> Sich seine Nahrung küsst, so bog ich mich
> In dunklen Stunden über seine Hände
> Um meiner Seele Nahrung: tiefen Traum.[23]

The speaker wants to do justice to Böcklin by filling the "pavilion" with "dream-shapes." The tiny play ("Spiel") grows out of the "mirror" or "reflected" image of Böcklin's "anxious dark hour." The German word *Spiegelbild* contains all the letters of *Spiel* and has a highly similar sound to that of the smaller word. The master's greatness is evoked by the "shadowy lips" of the actor:

> Es weise euch ein Spiel
> Das Spiegelbild der bangen, dunklen Stunde,
> Und grossen Meisters trauervollen Preis
> Vernehmet nun aus schattenhaftem Munde![24]

Hofmannsthal's playlet "Idyll" has a subtitle: "Nach einem antiken vasenbild: Zentaur mit verwundeter Frau am Rand eines Flusses." This work, stimulated by an image on a vase, then, is highly reminiscent of Mallarmé. A centaur now takes the place of the faun, the wounded woman replaces the nymphs. The shore of the river resembles the shores of Mallarmé's "marécage." The scene, Hofmannsthal writes, should be "in the style of Böcklin." An image generates the poem, but what kind of image? Both Rilke and Hofmannsthal draw upon paintings by Friedrich and Böcklin for inspiration. Indeed, Hofmannsthal wrote another lyric play, which he published in *Pan*, the fin-de-siècle review, that has the same title as an important painting by Friedrich: *Frau am Fenster*. Many of Hofmannsthal's characters are gazing out of the window as Claudio does, for example, in *Der Tor und der Tod*. Rilke's white princess, too, gazes out at the infinite expanse of the sea. Böcklin, furthermore, has a significant presence in *Pan*. Excerpts from his diaries and an article on his life and art are in the same issues as the works of Rilke and Hofmannsthal. Böcklin, of course, is much closer than Friedrich in temperament to the two writers, but Böcklin and Friedrich, simply speaking, are both painters of *Stimmung*.

If the lyric play and the tone poem slow down poetry and music in order to evoke a *Stimmung*, then Böcklin and Friedrich stir up painting to evoke a *Stimmung*. They do this by placing detached signifiers from old contexts in new settings. The new context invites interpretation. What, after all, does a monk have to do by the sea? Why is the woman looking out of the window? Do we need to answer these questions to admire the paintings? Certainly not. But we must understand that the ambiguity of the paintings makes us ask them anyway. Thus, the interest of Hofmannsthal in Böcklin or

Friedrich does not go against his interest in music. One aesthetic binds Hofmannsthal's favorite painters to the literature and music of his time: the amount of didactic information in works of art is decreased in order to create the subtleties of mood.

Character, in Hofmannsthal's lyric plays, is subservient to the word. Hofmannsthal illustrates this theoretically in his little dialogue "On Characters in Novels and Plays."[25] Here, Hofmannsthal creates a fictional dialogue between Balzac and Hammer-Purgstall. It is no accident that Hofmannsthal has Balzac, perhaps the greatest master of character in nineteenth-century fiction, actually debunk the importance of character in literature. "Characters in the theater," the Balzac figure says, "are nothing but contrapuntal necessities." For Hofmannsthal, Balzac did not care about the individual personae of his characters. "I don't see people," continues the fictional Balzac, "I see destinies." "My people are nothing but litmus paper which reacts by turning red or blue. The living, the great, the real, are the acids—the powers—the destinies."[26]

Of course, this says very little about the novelist Balzac but a great deal about the lyric playwright Hofmannsthal. Claudio, for example, in *Der Tor und der Tod*, is far less important as an individual who has been brought to life through his specific problems, than as a vehicle for Hofmannsthal's general philosophical views of the human condition. Claudio barely moves in *Der Tor und der Tod*. First, he sits by the window bathed in the dim light of the setting sun. Then he stands by the window, gazing outward. He looks at a painting. He stands by an armoire. He recounts his pointless past as he putters about the ornate room. We learn that he is a fool. Death comes. Claudio, too, learns that he is a fool. Claudio dies and the play ends. This lyric play, like the others we have discussed, has almost no plot.

As we meet Claudio alone in his study, musing over his wasted existence, so do we first see Faust, as depicted by Goethe, in his study. The Hofmannsthal play does not develop into a huge Romantic tragedy, though. There is no real action. Instead, Hofmannsthal uses the rich language of Symbolism to suggest the problematic inner psyche of Claudio. Claudio's lists of exhaustion are the lists of a tainted dandy, worthy of des Esseintes in Huysman's *A Rebours*.

> Ihr hölzern, ehern Schilderwerk,
> Verwirrend, formenquellend Bilderwerk

Ihr Kröten, Engel, Greife, Faunen,
Phantastische Vögel, goldnes Fruchtgeschlinge
Berauschende und ängstigende Dinge,
Ihr wart doch all einmal gefühlt . . .[27]

"All of these things were felt before"—the bewildering conglomeration of "toads, angels, monsters, fauns, fantastic birds, rings of fruit laced with gold." The exhausted dandy is even tired of the hedonistic indulgences in which he had originally sought relief from boredom ("umsonst bin ich, umsonst euch nachgegangen"). How different from the thwarted idealistic aspirations of Faust!

Habe nun, ach! Philosophie,
Juristerei und Medizin
Und leider auch Theologie
Durchaus studiert mit heissem Bemühn.
Da steh ich nun, ich armer Tor!
Und bin so klug als wie zuvor.[28]

When death appears, it is signified by the "sehnsüchtige und ergreifende Spiel einer Geige."[29] The Symbolist glow of language yields to the actual flow of the real music of the violin on the stage. The music helps, in this case, to capture the stillness, the absence of action (counteracted by the intricacies of language) that is characteristic of Symbolist drama. As the music grows, its presence provokes the turbulent workings of Claudio's inner mind: "Musik? und seltsam zu der Seele redende." The music rushes at Claudio in "long awaited paroxysms." It suggests "unending hope" and "unending regret." Can music suggest such things? We have learned that for a nineteenth-century Symbolist music certainly can do so. Claudio yields to the waves of music with waves of synesthetic responses.

Death is sensuous and beautiful in *Der Tor und der Tod*. The music is seductive, irresistible, and Death, when he finally appears, is a beautiful young god like Bacchus. Death himself tells us that he is most like Dionysius, god of passion, and Venus, goddess of beauty:

Ich bin nicht schauerlich, bin kein Gerippe!
Aus des Dionysos, der Venus Sippe
Ein grosser Gott der Seele steht vor dir.[30]

With his violin, Death conjures up visions of the Mother, the Lover, and the Friend (of the fool). These are not individualized characterizations, though each one is a symbolic cluster that suggests universal aspects of the Friend, the Lover, the Mother. Hofmannsthal makes them universal types without allowing them to become allegorical figures. If he had done this, he would have engaged in the simple sign-making process of the medieval mystery play, or in the simple symbolic system of the *Ring*. Because he stops short of this, he remains a Symbolist.

Fertility, ripeness, and death are linked together by music. "Von Lebenstraum wohl auf in Todeswachen" are Claudio's last words. They are words of recognition. Claudio's veiled life of the dream gives way to a transfiguration, to a state of knowledge via death. As the play ends, we see Claudio among the dead, following Death, who plays, once again, his violin. Death and transfiguration are evoked in *Der Tor und der Tod* just as they are evoked in the musical counterpart to Hofmannsthal's lyric play, Richard Strauss's tone poem *Tod und Verklärung*.

Like Hofmannsthal, Maurice Maeterlinck also wrote Symbolist lyrics before he emerged as a major playwright. Maeterlinck's important book of verse, *Serres chaudes* (1889), is rendered in an elliptical voice, with a carefully crafted texture of ambiguous actions and questions, with open-ended symbolic patterns. Maeterlinck's lyric plays show the same traits. *Les Aveugles* (1890), for example, is written in one sustained, through-composed movement, much like the tone poem, the characteristic musical form of the 1890s. The play seems almost plotless. There is little developed characterization. The dialogue, too, is fragmented and sparse. There are no long monologues. Indeed, each successive speaker utters scarcely more than a few words at a time. Although there is no argument or conflict, little interchange of wit, each interjection contributes to an overall atmosphere of anxiety. Maeterlinck's fractured phrases echo against each other. One utterance seems to flow from the other on the basis of pure sound rather than sense. The strands of dialogue resonate with the same "conscience de l'écho" that so fascinated Mallarmé when he saw Maeterlinck's *Pelléas et Mélisande* in 1893.

As *Les Aveugles* begins, we see six blind men and six blind women on either side of a frighteningly pale old priest who is wrapped in a long black robe. They are waiting, Maeterlinck tells us in the stage directions. One woman is unusually beautiful and has lovely hair. Another seems mute and insane. It is nighttime. Maeterlinck instantly establishes a cluster of signifiers that point in various directions. Why are there six of each sex? The symmetrical number seems important. Why are they dressed the same? Why are they blind? Why are they praying? These questions are evoked merely by the setting, even before the first words are uttered. The figures are placed in a strange context, and they are so strange themselves that we know from the first instant we see them that they stand for more than they really are in the flesh. A king in Shakespeare or Racine is simply a king. A fool is a fool. A ghost is a ghost. Maeterlinck's figures all have a symbolic presence that goes beyond the specificity of their position on the stage, but we cannot say what that symbolic presence is in a didactic way. The symbols are open-ended and ambiguous, not allegorical and specific.

Maeterlinck's blind ones are not sure about much, either. They are not sure where they are. They do not even know how many are present in their group. One wants to know where the beautiful girl is. Another asks about the madwoman. "I want to know who I am sitting next to," one blind man says. "I think I'm close to you," responds another.

Their blindness creates an ideal condition for synesthetic imagery. The blind try to hear and touch what they cannot see. "I feel the moonlight upon my hands," the young blind girl says. The old blind woman "hears" the stars. The blind do not know what they are waiting for. A flight of birds frightens them. They sense the birds as something that has passed between them and the night sky. This contributes to their anxious fears of suffocation and entrapment. The birds pass again. The old man cries out again. Sounds and dialogue interact as if they were musical motives of the fractured, segmented kind that tie post-Wagnerian compositions together.

As in the plays of Chekhov, natural sound takes center stage along with the dialogue of the characters. The birds are followed by the entrance of the sound of the wind, which is in turn followed by the falling of the leaves. A falling leaf becomes a significant event to the blind. "Who touched my hands?" asks a blind man as he is grazed by the leaves. The madwoman rubs her eyes violently. This is a hideous image, and perhaps it has more impact than any of the dialogue recited by the characters. Her mad act shows suffering, not suffering that is successfully borne by courage, but suffering that is intolerable and senseless. It creates a sense of fear in the others, who cannot see the rubbing of the blind eyes as we do, but can hear it.

The wind rises, the sea crashes against the cliffs. Still, the blind sit in fear. Footsteps are heard; a large dog enters. The tension mounts. Is someone coming to help them, we wonder? Why do they seem to be in such danger? No action has suggested the danger. Just the symbols themselves evoke the sense of dread. It is the old priest who has died. The dog was his, and it will not leave the side of its master. The death is untimely, silent, understated, not heroic and dramatically highlighted as it would have been in a Wagnerian *Gesamtkunstwerk*.

Suddenly the fear of the blind makes more sense. Will the death of the priest mean the death of the blind ones too? One of them hears the ice under the surf. Another is shivering. The cold may kill them. The wind contributes to their growing terror with a gust. It begins to snow. Footsteps are heard once again. Only the helpless young child can see. He seems to be staring at something. The blind think they hear the rustle of a robe against the leaves. They become convinced that the steps have carried the newcomer into their midst. Is it Death? Of course, Maeterlinck hints at this, but he does not make this a clear symbol one way or the other. Perhaps they are going to die from the cold, and their imagination has created the persona of Death, just as the birds were described as coming between them and the sky. Perhaps they will live and therefore suffer a little while longer. We will never know, though, for the play ends quietly at this point, with no sound except the weeping of the child.

Blinded Oedipus or blinded Gloucester in *King Lear* stimulate our pity and fear in the Aristotelian sense. But why do these blind figures of Maeterlinck disturb us so? Because they are devoid of fleshed-out characterization provided by a firm sense of time, place, and social position, they are Symbolistic. But they are symbols in a wide, ambiguous sense. By stripping his play of plot and character, Maeterlinck gains expressive power. With the connotations of meaning embodied in their suffering, these desperate blind ones reach outward until it becomes quite possible to believe that they may stand for us all.

We may equate the symbolic ambiguity of the lyric play with the harmonic suggestiveness of the tone poem. Strauss, Debussy writes, "thinks" in "colored images." Both composers, actually, gave music new contrast through enriched harmonies and imaginative orchestration. These innovations enabled the expression of the so-called "colored imagery" described by Debussy. Surely, harmony, for both composers, added to the suggestive power of music and balanced against the repetitiousness of symmetrical figurations. Harmonic inventiveness and enriched orchestral color enabled both composers to loosen up musical structure. Undoubtedly, the most successful new form for both composers was the tone poem.

At the same time, in the literary sphere, playwrights like Hofmannsthal, Strindberg, Yeats, Rilke, and Maeterlinck were able to weave together the old divisions of acts and scenes into a single, foreshortened structure. The specificity of clearly defined plot and character was sacrificed to gain greater symbolic potential. Meaning was implied through symbols that suggested large semantic areas. A little information became better than too much, and extensive explanation was deemed unnecessary. It was only natural that these changes in both music and drama would combine once again in a new kind of opera, but the tone poem and the lyric play stand out as two of the most innovative forms of artistic expression that emerged in the late nineteenth century.

7. Symbolist Opera

The Symbolist sensibility that was evident in the lyric play and the tone poem manifested itself, too, in the opera. Hugo von Hofmannsthal and Maurice Maeterlinck, two of the major figures who wrote Symbolist poetry and lyric plays, also contributed important opera libretti. Hofmannsthal worked with Richard Strauss over a period of many years, furnishing six libretti for the composer. Maeterlinck only allowed the fashioning of one of his plays, *Pelléas et Mélisande,* into an opera libretto for Claude Debussy. Maeterlinck's lyric play, though, retained its Symbolist qualities in its opera form. Hofmannsthal's libretti did not; they were overpowered by the late Romanticism of Richard Strauss.

In a way, it is tragic that Hofmannsthal did not have a composer with as fine a literary sensibility as Debussy to collaborate with on his opera projects. He had to settle for Richard Strauss. Alfred Einstein, musing about an English translation of the Strauss-Hofmannsthal correspondence, sums up the issue quite succinctly: "I have said that the title 'Richard Strauss: Correspondence with Hugo von Hofmannsthal' is incorrect. It should have run: 'Letters from Hofmannsthal on the Problem of Writing Opera Librettos for Richard Strauss, with some Answers from the Composer.' "[1] Of course, Strauss was a composer of genius, but he was a genius who expressed himself through eclecticism, whereas Hofmannsthal wrote in the unified and recondite voice of the Symbolist. Strauss and Hofmannsthal were a strange pair of collaborators. In the correspondence between the two, Strauss continuously keeps his eye and ear on the audience. He wants to build up massive effects the audience cannot miss. He wants the impact of the *Gesamtkunstwerk.* Hofmannsthal tries to go beyond this, to temper Strauss and pull him out of the nineteenth century and into the twentieth. Hofmannsthal is an artist of the elite; Strauss is an artist of the masses.

As the two men worked on *Ariadne auf Naxos,* this difference became a critical one. Strauss was afraid of the obtuse symbolism of the libretto, feeling that the public would not be able to understand it all. The opera, as Strauss saw it, would therefore be doomed to failure. Hofmannsthal wanted to challenge the audience. "There exists," the poet argued, "a certain productivity not only of creation, but also of reception."[2] The poetry, in other words, requires active participation, a creative and "heightened response," that is a responsibility not of those who write it, but of those who would understand it. Poetry, he writes later, should be difficult: "No, my dear friend, the essence of poetic meaning comes to be understood only gradually, very gradually. This understanding emanates from very few people who are in close touch with the world of poetry, and it takes decades to spread."[3] Might not this remark have been uttered, perhaps a little more enigmatically, by Mallarmé himself?

Hofmannsthal, as a librettist, was not totally removed from his original orientation as a Symbolist. *Ariadne auf Naxos* is a libretto made out of literary signifiers that have conflicting semantic information. The long *Vorspiel,* reminiscent, to a certain extent, of the kind of Romantic irony in Tieck's *Der gestiefelte Kater,* plays against the fictional reality of the *Oper* proper. The "Haushofmeister," the "Musiklehrer," the "Komponist," the tenor who will play Bacchus, Zerbinetta, the prima donna who will play Ariadne, and so on, are shown as they squabble over how to put on the opera. Because of this lengthy introduction, the opera is really act 2 and the *Vorspiel* is act 1.

When the opera itself starts, Ariadne is motionless at the mouth of a cave, waiting to die. She is spotted by nymphs and dryads who would comfort her. Is she sleeping or weeping, they ask? Ariadne awakens from a sleep of sorrow.

> Wo war ich? tot? und lebe, lebe wieder
> Und lebe noch?
> Und ist ja doch kein Leben, das ich lebe!
> Zerstückelt Herz, willst ewig weiter schlagen?
> Was hab' ich denn geträumt? Weh! schon
> vergessen![4]

Like the faun of Mallarmé, Ariadne asks the question: was it a dream? Illusion and reality intermingle in her mind.

As Mallarmé takes apart the myth of Pan, Hofmannsthal reworks the myth of Theseus and Ariadne. Theseus now exists only in her memory. She recreates the passion and suffering in her mind. As in much of the Symbolist theater, death is a realm of purity as opposed to the corruption of life. "There is a realm," Ariadne sings, "where all is pure—it has a name—the realm of death."[5] Ariadne—like her fellow sufferers in Rilke, Yeats, Maeterlinck—waits. "Du schöner, stiller Gott, sieh! Ariadne wartet," she exclaims in a warm mellifluous monologue.[6] With Yeats's Forgael and Dectora, with Villier's Axel and Sara, she waits for an alternative to life which looms in her mind as death. As in Hofmannsthal's *Des Tor und der Tod,* Death is a beautiful and sensuous image here. Ariadne, rejected by Theseus, must die because, as Hofmannsthal explains in a letter to Strauss, she "could be the wife of one man only, just as she can be only one man's widow, can be forsaken by only one man."[7] She is juxtaposed against Zerbinetta, who has known many men, who is "frivolous" and "merely human."[8]

Zerbinetta, a character from the *Vorspiel,* comes onstage shortly after Ariadne's monologue. Zerbinetta lists her faithless lovers: Pagliazzo, Mezubin, Cavicchio, Burattin, and others. Zerbinetta, Hofmannsthal writes, is "in her element drifting out of the arms of one man, into the arms of another."[9] Next, Arlecchino's flirtation with Zerbinetta contrasts, as an example of common love, like the love of the servants in *Axel,* with the higher love of Ariadne.[10]

Hofmannsthal himself best expresses his ultimate solution for Ariadne. "One thing, however, is still left even for her: the miracle, the God. To him she gives herself for she believes him to be Death: he is both Death and Life at once; he it is who reveals to her the immeasurable depths in her own nature, who makes of her an enchantress, the sorceress who herself transforms the poor little Ariadne; he it is who conjures up for her in this world another world beyond, who preserves her for us and at the same time transforms her."[11] Bacchus, the beautiful God, comes for Ariadne. He takes the place of Theseus. Bacchus also has had a lover—Circe. But upon witnessing the sweetness of Ariadne as she offers herself to him and mistakes him for "the messenger of death," he falls in love with her. Ariadne wants to go on a ship into the night with her god. She expects to be taken into a "shadowy land," a realm above the material baseness of the "temporal world."[12]

> Du Zauberer, du! Verwandler, du!
> Blickt nicht aus dem Schatten deines Mantels
> Der Mutter Auge auf mich her?

Ist so dein Schattenland! also gesegnet!
So unbedürftig der irdischen Welt?[13]

Shadows and waters intermingle to evoke death in Hofmannsthal as they do in Yeats.

Bacchus immortalizes Ariadne. In a sense she dies because her human existence is gone, and she asks, "Was bleibt von Ariadne?" She dies in one sense, and does not in another. Hofmannsthal is intentionally ambiguous. Zerbinetta, too, complicates matters further. She cancels out the divine purity of the immortal lovers. The libretto ends, Hofmannsthal claims, in ironic ambiguity.

> But what to divine souls is a real miracle, is to the earth-bound nature of Zerbinetta just an everyday love-affair. She sees in Ariadne's experience the only thing she *can* see: the exchange of an old lover for a new one. And so these two spiritual worlds are in the end ironically brought together in the only way in which they can be brought together: in non-comprehension.[14]

There is little action in the opera. Ariadne waits. Bacchus comes. The opera is over. Character is not developed. Symbols clash and are not reconciled, especially in terms of the two worlds of the *Vorspiel* and the main act. The libretto has the hallmarks of the lyric play, and yet it serves as a vehicle for Strauss's lush, chromatic style. The coloristic music fits in where the ambiguous text leaves off, filling out Hofmannsthal's elusive dramatic material with the full-blown sound of Romantic opera.

The paradoxical nature of this odd wedding of dramatic and musical styles becomes far clearer when viewed in the context of the more harmonious union achieved in *Pelléas et Mélisande.* In *Pelléas et Mélisande,* the main characters are nobles. However, they reign in a land that is gloomy and remote, afflicted by inexplicable famine, located in a place that is of no particular importance. In short, the play could take place anywhere, and Golaud, Pelléas, Mélisande, and Arkel are not aristocratic personages as much as they *could be* anyone. In act 4, Arkel refers to the sickroom atmosphere of the castle. It is too much, he feels, for a young and beautiful girl to sit in an atmosphere of death: "For you are too young and too beautiful to live already, day and night, under the shadow of death."[15]

Maeterlinck intensifies the sense of dread with the detached signifiers of Symbolism. Golaud, who is by now as jealous as Othello, searches for his sword, but he has, inexplicably, blood upon his brow. As Mélisande fetches the sword, he mentions the evidence of famine, which in turn evokes the impending sense of catastrophe in his troubled kingdom. "They just found a peasant who starved to death by the sea. One could say that they are all dying right under our noses."[16] Mélisande, upon bearing the brunt of Golaud's rage, openly admits her unhappiness to Arkel. However, she simply says, "I am not happy"; she does not give any reason for her misery. She is, as always, ambiguous and secretive. In a similar fashion, Arkel replies in a way that does not apply to the tragic dignity of a specific princess so much as to the general unhappiness of men: "If I were God, I'd have pity for the hearts of men."[17] Yniold also contributes to the evocation of unhappiness as a tenebrous but universal entity. His arm is not long enough to throw a rock, he complains. The sheep that he sees are hurrying and afraid. They are even weeping, and the shepherds are throwing stones at them.

Obviously, the characters and symbols of *Pelléas et Mélisande* are rather familiar, but it is the way in which Maeterlinck empties the old signs of their excess meaning that makes him original. Consider the specificity of Brünnhilde or Isolde in comparison with Mélisande. We know who the Wagnerian heroines are. Mélisande simply appears in the forest before Golaud. We know nothing of her past, her lineage, her place of origin. And who is Pelléas when we place him next to his Wagnerian counterpart, the great warrior Tristan? Clearly, he is a young and innocent fool, a nobody, and certainly not a great hero. The "anneau" of Golaud, too, which Mélisande drops mistakenly into a "fontaine" in a park merely hints at the betrayal that is to come. But the adultery never really takes place in Maeterlinck, whereas in Wagner it always does. Wagner's ring, moreover, signifies absolute power, and it comes from and returns to a mighty river, whereas Mélisande's ring merely stands for her unfortunate marriage to Golaud and it falls into a little fountain.

The summa of the interrelated aesthetic of Symbolist poetry and music is the opera *Pelléas et Mélisande*. Debussy's music, furthermore, has kept large audiences in touch, at least tangentially, with the much neglected theater of the Symbolists. Although Maeterlinck's play was written in five acts and thus is not a lyric play in the strictest sense, it has all of the other features of the Symbolist theater that we have discerned. Debussy's music, too, has the familial traits of the tone poem. The music is almost entirely devoid of melody in the standard sense. The text is heightened by the subtle evolution of Debussy's harmonic adventure, but there is little melodic movement throughout the entire opera. Debussy saw melody as intruding upon the emotion of characters in the drama. He intentionally cut out the old square melodic phrases even more extensively than Wagner did. Wagner replaced the old periodicity with a new norm of irregularity. Debussy eliminated periodic melody altogether. The music for *Pelléas et Mélisande* was intended to evoke only the dramatic content of Maeterlinck's play. The music was never allowed to speed up or slow down the various attitudes or passions of the characters:

> Les sentiments d'un personnage ne peuvent s'exprimer continuellement d'une façon mélodique; puis la mélodie dramatique doit être tout autre que la mélodie en général.... A l'audition d'une oeuvre, le spectateur est accoutumé à éprouver deux sortes d'émotions bien distinctes: l'émotion musicale d'une part, l'émotion du personnage de l'autre; généralement il les ressent successivement. J'ai essayé que ces deux émotions fussent parfaitement fondues et simultanées.[18]

This statement is as helpful in illuminating what Strauss does not do as it is in showing how clearly Debussy realized his own self-imposed goals.

Strauss continually molds his text so that the "musical emotion" outweighs the "emotion of the character." Strauss, too, builds his music upon the foundations of Germanic music composition that go back way before Wagner, all the way to Mozart and Haydn. When Strauss needs Mozartian symmetry, he uses it. When he needs the coloristic texture of a Beethoven symphony, he writes like Beethoven. When he needs Wagnerian freedom, he takes it. Obviously, both Strauss and Hofmannsthal were keenly aware of the similarity between the sound of Zerbinetta's Italianate name and that of innummerable characters in the operas of Mozart: Zerlina in *Don Giovanni*, Suzanna in *Le Nozze di Figaro*, and Papagena in *Die Zauberflöte* (to name only a few). For Hofmannsthal, Zerbinetta "cancels out" the pathos of Ariadne; she exists in the play in Symbolic contradistinction to Ariadne's role.

Strauss realizes this complex concept in music by frequently writing like Mozart when Zerbinetta sings in the opera. As Zer-

binetta names her lovers, Strauss resorts to the old musical couplings of rhythmic pulse, harmonic movement, and melodic structure. At times, the rhythm of the musical thought is the same as in
Mozart. Even the texture is similar. We are far from the everlasting
love of Tristan, or the nihilistic absolute of Axel. We are back in the
elegant, coquettish world of *Le Nozze di Figaro,* or *Cosi Fan Tutte,* or
Don Giovanni (see figure 7-1). "Like a god came each one of my lovers," sings Zerbinetta, "and his footstep left me speechless."[19] This
does not last, though. Soon another "god" comes. All of this is in
contrast to Ariadne, who really does await her god, Bacchus.

Admittedly, Strauss draws upon a Mozart viewed through the
misty forests of Wagner. Strauss pulls apart his periodic structure
by sliding into numerous harmonic progressions within the
phrase, as Wagner does in *Lohengrin.* He also adds a few extra measures to his period here, thereby disguising his borrowings from
musical classicism. Nevertheless, Strauss forms the Symbolist text
to fit the needs of bel canto opera, to provide the recognizable musical environment of coloratura singing.

With these virtuoso passages from *Ariadne auf Naxos,* compare
the understated intensity of Debussy's music for Maeterlinck's text
in act 3 of *Pelléas et Mélisande.* At the beginning of the act, the sparse
octave ostinato of the harp, which resembles the opening of the piano piece "La Soirée dans Grenade," is given the barest amount of
harmonic flesh. Here, less is more. The A, F-sharp, and D, played
by the first violins, leave the ostinato hovering ambiguously in the
air (see figure 7-2). The B chord of the sixth measure initiates another ostinato, which alternates between the augmented sound
provided by the G-natural–F-sharp–D-sharp pattern and the major sound of the G-sharp–F-sharp–D-sharp pattern.

When Mélisande finally enters, she sings alone. Her melodic
line, which is unusually tuneful for this opera, flirts with a lydian
mode built on G. The tonal suspense created by this flirtation with
the modal scale, played off against the more familiar sound of an
E-minor scale, contributes brilliantly to the tension of the text as
Mélisande lowers her long tresses to the threshold of the tower (see
figure 7-3). Debussy barely touches his text. No long melisma or
ornamented passagework is needed. An absolute minimum of harmonic support is supplied. Only an atmosphere is created. In fact,
in setting the text, Debussy does little else here except write a single
note for each syllable. The music does not intrude upon the words.

7-1. Strauss, *Ariadne auf Naxos,* act 2, measures 1–2

7-2. Debussy, *Pélleas et Mélisande,* act 3, scene 1, measures 1–10. Copyright © 1907, Durand S. A. Editions Musicales (and/or United Music Publishers). Used by permission of the publisher. Theodore Presser Company, sole representative U.S.A.

7-3. *Pelléas et Mélisande*, act 3, scene 1, measures 18–23. Copyright © 1907, Durand S. A. Editions Musicales (and/or United Music Publishers). Used by permission of the publisher. Theodore Presser Company, sole representative U.S.A.

The contrast between the eclectic style of Strauss and the unified Symbolist treatment of Maeterlinck by Debussy becomes still more apparent when we compare Golaud's discovery of Mélisande in the forest to the meeting of Ariadne and Bacchus. Strauss finds sustenance in the vast storehouse of musical experience encompassed by Mozart, Beethoven, Wagner, and Brahms, which enables him to intensify the drama of the moment. Debussy writes a thin series of antifunctional harmonies. His music is comparatively abstract and pure. It does little except support Maeterlinck's poetry.

These are moments of great dramatic portent in both operas. Debussy needed to write music that would in some way link these expository events in the drama to the catastrophe resulting from the marriage of Golaud and Mélisande. Strauss had to render in music the abstract concepts of Hofmannsthal—Ariadne's awakening to death, which is really eternal life realized through the love of Bacchus ("both death and life at once"). Strauss takes advantage of the natural stresses of German in Hofmannsthal's verse to set up a highly symmetrical series of musical phrases:

I. Circe! Circe!
    Circe! Ich konnte fliehen!

II. Circe, du hast mir
     fast nichts getan?

III. Circe, ich konnte fliehen
      Sieh, ich kann lächeln und ruhen

IV. Circe! Circe!
     Was war dein Wille an mir zu tun?[20]

These words are set to four eight-bar periods. Within the periods, one finds Strauss's eclecticism. On "Circe! Circe!" Strauss writes huge declamatory intervals, creating musical cries reminiscent of those of Wagner's most heroic characters (see figure 7-4). This is not a Beethovenian period, but a Wagnerian one, for it wanders, during the consequent part of the phrase, from the original B-flat major to G major. In the next period, too, Strauss slips away from G major by the seventh bar, ending up on the foreign pitch of D-sharp (see figure 7-5). The third of the four periods combines two disparate musical styles. In the first four bars we hear the parallel thirds of Brahms (see figure 7-6). These glimmerings of a Brahmsian C-sharp minor are dropped quickly, though. Strauss closes the phrase with an extraordinarily simple I-V-I cadence in C-sharp major that could have been written by Mozart or a young Beethoven. Only the coloristic use of the harp marks this excerpt as a late Romantic passage (see figure 7-7).

7-4. *Ariadne auf Naxos,* act 2, scene 3, measures 389–96

7-5. *Ariadne auf Naxos,* act 2, scene 3, measures 397–404

7-6. *Ariadne auf Naxos,* act 2, scene 3, measures 405–08

7-7. *Ariadne auf Naxos,* act 2, scene 3, measures 409–12

When Ariadne responds to Bacchus's cries, she also answers in a periodic structure: "Belade nicht zu üppig / mit nächtlichem Entzücken."[21] It is the parallelism of the harmonies that enables us to identify this passage as the work of a composer steeped in late nineteenth-century practices. The rhythm of the harmonies, though, is neoclassical and divides the passage into neatly defined antecedent and consequent sections; and the phrase is held together tonally by the resounding A pedal in the basses and cellos (see figure 7-8).

7-8. *Ariadne auf Naxos,* act 2, scene 3, measures 420–28

Ariadne's first encounter with Bacchus is rendered in eclectic yet tonal and symmetrical phrases. In Debussy's opera, when Golaud meets Mélisande in the forest, they are both lost. Golaud's meanderings are signified in the music, too, for the music is without specific tonal orientation or symmetrical regularity in phrase structure. Here Debussy's success lies in his vagueness. The French composer masterfully realized in music the thematic ambiguity in Maeterlinck's writing. Consider, once again, the obscurities that confronted the composer in the play.

Golaud and Mélisande are estranged and disoriented from the first moments of Maeterlinck's work. Golaud discovers Mélisande weeping by a well. She is cloaked in Symbolist *mystère*. Who is she? Why is she weeping? Whose is the lovely crown that she has dropped in the well? We only know that it was given to her by a man ("it's the crown that *he* gave me") and that she would rather die than have it back ("I don't want it anymore. I prefer to die.")[22] A true Wagnerian would have attributed a specific cause of Mélisande's woes to a specific symbol or character. Perhaps an evil prince or a wicked knight could have served as a villainous equivalent for Wagnerian trolls and black princes. Maeterlinck leaves Mélisande as a victim of ambiguous evils. Who has harmed her? "Tous," she answers, and when Golaud asks what bad things have been done to her by "tous," she refuses to explain—"I don't want to say, I can't say."[23] The pattern of evasion continues. To the question "Where are you from?" she only answers that she ran away, that she is lost, that she comes from far away.[24] That is all we learn about the mysterious Mélisande. Seemingly brought together by chance, Golaud and Mélisande wander off together into the forest, still lost. In the next scene, we learn that they have been married. Maeterlinck has absorbed techniques we have identified in Symbolist lyrics into his dramatic writing. The lack of detailed semantic context increases the sense of ambiguity in the play. The unanswered questions, though, give the writing a unique power and universal significance.

In Debussy's music, the lack of tonal orientation generates the appropriate atmosphere of the mysterious, the unknown. This is achieved by rising whole-tone scales and interlocking chains of unresolved seventh and ninth chords. As the lovers sing, the concatenation of sevenths and ninths continues and the luxuriant chord pattern is held in check by a limpid and subdued orchestration. While Mélisande evades Golaud's questions, the music wanders tonally. The thematic evasion in the play, the ambiguous treatment of the codes of actions and questions, is equated by the composer with the denial of conventional aural expectations.

The whole-tone scale is made up of equidistant intervals that tend to negate the aural dominance of a single pitch. Out of the last bars of the short orchestral prelude in act 1, the scale rises. It prepares Golaud's entrance with a wash of ambiguous sound (see figure 7-9). The harmonies here, built upon that whole-tone scale, are no longer functional in the traditional sense, yet they have a valid coloristic purpose. Note, too, Golaud's stagnant asymmetrical melodic line and the frequent use of the same pitch for four or five syllables in a row. Debussy, unlike Strauss, does not allow the symmetrical phrases, a characteristic of traditional melody, to intrude upon the words. Symmetrical phrases create that foreign element, "the musical emotion," which Debussy wishes to avoid. He wants the character's emotion to dominate (see figure 7-10). Golaud rarely begins his asymmetrical phrases on a strong beat; he often enters on a weak beat in the middle of a bar. Even the points of entry change continuously. Debussy has written *vers libre* in music to go with the *vers libre* of Maeterlinck's poetry. The grouping of repeated note patterns in unequal, asymmetrical units creates Debussy's antimelodic style, a style that is maintained by the composer from Golaud's first utterances through the entire opera.

Debussy's manner is one of understatement. When Ariadne responds to the cries of Bacchus, Strauss uses a full orchestra to create excitement. But when Golaud first addresses Mélisande, Debussy needs almost no sound at all (see figure 7-11). As in Golaud's opening phrases, Debussy uses his asymmetrical style to facilitate the rendering of the dialogue in music. Mélisande's short exclamations on "Ne me touchez pas" are in response to Golaud's "Pourquoi pleurez-vous, ici, toute seule?" The disjunct interjections of the poetry are realized in the uneven phrases in the music, and the vocal lines are supported by chains of seventh and ninth chords. The rich, unresolved sonority on Golaud's "belle," for example, sounds like an old dominant function. Here, however, it dissolves into silence. Mélisande sings alone as she threatens to throw herself into the water if Golaud touches her. All expectations of an A cadence are finally thwarted a few bars later, as Golaud informs Mélisande that he will not bother her, but he will remain there, resting harmlessly against a tree. Now the accompaniment moves back to a reiteration of the forest motive, a tiny motivic kernel made up of open fifths and parallel octaves.

Debussy builds this deceptive resolution, which to a certain extent resembles the old deceptive cadence of traditional practice, not on the expected pitch of A, but on C-sharp. The old deceptive cadence relied on a firm set of expected resolutions in relation to symmetrical phrase structures to be truly deceptive. In Debussy, deception is the norm, not the exception. Nevertheless, Debussy shows his command of older practices here and throughout the opera, as he turns them around, even upside down, while developing his own unique voice.

7-9. *Pelléas et Mélisande,* act 1, scene 1, measures 24–25. Copyright © 1907, Durand S. A. Editions Musicales (and/or United Music Publishers). Used by permission of the publisher. Theodore Presser Company, sole representative U.S.A.

Figure 7–10 *(continued)*

crois que je me suis per - du   moi - même   et mes chiens ne me re -

trouvent plus   je vais re - ve - nir sur mes pas

7-10. *Pelléas et Mélisande*, act 1, scene 1, measures 25–41. Copyright © 1907, Durand S. A. Editions Musicales (and/or United Music Publishers). Used by permission of the publisher. Theodore Presser Company, sole representative U.S.A.

7-11. *Pelléas et Mélisande*, act 1, scene 1, measures 61–64. Copyright © 1904, Durand S. A. Editions Musicales (and/or United Music Publishers). Used by permission of the publisher. Theodore Presser Company, sole representative U.S.A.

  In the Strauss excerpt, harmonic events are linked to the even phrase structures. In Debussy, harmonic events are isolated and independent. The pressure of the cadence no longer holds harmonic movement in check. Debussy uses familiar sonorities in his opera, but the different contexts make them fresh. They exist in a new pattern of musical thought. Two especially important examples are the major triads that are used when Golaud and Mélisande identify themselves within the dramatic text. These are acts of naming, major instances of signification. As Maeterlinck allows his characters to name themselves in the drama, he provides a much-needed point of access into his ambiguous text. Debussy, accordingly, provides the familiar sound of the triad, the mainstay of the old style, as a basis for the uttering of the names in musical sound (see figures 7-12 and 7-13). These are major triads thwarted by their contexts, though. The strong B-flattish sound of Golaud is blurred by the F-sharp major chord in the next bar. Mélisande's G-flat major chord has little or nothing to do with G-flat major. Debussy builds harmonies on yet another whole-tone scale—one with a point of origin on G-flat—in the measures that follow it. The major triads are isolated events in Debussy's loose harmonic chains just as the two characters are lost in the forest.

Mé - li - san - de

7-12. *Pelléas et Mélisande*, act 1, scene 1, measure 136. Copyright © 1907, Durand S. A.Editions Musicales (and/or United Music Publishers). Used by permission of the publisher. Theodore Presser Company, sole representative U.S.A.

Je suis le   prin-ce Golaud   le pe - tit   fils d'Arkel   le vieux roi d'Allemon - de

7-13. *Pelléas et Mélisande*, act 1, scene 1, measures 125–26. Copyright © 1907, Durand S. A. Editions Musicales (and/or United Music Publishers). Used by permission of the publisher. Theodore Presser Company, sole representative U.S.A.

The crown Mélisande has allowed to fall into the water also receives a tiny spark of Wagnerism, a C-majorish triadic structure played pianissimo by the French horns (see figure 7-14). This is only a momentary flourish of tribute to the past that intimates the symbolic potential of the crown. Debussy leaves the crown stranded in the music just as Maeterlinck does in the text. Mélisande will not have the crown back, and she panics when Golaud offers to retrieve it. She would rather die than have it back, she claims. As she cries that she will not have the crown, the whole-tone scales rise again in the orchestra, signifying her distraught state with tonal ambiguity. The crown, which intimates explanation in the text, is attached to a triadic sound. Mélisande's consternation, the real subject of the text, an entity in itself that needs no explanation, is given the revolutionary freedom of the whole-tone scale, and the liberated sonorities that stem from the scale's harmonic implications.

Although the crown and its musical signifier appear once more as Golaud casts a final glance at it, the symbol does not survive. Golaud now turns his full attention to Mélisande, who captivates him more intensely with each passing beat of the music. The Romantic residue of the crown is dropped for good, isolated, embedded yet unresolved in both text and music.

Certainly, Wagner made this kind of writing possible, but Debussy, in his opera, is anything but a Wagnerian. Whereas Wagner worked up heavy, aurally overwhelming textures, Debussy uses his harmonic innovations in a sparse, diaphonous score. In the same way Maeterlinck uses Wagnerian symbols in an anti-Wagnerian manner, Debussy defuses Wagner in his music. The French composer uses the familiar leitmotif, but he uses it in a uniquely French way. Of course, some passages in Debussy's opera, taken out of context, are highly similar to Wagner's music. The chain of thirds just before act 1, scene 3, is a case in point. It is almost identical to Wagner's "ring" motive (see figure 7-15).

7-14. *Pelléas et Mélisande*, act 1, scene 1, measure 94. Copyright © 1907, Durand S. A. Editions Musicales (and/or United Music Publishers). Used by permission of the publisher. Theodore Presser Company, sole representative U.S.A.

7-15. *Pelléas et Mélisande*, act 1, scene 2, measures 140–42. Copyright © 1907, Durand S. A. Editions Musicales (and/or United Music Publishers). Used by permission of the publisher. Theodore Presser Company, sole representative U.S.A.

Nevertheless, *Pelléas et Mélisande* is in no way derivative. Although Debussy has learned from his predecessor, he has absorbed his lessons into his own style. One finds leitmotifs in *Pelléas et Mélisande,* but they are so small and so carefully woven into the texture that it has become almost impossible to unravel them all. For example, Debussy's "fate" motive is built out of an oscillating two-note pattern that can fit literally anywhere into the musical patterns (see figure 7-16). It is highly similar to the simple "forest" motive (see figure 7-17) and to Pelléas's motive (see figure 7-18) or to Mélisande's motive (see figure 7-19). It is really the varied *Stimmungen* created by Debussy's rich harmonization and his ingenious use of the coloristic possibilities of the orchestra that set these tiny sparks of musical ideas apart. They are, in fact, almost identical.

Whether we consider Debussy's tone poem on Mallarmé's "Après-midi d'un faune," his songs, or his opera, we can identify his style in a few bars. Debussy is distinguished by the interplay of his innovations with his command of musical conventions. Debussy

7-16. *Pelléas et Mélisande,* act 1, scene 1, measures 5–6: the "fate" motive. Copyright © 1907, Durand S. A. Editions Musicales (and/or United Music Publishers). Used by permission of the publisher. Theodore Presser Company, sole representative U.S.A.

7-17. *Pelléas et Mélisande,* act 1, scene 1, measures 1–4: the "forest" motive. Copyright © 1907, Durand S. A. Editions Musicales (and/or United Music Publishers). Used by permission of the publisher. Theodore Presser Company, sole representative U.S.A.

7-18. *Pelléas et Mélisande*, act 1, scene 2, measures 92–93: Pelléas's motive. Copyright ©1907, Durand S. A. Editions Musicales (and/or United Music Publishers). Used by permission of the publisher. Theodore Presser Company, sole representative U.S.A.

7-19. *Pelléas et Mélisande*, act 1, scene 1, measure 13: Mélisande's motive. Copyright © 1907, Durand S. A. Editions Musicales (and/or United Music Publishers). Used by permission of the publisher. Theodore Presser Company, sole representative U.S.A.

always breaks rules from a position of knowledge and authority, and never out of ignorance. His musical style is rooted in the experimental voice of Mallarmé, a poet whose ambiguities result from absolute linguistic mastery rather than amateurish accident. Mallarmé, though, did not produce a dramatic text suitable for a Symbolist opera, in spite of his theoretical interest in the theater. Debussy, accordingly, turned to Maeterlinck. The norm in Debussy is to displace conventional sounds into unexpected positions, to pull apart old patterns of musical expression and leave them enhanced in isolation, invigorated by fresh contexts.

While Strauss, in many respects, treats texts touched by Symbolist influences with conventional approaches, Debussy's keen understanding of the literary culture of his time makes him unique. Debussy's delicate undermining of compositional rule expresses in music the highest ideals of the Symbolist—disdain for the didactic, realization of the evocative, intellectual challenge, great impact achieved through understatement. As Debussy returns to the D-flat tonality at the close of his *Feux d'artifice* piano prelude or acknowledges E major in his prelude to Mallarmé's "Après-midi d'un faune," he returns to D minor at the close of the first scene of his opera. The "forest" motive, which begins the opera, returns replete with its original pitches (see figure 7-20). Tonal unity is recognized, but it is not needed, and there is irony in Debussy's impish concession to musical orthodoxy. The return to the tonality is hidden, veiled by too many excursions into remote regions of harmonic possibility. It is in no way prepared by the spinning out of the music as Debussy sets the text. There is no aural resolution because there is no adequate preparation (in spite of the dominant on A in the preceding two bars).

When Debussy speaks of "musical emotion" and the "emotion of character" as two contradistinct entities that should not clash in an ideal opera, he shows that he understands how the dictates of standard musical phrase structures impose upon dramatic material. His great achievement in *Pelléas et Mélisande* is that he does not allow this imposition to take place. Strauss had different, equally valid intentions, but his writing for Hofmannsthal's libretto is outside the sphere of influence of the Mallarméan aesthetic. Debussy gave something new, something revolutionary to the world of opera. In his operas Strauss merely added enriched colors to the old rhythm of musical thought; the basic skeleton remained the same. Debussy was the composer who displaced the old rhythm of musical thought with a new pattern. For this reason, Debussy, who was sparked by Symbolist theories, was more instrumental than Strauss in the development of modern styles in art.

7-20. *Pelléas et Mélisande*, act 1, scene 1, measures 148–51. Copyright © 1904, Durand S. A. Editions Musicales (and/or United Music Publishers). Used by permission of the publisher. Theodore Presser Company, sole representative U.S.A.

Conclusion

To uncover the interfusion of literature and music in the late nineteenth century is not only to trace the mutual *Zeitgeist* shared by artists who worked in different media but also to examine technical parallels and influences in specific works of art. If one artist did dominate both the musical and literary scenes, it was Wagner, but he was often misunderstood by those who admired him most and he eventually inspired hostility in those who understood him best. Actually, the true progress of musico-literary interrelationships was paradoxical and contradictory. Wagner instilled a canon of asymmetrical freedom and ambiguity in French posts, literary theorists, and musicians, yet Baudelaire, who was one of the first to praise Wagner in the 1860s, was a practitioner of formalized classical symmetry in his poetry. Mallarmé, on the other hand, who probably understood Wagner less adequately than Baudelaire, did loosen the old syntactic and semantic ties of poetry and generated an entirely fresh series of developments in the arts. Debussy, finally, grasped both Wagner and Mallarmé with extraordinary perspicacity. Debussy, building upon Wagner's innovations, was also able to turn to Mallarmé as a model for a fresh, anti-Romantic sensibility.

Mallarmé was thus a common source of an antisentimental attitude that called for the cleansing of the sign systems of both music and poetry. Although Wagner had already loosened the old sign systems, his excessively didactic manner of constructing meanings proved to be unattractive to French taste in both the literary and musical arts. Thus, Mallarmé was the key. Without his influence, Debussy might have been an entirely different composer. Perhaps the most mysterious aspect of this deeply penetrating interrelationship between the arts of poetry and music is that Debussy's response to the Mallarméan aesthetic was clearly formed at the same time or even before major poets—poets like Hofmannsthal, Rilke, Yeats, or Maeterlinck—had realized the intrinsic value of Mallarmé's thought.

Mallarmé played against the logical ordering of actions and

questions that were traditionally housed, in verse, in symmetrical couplings and stanzaic blocks. Debussy also discarded the periodic phrase structures of pre-Wagnerian music, phrase structures which were housed within the functional system of tonal harmony. Although Debussy retained tonal harmony, he played against it and explored its coloristic possibilities to an unprecedented extent. It was this conscious awareness of the need to systematically challenge the old languages of poetry and music that bound "L'Après-midi d'un faune" to its musical counterpart, Debussy's *Prélude*.

The new attitude was more important than genre, medium, or scope in both music and literature. It held true for small lyrics and musical settings of those lyrics. The way in which a composer responds to a literary text is another means of gauging musico-literary interrelationships. In the case of Debussy, his manner of dealing with Baudelaire, Verlaine, and Mallarmé lyrics shows a remarkable awareness of the innovations of literary Symbolism and also reflects his evolution as a composer. His Baudelaire songs are undeniably the most Wagnerian pieces in his oeuvre, and his Mallarmé songs are the most elliptical, hermetic, and understated. Schoenberg, too, turned to the Symbolist aesthetic as he was wrestling with the overbearing presence of Wagnerism in Viennese musical culture. George stimulated Schoenberg's movement away from the old tonal hierarchy into a style of complete atonality. Eventually, the *Georgelieder* led to the total abstraction of Schoenbergian serialism in the 1920s, a musical style that resembles the extreme abstraction of Mondrian and the Bauhaus movement.

Both small and large forms, then, were affected by the new aesthetic. The lyric, the song, the cycle of poems, the song cycle, the tone poem, and the lyric play all were touched by the musico-literary aesthetic of Mallarmé. Finally, even the opera became a medium of expression for the Symbolist aesthetic through the libretti of both Hofmannsthal and Maeterlinck, but only in the hands of Debussy did a Symbolist playwright find a realization of his literary sensibility in a musical voice.

The most remarkable and representative of the new subgenres of the era were the one-act lyric play of the Symbolist theater and its corresponding musical form—the one-movement tone poem. Both the tone poem and the lyric play were relatively short-lived forms that did not survive much beyond the first decade of the twentieth century. Thus, they were uniquely characteristic of their age.

Notes

Introduction

1. See the commentary by Walter Kaufmann in his translation of *The Birth of Tragedy and the Case of Wagner* (New York: Random House, 1967), p. 15.

2. (Princeton: Princeton University Press, 1961).

3. Both Arthur Wenk and Robin Holloway have made similar observations. This distinction is undeniable and vitally important. See Arthur Wenk, *Claude Debussy and the Poets* (Berkeley: University of California Press, 1976), pp. 246–47; Robin Holloway, *Debussy and Wagner* (London: Eulenburg, 1979), p. 43.

1. Periodicity and Correspondences in Poetry and Music

1. Walter Pater, *The Renaissance: Studies in Art and Poetry,* ed. Donald L. Hill (Berkeley: University of California Press, 1980), p. 106.

2. See Stéphane Mallarmé, *Oeuvres complètes* (Paris: Gallimard, 1945), p. 156.

3. Edward Lockspeiser, *Music and Painting* (London: Cassell, 1973), p. 15. For Wagner's ideas on the unconscious, see Richard Wagner, *Sämtliche Schriften und Dichtungen,* vol. 9, *Beethoven* (Leipzig: Siegel, 1900), pp. 75–85.

4. Two of the newest studies are Rudolf Arnheim, *The Power of the Center* (Berkeley: University of California Press, 1982) and E. H. Gombrich, *The Image and the Eye* (Ithaca: Cornell University Press, 1982).

5. *New Grove Dictionary of Music and Musicians,* 1980, s.v. "rhythm," by Walther Dürr and Walter Gerstenberg; *Harvard Dictionary of Music,* 2nd ed., s.v. "rhythm"; *Oxford English Dictionary,* 1926 ed., s.v. "rhythm"; *Webster's Third New International Dictionary* (unabridged), s.v. "rhythm."

6. "L'Ancienne rhétorique," *Communications* 16 (1970): 222.

7. Trans. W. Rhys Roberts (New York: Random House, 1954), p. 182.

8. Barthes, "L'Ancienne rhétorique," p. 222.

9. (London: Oxford University Press, 1971).

10. Ibid., p. 21.

11. Ibid.

12. Harold S. Powers, "Language Models and Musical Analysis," *Ethnomusicology* (January 1980): 51.

13. Ibid.

14. as quoted in Powers.

15. *New Grove Dictionary,* s.v. "rhythm."

16. *Die Welt als Wille und Vorstellung* (Leipzig: Brodhaus, 1888), pp. 518–19.

The musical period consists of several bars, and it has also two equal parts, one rising, aspiring, generally going to the dominant, and one sinking, quieting, returning to the fundamental note. Two or several periods constitute a part, which in general is also symmetrically doubled by the sign of repetition; two parts make a small piece of music, or only a movement of a larger piece; and thus a concerto or sonata usually consists of three movements, a symphony of four, and a mass of five. Thus we see the musical composition bound together and rounded off as a whole, by symmetrical distribution and repeated division, down to the beats and their fractions, with thorough subordination, superordination, and co-ordination of its members, just as a building is connected and rounded off by its symmetry. Only in the latter that is exclusively in space which in the former is exclusively in time.

Arthur Schopenhauer, *The World as Will and Idea,* trans. R. B. Haldane and R. Kemp (London: Routledge and Kegan Paul, 1964), pp. 239–40.

17. As quoted in Carl Dahlhaus, *Between Romanticism and Modernism,* trans. Mary Whittall (Berkeley: University of California Press, 1980), p. 53.

18. *New Grove,* s.v. "rhythm," p. 819.

19. Hugo Riemann, *System der musikalischen Rhythmik und Metrik* (Leipzig: Breitkopf und Hartel, 1903), p. 196.

20. *New Grove,* s.v. "rhythm," p. 819.

21. Dahlhaus, *Between Romanticism,* p. 59.

22. S. R. Levin, *Linguistic Structures in Poetry* (Mouton: The Hague, 1967), p. 42; Sandra Bermann, "The Sonnet: Repetition with a Difference," paper presented at the 10th ICLA Congress held in August 1982 at New York University.

23. Levin, *Linguistic Structures in Poetry,* p. 34.

24. Ibid., p. 42.

25. Ibid.

26. Ibid.

27. Ibid.

28. Ibid., p. 43.

29. Hermann von Helmholtz, *On the Sensations of Tone,* trans. Alexander J. Ellis (New York: Dover, 1954), p. 8.

30. Bermann, "The Sonnet," p. 1.

31. Jakobson as quoted in Levin, *Linguistic Structures,* p. 52.

32. *New Grove,* 1980, s.v. "tonality," by Carl Dahlhaus, p. 51.

33. Here I follow the arguments presented by Carl Dahlhaus in his article on "harmony" in the *New Grove Dictionary,* 1980, p. 183.

34. Levin, *Linguistic Structures,* p. 9.

35. Baudelaire, *Oeuvres complètes* (Paris: Edition du Seuil, 1968), p. 88.

36. Henri Peyre, ed., *Baudelaire: A Collection of Critical Essays* (Englewood Cliffs, NJ: Prentice Hall, 1962), pp. 150–55.

37. René Wellek, *Theory of Literature* (New York: Harcourt, Brace, *1956*), pp. 129–45.

38. Mallarmé, *Oeuvres complètes*, p. 27.

39. Baudelaire, *Oeuvres complètes*, p. 46.

40. Arnold Schoenberg, *The Structural Functions of Harmony* (New York: Norton, 1954), p. 44.

41. Baudelaire, *Oeuvres complètes*, p. 46.

42. See also the discussion by the linguist Stephen Ullmann, *The Principles of Semantics* (Oxford: Basil Blackwell, 1957), pp. 266–88.

43. *Meditations on a Hobby Horse* (New York: Phaidon, 1963), p. 14.

44. Ibid.

45. The subsequent summary of Barthes's ideas is taken from *S/Z* (Paris: Edition du Seuil, 1970), p. 37.

46. Baudelaire, *Oeuvres complètes*, p. 512.

From the very first bars the soul of the pious wanderer who is awaiting the holy vessel *plunges into an infinity of space.* Little by little there forms before his eyes a strange vision which takes a body and a face. The vision becomes clearer, and the *miraculous host of angels* passes before him, bearing the holy cup in their midst. The sacred procession draws nearer; the heart of the elect of God gradually stirs; it swells, it expands; ineffable yearnings awaken within him; *he yields to a growing feeling of bliss* as the *radiant vision* comes ever closer, and when at last the Holy Grail itself appears in the midst of the sacred procession, *he is swallowed up in an ecstasy of adoration, as if the whole world had suddenly disappeared.*

Meanwhile the Holy Grail pours its blessings upon the saint in prayer, consecrating him its knight. Then the *burning flames gradually mitigate their brilliance*: in holy joy, the angelic host, smiling upon the earth that they are leaving, returns to the heavenly heights. They have left the Holy Grail in the care of pure men, *into whose hearts the divine essence has flowed,* and the majestic company vanishes *into the infinities of space* in the same way that it first appeared.

Id., *The Painter of Modern Life and Other Essays,* trans. Jonathan Mayne (London: Phaidon, *1965*), p. *114.*

47. Baudelaire, *Oeuvre complètes*, pp. 512–13.

48. Ibid., p. 513.

The prelude contains and reveals that *mystical element* which is always present and always latent in the work. . . . To teach us the untellable power of this secret, Wagner shows us first of all the *ineffable beauty of the sanctuary,* the dwelling-place of a God who avenges the oppressed and asks no more than *faith and love* from his followers. He introduces us to the Holy Grail; we are made to see glimmering before our eyes the temple of incorruptible wood, with its sweet-smelling walls, its doors of *gold,* its joists of *asbestos,* its columns of *opal,* its partitions of *cymophane,* and its porticoes, which may only be approached by those whose hearts are uplifted and whose hands pure. He is very careful not to present it to us in all its awe-inspiring reality, but, as though to spare our feeble senses, he shows it first of all reflected in *some azure wave* or mirrored by *some iridescent cloud*.

At the beginning it is a *vast, slumbering lake* of melody, a *vaporous extending ether,* on which the holy picture may take form before our profane eyes: this is a passage given exclusively to the violins, divided into eight different desks, which, after several bars of harmonious chords, is then taken up by the mellowest of the wind instruments; the horns and the bassoons join in to prepare for the entrance of the trumpets and the trombones which repeat the melody for the fourth time *with a dazzling burst of colour,* as if at this unique moment the holy edifice had *blazed forth* before our *blinded eyes,* in *all its radiant and luminous magnificence.* But the vivid sparkle which has been gradually raised to this *intensity of solar effulgence* dies away swiftly, like a *celestial glimmer.* The *diaphonous vapour* of the clouds closes in once more, the vision dissolves little by little amid the same iridescent incense in which it first appeared and the piece concludes with a repetition of the first six bars, only *more ethereal still.* The *ideally mystical* quality which characterizes it is conveyed not least by the *pianissimo* which is always preserved by the orchestra and which is barely interrupted by the brief moment in which the *brass bursts forth* with the marvellous phrases of the prelude's single motive. Such is the image which stirs our senses at a first hearing of this sublime agadio.

ID *Painter of Modern Life and other Essays,* pp. 115–16.

    49. Baudelaire, *Oeuvres complètes,* p. 513.

    50. Ibid.

However it would be by no means absurd at this point to argue *a priori*; for what would be truly surprising would be to find that sound *could not* suggest colour, that colours *could not* evoke the idea of a melody, and that sound and colour were *unsuitable* for the translation of ideas, seeing that things have always found their expression through a system of reciprocal analogy ever since the day when God uttered the world like a complex and indivisible statement.

Id., *The Painter of Modern Life,* p. 116.

    51. Baudelaire, *Oeuvres complètes,* pp. 513–14.

I remember that from the very first bars I suffered one of those happy impressions that almost all imaginative men have known, through dreams, in sleep. I felt myself released from the *bonds of gravity,* and I rediscovered in memory that extraordinary *thrill of pleasure* which dwells in *high places* (be it noted in passing that I was as yet ignorant of the programme quoted a moment ago). Next I found myself imagining the delicious state of a man in the grip of a profound reverie, in an absolute solitude, a solitude with an *immense horizon* and a *wide diffusion of light; an immensity with no other decor but itself.* Soon I experienced the

sensation of a *brightness* more vivid, an *intensity of light* growing so
swiftly that not all the nuances provided by the dictionary would be
sufficient to express *this ever-renewing increase of incandescence and heat.*
Then I came to the full conception of the idea of a soul moving about
in a luminous medium, of an ecstasy *composed of knowledge and joy,* hovering high above the natural world.

Id., *Painter of Modern Life,* pp. 116–17.

    52. Baudelaire, *Oeuvres complètes,* p. 514. "In all three interpretations we
find a sensation of *spiritual and physical bliss*; of *isolation*; of the contemplation of
something infinitely great and infinitely beautiful; of an *intensity of light* which rejoices *the eyes and the soul until they swoon*; and finally a sensation of *space reaching
to the furthest conceivable limits.*" Id., *Painter of Modern Life,* p. 117.

    53. Gombrich, *Meditations,* p. 7.

    54. Ibid.

    55. Walter Benjamin, *Illuminations,* trans. Harry Zohn (New York:
Schocken, 1969), p. 163.

    56. Baudelaire, *Oeuvres complètes, p.* 82.

2. Wagner and the French

    1. Richard Wagner, *Lohengrin* (New York: Kalmus), pp. 27–8.

    2. Ibid.

    3. Richard Wagner, *Sämtliche Schriften und Dichtungen,* vol. 10, *Über die
Anwendung der Musik auf das Drama* (Leipzig: Siegel, 1900), p. 191.

    4. Ibid., p. 192.

    5. Schoenberg, *Structural Functions of Harmony,* pp. 77–78.

    6. Wagner, *Schriften,* vol. 7, *Zukunftsmusik,* p. 121.

    7. Dahlhaus quotes this expression of Wagner's in *Between Romanticism,*
p. 53.

    8. Wagner, *Schriften,* vol. 7, pp. 87–137.

    9. Ibid., p. 122.

    10. Ibid., p. 123.

    11. Wagner, *Schriften,* vol. 9, *Beethoven,* p. 78.

    12. Ibid., p. 79.

    13. Ibid.

    14. Ibid.

    15. Ibid., pp. 83–84.

    16. Ibid.

The *Vernunft* of his art he found in that spirit which had built the formal framework of its outer scaffolding. And what a scant *Vernunft* it
was that spoke to him from that architectonic poise of periods, when
he saw how even the greatest masters of his youth bestirred themselves with banal repetition of flourishes and phrases, with mathematical
distribution of loud and soft, with regulation introductions of just so
many solemn bars, and the inevitable passages through the gate of
just so many half-closes to the saving uproar of the final cadence!
'Twas the *Vernunft* that had formed the operatic aria, dictated the

stringing-together of operatic numbers, the logic that made Haydn chain his genie to an everlasting counting of his rosary beads.

Id., *Richard Wagner's Prose Works*, vol. 5, *Beethoven*, trans. William Ashton Ellis (London: Kegan, Paul, Trench, Trubner, 1896), pp. 83–84.

17. Wagner, *Beethoven*, p. 109.

18. Ibid., p. 80.

19. Wagner did not use the expression "musical prose," but Schoenberg did when speaking of Wagner's approach to composition. See the discussion in Dahlhaus, *Between Romanticism*, pp. 52–71. See also Arnold Schoenberg, *Style and Idea* (New York: St. Martin's Press, 1950), p. 72.

20. Wagner, *Schriften* vol. 4, *Oper und Drama*, pp. 91–92. The ensuing account of *Stabreim* is taken from pp. 92–100.

21. Ibid., p. 120.

22. Ibid.

23. Ibid., vol. 9, 84.

24. Charles Rosen and Henri Zerner, "Enemies of Realism," *New York Review of Books* 29 (March, 1982): 33.

25. Wagner, *Schriften*, vol. 4, p. 121.

26. Wagner, *Schriften*, vol. 9, pp. 68–69.

27. Ibid.

28. Nietzsche, *The Birth of Tragedy and the Case of Wagner*, p. 171.

29. Dahlhaus, *Between Romanticism*, pp. 58–9.

30. *Revue Wagnérienne* 1 (January, 1886): 371–79. The *Revue Wagnérienne* is collected in three volumes. Volume 1 goes from 1885–86; volume 2, from 1886–87; volume 3, from 1887–88. The periodical is hereafter referred to as RW.

31. RW, 1 (February, 1885): 7.

32. RW, 1 (May, 1885): 109.

33. RW, 1 (May, June, July, August, 1885): 104–15, 142–48, 182–86, 211–13.

34. RW, 1 (February, 1885): 6–7.

35. RW, 1 (May, 1885): 105.

36. RW, 3 (November-December, 1887): 255.

37. Ibid.

38. Ibid.

39. RW, 2 (September, 1886): 259–60.

40. Ibid.

41. RW, 3 (July-August, 1888): 182–84.

42. RW, 3 (September-October, 1887): 211.

43. RW, 2 (February, 1886): 8–9.

44. See Mallarmé's preface to René Ghil's *Traité du verbe*, ed. Tizianna Goruppi (Paris: Nizet, 1978), p. 82.

45. RW, 2 (February, 1886): 22.

46. RW, 1 (April, 1885): 6–7.

47. RW, 1 (June, 1885): 131.

48. Ibid., p. 133.

49. Ibid., p. 134.

50. Ibid., p. 135.
51. Ibid.
52. Ibid.
53. Ibid.
54. Ibid.
55. RW, 2 (September, 1886): 266.
56. RW, 1 (January, 1886): 352.
57. Ibid., p. 353.
58. Ibid.
59. Ibid., p. 354.
60. Ibid.
61. Ibid., p. 355.
62. Ibid., pp. 354–55.
63. Ibid.
64. Ibid., p. 354.
65. Ibid., p. 354.
66. Ibid., p. 355.
67. All of the material recounted in this passages was taken from RW, 2 (June, 1886): 150–71.
68. RW, 3 (July, 1886): 184.
69. Ibid.
70. Ibid., p. 187.
71. RW, 2 (March, 1886): 33–35.
72. RW, 3 (February, 1887): 22.
73. RW, 1 (August, 1885): 194.
74. Ibid.
75. Ibid.
76. Ibid.
77. Ibid., p. 195.
78. Ibid.
79. RW, 3 (April, 1887): 65.
80. RW, 3 (July-August, 1887): 153–54.
81. Ibid.
82. RW, 3 (no month given, 1888): 294.
83. Ibid., p. 299.
84. Mallarmé, *Oeuvres complètes,* p. 71.

3. Mallarmé and Debussy

1. *Meditations,* p. 16.
2. Ibid.
3. Ibid., p. 17.
4. Mallarmé, *Oeuvres complètes,* p. 365.
5. Ibid., pp. 365–66.

The Decadent or Mystic Schools (as they call themselves or as they were hastily labeled by the public press) find their common meeting-ground in an Idealism which (as in the case of fugues and sonatas) shuns the materials in nature, avoids any thought that might tend to arrange them too directly or precisely, and retains only the suggestiveness of things. The poet must establish a careful relationship between two images, from which a third element, clear and fusible, will be distilled and caught by our imagination. We renounce that erroneous esthetic (even though it has been responsible for certain masterpieces) which would have the poet fill the delicate pages of his book with the actual and palpable wood of trees, rather than with the forest's shuddering or the silent scattering of thunder through the foliage. A few well-chosen sounds blown heavenward on the trumpet of true majesty will suffice to conjure up the architecture of the ideal and only habitable palace—palace of no palpable stone, else the book could not be properly closed.

Id., *Selected Prose Poems, Essays, and Letters,* trans. Bradford Cook (Baltimore: Johns Hopkins, 1956), pp. 39–40.

    6. Mallarmé, *Oeuvres complètes,* p. 366. "It is not *description* which can unveil the efficacy and beauty of monuments, seas, or the human face in all their maturity and native state, but rather evocation, *allusion, suggestion.*" Id., *Selected Prose Poems, Essays,* p. 40.

    7. Mallarmé, *Oeuvres complètes,* pp. 367–68.

    8. Ibid.

    9. Ibid.

    10. Ibid. "Everything will be hesitation, disposition of parts, their alternations and relationships—all this contributing to the rhythmic totality, which will be the very silence of the poem, in its blank spaces, as that silence is translated by each structural element in its own way." Id., *Selected Prose Poems, Essays,* p. 41.

    11. Ibid., pp. 455–56.

    12. Ibid.

    13. Ibid.

    14. Ibid.

    15. Ibid.

    16. Richard Wagner, *Parsifal Libretto,* (New York: Rullman, n.d.), p. 5.

    17. Ibid., p. 10.

    18. Mallarmé, *Oeuvres complètes,* p. 68.

    19. Robert Greer Cohn, *Towards the Poems of Mallarmé* (Berkeley: University of California Press, 1965), p. 127.

    20. Mallarmé, *Oeuvres complètes,* p. 68.

    21. Mallarmé, "Richard Wagner: Rêverie d'un poète français," *Oeuvres complètes,* p. 545.

    22. Calvin Brown, "The Musical Analogies in Mallarmé's *Un Coup de dés,*" *Comparative Literature Studies* 10 (1967): 72.

    23. Cohn, *Towards the Poems,* pp. 265–80.

    24. Mallarmé, *Oeuvres complètes,* p. 887.

    25. Wagner, *Schriften,* vol. 4, pp. 91–92.

    26. Ibid.

27. Barthes, *S/Z*, p. 37.

28. Ibid.

29. Ovid, *Metamorphoses*, trans. Rolfe Humphries (Bloomington: Indiana University Press, 1955), pp. 24–25.

30. Mallarmé, *Oeuvres complètes*, p. 1450.

31. Ibid.

32. Ibid., p. 1456.

33. Ibid., p. 50.

34. Suzanne Bernard, *Mallarmé et la musique* (Paris: Nizet, 1959), pp. 113–14.

35. Arthur Wenk, *Claude Debussy and the Poets* (Berkeley: University of California Press, 1976), pp. 148–70.

36. As quoted in Wenk, *Claude Debussy*, p. 152.

37. Mallarmé, *Oeuvres complètes, p.* 50.

38. Ibid., p. 870.

Later on, around 1875, all the Parnassians (except for a few friends such as Mendès, Dierx, and Cladel) shrieked with horror at my *Afternoon of a Faun*, and all together, they threw it out. For I *was* trying, actually, to make a sort of running pianistic commentary upon the fully preserved and dignified alexandrine—a sort of musical accompaniment which the poet composes himself, so that the official verse will appear only on the really important occasions.

Id., *Prose Poems, Essays*, p. 22.

39. Mallarmé, *Oeuvres complètes*, p. 51.

40. Ibid., pp. 50–51.

41. *Grand Larousse de la langue française*, 1975, s.v. "conter"; E. Littré, *Dictionnaire de la langue française*, 1878, s.v. "conter."

42. Bernard, pp. 113–14.

43. Ibid.

44. Nicholas Ruwet, *Langue, musique, poésie* (Paris: Editions du Seuil, 1972), pp. 159–60.

45. Mallarmé, *Oeuvres complètes*, pp. 50–53.

46. Ruwet, pp. 176–80. Ruwet analyzes this example.

47. Mallarmé, *Oeuvres complètes*, p. 51.

48. Claude Debussy, *Monsieur Croche et autres écrits* (Paris: Gallimard, 1971), p. 175. "My lord! How intolerable these men in helmets and animal skins become by the fourth evening. . . . Remember they never appear unless accompanied by their damnable leitmotiv, and there are even those who sing it! It's rather like those silly people who hand you their visiting cards and then lyrically recite key information they contain. Most annoying to hear everything twice!" Id., *Debussy On Music*, trans. Richard Langham Smith (New York: Knopf, 1977), p. 203.

49. As quoted in Edward Lockspeiser, *Debussy: His Life and Mind, vol.* 1 (New York: Macmillan, 1962), pp. 204–8.

4. The Song Form and the Symbolist Aesthetic

1. See *New Grove Dictionary*, s.v. "Debussy," for a complete catalog of Debussy's works.

2. Debussy, *Debussy on Music,* trans. Richard Langham Smith (New York: Knopf, 1977), p. 77.

3. Paul Verlaine, *Oeuvres complètes* (Paris: Vanier, 1907), p. 311.

4. Claude Debussy, *Songs: 1880–1904,* ed. Rita Benton (New York: Dover, 1981), pp. 171–73.

5. Debussy, *Monsieur Croche,* p. 270.

6. Robin Holloway, DEBUSSY AND WAGNER (London: Eulenburg, 1979), p. 43.

7. Debussy, *Monsieur Croche,* pp. 201–2.

8. Ibid.

Good poetry has a rhythm of its own, which makes it very difficult for us. One minute, though: recently, I set to music (I don't know why) three of Villon's ballads. But I do know why: because I have wanted to for a long time. It is very difficult to follow and to cast the rhythms in a suitable mold, still preserving one's inspiration. If one cheats and is content with a mere juxtaposition of the two arts, it is not too difficult, but is it worth the trouble? Classic poetry has a life of its own, an "interior dynamism," as the Germans would say. But then that is not our concern.

Blank verse is a little easier; we can turn to the world of the senses. But why should the musician not write his own blank verse? What is he waiting for? Wagner did it. But then his poems, like his music, are not an example that should be followed. His texts are no better than any others, but for him they are the best, and that's the main thing.

Id., *Debussy on Music,* pp. 250–51.

9. Debussy, *Songs,* pp. 172–73.

10. The symbols used here are those of the International Phonetic Association. The same symbols are used throughout this study to show phonological aspects of language.

11. Verlaine, *Oeuvres complètes,* p. 155.

12. Debussy, *Songs,* p. 173.

13. Verlaine, *Oeuvres complètes,* p. 33.

14. Debussy, *Songs,* p. 173.

15. Ibid.

16. Verlaine, *Oeuvres complètes,* p. 33.

17. Ibid., p. 155.

18. Debussy, *Songs,* p. 173.

19. Debussy, *Monsieur Croche,* pp. 45–46.

20. Wenk, *Claude Debussy,* p. 22.

21. Verlaine, *Oeuvres complètes,* p. 112.

22. Ghil, *Traité,* p. 109.

23. Gombrich, *Meditations,* p. 14.

24. John Keats, *The Norton Anthology of Poetry* (New York: Norton, 1975), pp. 712–13.

25. Verlaine, *Oeuvres complètes,* p. 153.

26. Ibid., p. 155.

27. Wenk, p. 134.

28. Mallarmé, *Oeuvres complètes,* p. 870.

He was the first to react against the impeccable and impassible Parnassian attitudes. His fluid verse and certain of his intentional dissonances were already evident in *Sagesse.* . . .

But the father, the real father of all the young poets is Verlaine, the magnificent Verlaine. The attitude of the man is just as noble as the attitude of the writer. For it is the only possible attitude at a time when all poets are outlaws. Think of absorbing all the grief that he has—and with his pride and his tremendous pluck!

Id., *Prose Poems, Essays,* pp. 22–23.

29. Wenk, p. 245.

30. See Wenk, pp. 246–47; Holloway, p. 43.

31. Wenk, p. 248.

32. Littré, *Dictionnaire,* s.v. "soupire" and "soupirer."

33. Ibid.

34. Ibid.

35. Ibid.

36. Mallarmé, *Oeuvres complètes, p.* 39.

37. Wenk, pp. 246–47.

38. Littré, s.v. "soupirer."

39. Wenk, p. 166.

40. Debussy, *Monsieur Croche,* pp. 45–46.

41. Littré, s.v. "Sèvres."

42. Ibid., s.v. "placet" and "placer."

43. Ibid.

44. Mallarmé, *Oeuvres complètes,* p. 1415.

45. Ibid., pp. 30–31.

46. Ibid., p. 58.

47. Littré, s.v. "mensonge."

48. Ibid., s.v. "vertige."

49. Ibid., s.v. "sceptre."

5. The Book of the Hanging Gardens

1. Carl Schorske, *Fin-de-Siècle Vienna* (New York: Random House, 1979), p. 322.

2. Ibid., p. 345.

3. Ibid., p. 346.

4. Ibid.

5. Ibid.

6. Ibid.

7. Ibid.

8. Ibid.

9. Stefan George, "Fünfzehn Gedichte aus *Das Buch der hängenden Gärten*," *The Penguin Book of Lieder,* ed. and trans. S. S. Prawer (Baltimore: Penguin, 1965), pp. 158–59.

10. As quoted in Arnold Schoenberg, *Das Buch der hängenden Gärten* (Vienna: Universal, n.d.).

11. Theodor W. Adorno, *Philosophy of Modern Music,* trans. Anne G. Mitchell and Wesley Blomster (New York: Seabury, 1973), pp. 36–39.

12. Ibid., p. 37.

13. Ibid., p. 39.

14. George, "Fünfzehn Gedichte," p. 159.

15. Schoenberg, *Das Buch,* p. 1.

16. George, "Fünfzehn Gedichte," p. 159.

17. Ibid.

18. Ibid.

19. Adorno, *Prisms,* trans. Samuel Weber and Shierry Weber (Cambridge: MIT Press, 1982), pp. 159–60.

20. George, "Fünfzehn Gedichte," p. 159.

21. Ibid., p. 160.

22. Ibid.

23. Adorno, *Prisms,* p. 160.

24. George, "Fünfzehn Gedichte," p. 159.

25. Ibid.

26. Ibid.

27. Ibid.

6. The Lyric Play and the Tone Poem

1. Lockspeiser, *Debussy,* vol. 1, pp. 189–90.

2. Ibid.

3. Ibid.

4. Debussy, *Monsieur Croche,* p. 139.

5. Lockspeiser, *Debussy,* vol. 1, p. 215.

6. Ibid., p. 220.

7. Ibid., p. 221.

8. Jean Marnold, *Mercure de France* 6 (1907): 734–36.

9. Ibid., p. 735.

10. Schorske points this out in *Fin-de-Siècle Vienna,* p. 347.

11. Anton Chekhov, *The Best Plays of Chekhov,* trans. Stark Young (New York: Random House, 1950), p. 14.

12. Maynard Solomon, *Beethoven* (New York: Macmillan, 1977), p. 193. Actually, this analogy was not made by Solomon. He credits the comparison to Lacépède, who in 1787 compared "the three movements of a sonata or symphony to the 'noble' first act, 'more pathetic' second act, and 'more tumultuous' third act of a drama."

13. Leo Spitzer, *Classical and Christian Ideas of World Harmony* (Baltimore: Johns Hopkins University Press, 1963), p. 5.

14. *New Grove Dictionary,* s.v. "symphonic poem," by Hugh MacDonald.

15. Ibid.

16. Debussy, *Monsieur Croche,* p. 214. "There are curious similarities between the art of Böcklin and that of Richard Strauss. There is a similar disregard for any kind of preconceived form, even a taste for a form derived directly from the color itself and a drawing of dramatic pictures with these very same colors." Id., *Debussy on Music,* p. 270.

17. Debussy, *Monsieur Croche,* p. 215.

Tod und Verklärung, without having the sparkling clarity of *Till Eulenspiegel* or the grandeur of *Don Juan,* nonetheless contains many of the original effects so dear to Strauss's heart, although he has improved on them in the meantime.

At the beginning one senses one is in a sepulcher in which the souls of the dead move uneasily around. . . . The spirit undergoes great torments, struggling as hard as it can to break free from its fleshly chains, the body that binds it to the earth. But then an oboe comes in with a singing melody reminiscent of an Italian cantilena. At first one does not quite understand why, because one's mind is still full of all those mysteriously migrating souls. Besides, even if one is concerned about what is actually happening in a symphonic poem it is better to refrain from writing about it. It is certainly not the reading of those little guides that will prevent the frequent misunderstandings between composer and audience.

Id., *Debussy on Music,* pp. 270–71.

18. Debussy, *Monsieur Croche,* p. 134.

The art of M. Richard Strauss is not always quite so fantastic but he definitely thinks in colored images, and he seems to draw the outline of his ideas with the orchestra. It's no mean way of doing things, but it's rarely used. What's more, M. Richard Strauss has found a highly individual way of handling the development. He no longer uses the rigorous architectural methods of a Bach or a Beethoven. Instead, he develops with rhythmic colors. He juxtaposes the strangest tonalities as if it were quite normal, for he is not concerned with what he has "abused" but only with what "new life" he has gained.

Id., *Debussy on Music,* p. 160.

19. Bertrand as quoted in Maurice Ravel, *Gaspard de la nuit* (Paris: Durand, n.d.), p. 16.

20. See the brief account of Rilke's evolution as a playwright by Klaus Phillips in Rilke, *Nine Plays,* trans. Klaus Phillips and John Locke (New York: Ungar, 1979), pp. ix–xv.

21. Ibid., p. 177.

22. Hofmannsthal, *Gesammelte Werke,* vol. 1 (Stockholm: Fischer, 1946), pp. 49–51.

23. Ibid.

24. Ibid.

25. Hofmannsthal, *Selected Prose,* trans. Mary Hottinger, Tanya Stern,

and James Stern, Bollingen series 33 (New York: Pantheon, 1952), p. 290.

26. Ibid.

27. Hofmannsthal, *Werke*, vol. 1: p. 273.

28. Goethe, *Faust*, trans. Walter Kaufmann (New York: Doubleday, 1963), pp. 92–93.

29. Hofmannsthal, *Werke*, vol. 1, p. 277.

30. Ibid., p. 279.

7. Symbolist Opera

1. Alfred Einstein, *Essays on Music* (New York: Norton, 1966), p. 252.

2. As quoted in Donald G. Daviau and George J. Buelow, *The Ariadne auf Naxos of Hugo von Hofmannsthal and Richard Strauss* (Chapel Hill: University of North Carolina Press, 1975), p. 42.

3. Ibid., p. 43.

4. Hugo von Hofmannsthal, *Ariadne auf Naxos*, libretto (New York: Boosey and Hawkes, 1943), p. 28.

5. Ibid., p. 30.

6. Ibid., p. 31.

7. Daviau and Buelow, *Ariadne of Hofmannsthal and Strauss*, p. 125.

8. Ibid., p. 124.

9. Ibid.

10. Ibid.

11. Ibid.

12. Hofmannsthal, *Ariadne*, p. 48.

13. Ibid.

14. Daviau and Buelow, *Ariadne of Hofmannsthal and Strauss*, p. 124.

15. Maeterlinck, *Pelléas et Mélisande* (New York: Schirmer, 1907), p. 37.

16. Ibid., p. 38.

17. Ibid., p. 40.

18. Debussy, *Monsieur Croche*, p. 62 and p. 270.

> A character cannot always express himself melodically: the dramatic melody has to be quite different from what is generally called melody. . . . On hearing opera, the spectator is accustomed to experiencing two distinct sorts of emotion: on the one hand the *musical emotion*, and on the other the emotion of the characters—usually he experiences them in succession. I tried to ensure that the two were perfectly merged and simultaneous.

Id., *Debussy on Music*, pp. 75, 80.

19. Hofmannsthal, *Ariadne*, p. 35.

20. Ibid., p. 45.

21. Ibid.

22. Maeterlinck, *Pelléas*, p. 8.

23. Ibid., p. 7.

24. Ibid., p. 8.

Bibliography

ADORNO, THEODORE W. *Philosophy of Modern Music.* Translated by Anne G. MITCHELL and WESLEY BLOMSTER. New York: Seabury, 1973.

———. *Prisms.* Translated by Samuel Weber and Shierry Weber. Cambridge: MIT Press, 1982.

ARMITAGE, MERLE. *Schoenberg.* New York: Schirmer, 1937.

ARNHEIM, RUDOLF. *The Power of the Center.* Berkeley: University of California Press, 1982.

ASCHER, GLORIA J. *"Die Zauberflöte" und "Die Frau ohne Schatten."* Berne: Francke, 1972.

BALAKIAN, ANNA. *The Symbolist Movement.* New York: New York University Press, 1977.

BANVILLE, THEODORE DE. *Oeuvres.* Geneva: Slatkine, 1972.

BARRICELLI, JEAN-PIERRE, and GIBALDI, JOSEPH, eds. *Interrelations of Literature.* New York: Modern Language Association, 1982.

BARTHES, ROLAND. *S/Z.* Paris: Editions du Seuil, 1970.

———. *S/Z.* Translated by Richard Miller. New York: Farrar, Straus and Giroux, 1974.

BAUDELAIRE, CHARLES. *Oeuvres complètes.* Paris: Editions du Seuil, 1968.

BEGUIN, ALBERT. *L'Ame romantique et le rêve.* Paris: Corti, 1939.

BENJAMIN, WALTER. *Illuminations.* Translated by Harry Zohn. New York: Schocken, 1978.

BERMANN, SANDRA. "The Sonnet: Repetition with a Difference." Paper presented at the 10th ICLA Congress held at New York University in August 1982.

BERNARD, SUZANNE. *Mallarmé et la musique.* Paris: Nizet, 1959.

BERNSTEIN, LEONARD. *The Unanswered Question.* Charles Eliot Norton Lectures, 1973. Cambridge: Harvard University Press, 1976.

BROWN, CALVIN. *Music and Literature.* Athens: University of George Press, 1948.

———. "The Musical Analogies in Mallarmé's *Un Coup de dés*." *Comparative Literature Studies* 10 (1967): 69–79

———. "The Relations between Music and Literature as a Field of Study." *Comparative Literature Studies* 22 (1970): 19–34.

BURROWS, DAVID. "Style in Culture: Vivaldi, Zeno, and Ricci." *Journal of Interdisciplinary History* (Summer, 1973): 1–23.

CHASSÉ, CHARLES. *Les Clés de Mallarmé.* Paris: Montaigne, 1954.

CLAUDON, FRANCIS. *Hofmannsthal et la France.* Berne: Peter Lang, 1979.

COHN, ROBERT GREER. *Toward the Poems of Mallarmé.* Berkeley: University of California Press, 1965.

———. *Mallarmé's "Un Coup de dés."* Yale French Studies, no. 6. New Haven: Yale University Press, 1959.

COOKE, DEREYCK. *Language of Music.* New York: Oxford University Press, 1959.

CURTIUS, ERNST ROBERT. *Essays on European Literature.* Translated by Michael Kowal. Princeton: Princeton University Press, 1973.

DAHLHAUS, CARL. *Between Romanticism and Modernism.* Translated by Mary Whittall. Berkeley: University of California Press, 1980.

———. "Wagner's Begriff der 'dichterisch-musikalischen Periode.'" In *Beiträge zur Geschichte der Musikanschauung im 19. Jahrhundert.* Edited by Walter Salmen. Regensburg: Bosse, 1965.

DAVIAU, DONALD G., and BUELOW, GEORGE J. *The Ariadne auf Naxos of Hugo von Hofmannsthal and Richard Strauss.* Chapel Hill: University of North Carolina Press, 1975.

DEBUSSY, CLAUDE. *Debussy on Music.* Translated by Richard Langham Smith. New York: Knopf, 1977.

———. *Lettres à son éditeur.* Paris: Durand, 1927.

———. *Monsieur Croche et autres écrits.* Paris: Gallimard, 1971.

———. *Prelude to "The Afternoon of a Faun."* Edited by William W. Austin. New York: Norton, 1970.

DONOGHUE, DENIS. *William Butler Yeats.* New York: Viking, 1971.

EHRENFORTH, KARL HEINRICH VON. *Ausdruck und Form: Schoenbergs Durchbruch zur Atonalität in den Georgeliedern, op. 15.* Bonn: Bouvier, 1963.

EINSTEIN, ALFRED. *Essays on Music.* New York: Norton, 1966.

ELLMAN, RICHARD. *The Identity of Yeats.* New York: Oxford University Press, 1964.

———. *Yeats: The Man, the Masks.* New York: Dutton, 1948.

EMPSON, WILLIAM. *Seven Types of Ambiguity.* New York: New Directions, 1947.

———. *The Structure of Complex Words.* New York: New Directions, 1951.

FISER, EMERIC. *Le Symbole littéraire: Essai sur la signification du symbole chez Wagner, Baudelaire, Mallarmé, Bergson.* Paris: Corti, 1941.

FREUD, SIGMUND. *Die Traumbedeutung.* Vienna: Deuticke, 1909.

———. *The Interpretation of Dreams.* Translated by James Strachey. New York: Avon, 1965.

FRYE, NORTHROP. *Anatomy of Criticism.* Princeton: Princeton University Press, 1973.

———, ed. *Sound and Poetry.* English Institute Essays, 1956. New York: Columbia University Press, 1967.

GEORGE, STEFAN. *Gesamt-Ausgabe der Werke.* Berlin: Bondi.

GHIL, RENÉ. *Traité du verbe.* Edited by Tizianna Goruppi. Paris: Nizet, 1978.

GOMBRICH, E. H. *Art and Illusion.* New York: Pantheon, 1960.

———. *The Image and the Eye.* Ithaca: Cornell University Press, 1982.

———. *Meditations on a Hobby Horse and Other Essays on the Theory of Art.* New York: Phaidon, 1963.

GREGORY, AUGUSTA, ed. and trans. *Cuchulain of Muirthemne.* New York: Scribner, 1903.

———, ed. and trans. *Gods and Fighting Men.* Toronto: Macmillan, 1976.

HANSLICK, EDUARD. *The Beautiful in Music.* Translated by Gustav Cohen. New York: Bobbs-Merrill, 1957.

HAUPTMANN, GERHART. *The Sunken Bell.* Translated by Charles Henry Meltzer. New York: Doubleday, 1930.

HAUSER, ARNOLD. *The Philosophy of Art History.* New York: Knopf, 1959.

———. *The Social History of Art,* 2 vols. New York: Knopf, 1951.

HELMHOLTZ, HERMANN VON. *Die Lehre von den Tonempfindungen.* Hildesheim: Olms, 1968.

———. *On the Sensations of Tone.* Translated by Alexander J. Ellis. New York: Dover, 1954.

HOFMANNSTHAL, HUGO VON. *Ariadne auf Naxos.* New York: Boosey and Hawkes, 1943.

———. *Gesammelte Werke.* Stockholm: Fischer, 1946.

———. *Plays and Librettos.* Edited by Michael Hamburger. Bollingen series, 33. New York: Pantheon, 1952.

———. *Selected Prose.* Translated by Mary Hottinger, Tanya Stern, and James Stern. Bollingen series, 33. New York: Pantheon, 1952.

Hollander, John. *The Untuning of the Sky: Ideas of Music in English Poetry, 1500–1700.* Princeton: Princeton University Press, 1961.

———. *Vision and Resonance.* New York: Oxford University Press, 1975.

HOLLOWAY, ROBIN. *Debussy and Wagner.* London: Eulenburg, 1979.

JACKENDOFF, RAY. "Leonard Bernstein's Harvard Lectures." *High Fidelity* 24 (April 1974): 8–10.

JANKELEVITCH, VLADIMIR. *La Vie et la mort dans la musique de Debussy.* Neuchâtel: Baconniere, 1968.

KEILER, ALLAN. "Bernstein's *The Unanswered Question* and the Problem of Musical Competence." *Musical Quarterly* 64 (2): 195–222.

KENNER, HUGH. "Some Post-Symbolist Structures." In *Literary Theory and Structure.* Edited by Frank Brady, John Palmer, and Martin Price. New Haven: Yale University Press, 1973.

KERMAN, JOSEPH. *Opera as Drama.* New York: Knopf, 1956.

LENHART, CHARMENZ. *Musical Influence on American Poetry.* Athens: University of Georgia Press, 1956.

LEVIN, SAMUEL R. *Linguistic Structure in Poetry.* Mouton: The Hague, 1967.

———. *The Semantics of Metaphor.* Baltimore: Johns Hopkins University Press, 1977.

LOCKSPEISER, EDWARD. *Debussy: His Life and Mind,* 2 vols. New York: Cambridge University Press, 1978.

———. *Music and Painting.* London: Cassell, 1973.

LOEVGRAN, SVEN. *The Genesis of Modernism: Seurat, Gaugin, Van Gogh and French Symbolism in the 1880's.* Bloomington: Indiana University Press, 1971.

LOVEJOY, ARTHUR O. *Essays in the History of Ideas.* Baltimore: Johns Hopkins Press, 1948.

MCGRATH, WILLIAM J. *"Volksseelenpolitik* and Psychological Rebirth: Mahler and Hofmannsthal." *Journal of Interdisciplinary History* (Summer, 1973): 53–71.

MCKILLIGAN, KATHLEEN M. *Edouard Dujardin: "Les Lauriers sont coupés" and the interior monologue.* Leeds: The University of Hull Publications, 1977.

MAETERLINCK, MAURICE. *The Plays of Maurice Maeterlinck.* Translated by Richard Hovery. Greak Neck: Core Collection, 1977.

———. *Serres chaudes.* Brussels: Lacomblez, 1900.

———. *Théâtre.* Brussels: Lacomblez, 1905.

MALLARMÉ, STÉPHANE. *Oeuvres complètes.* Paris: Gallimard, 1945.

———. *The Poems.* Translated by Keith Bosley. New York: Penguin, 1977.

———. *The Poems of Mallarmé.* Translated by Roger Fry. New York: New Directions, 1951.

———. *Selected Prose Poems, Essays and Letters.* Translated by Bradford Cook. Baltimore: Johns Hopkins University Press, 1956.

MAURON, CHARLES. *Introduction to the Psychoanalysis of Mallarmé.* Translated by A. Henderson and W. McLendon. Berkeley: University of California Press, 1963.

MEYER, LEONARD. *Music, the Arts and Ideas.* Chicago: University of Chicago Press, 1973.

MICHAUD, GUY. *Mallarmé.* Translated by Marie Collins and Bertha Humez. New York: New York University Press, 1965.

———. *Message poétique du symbolisme.* Paris: Nizet, 1947.

MICHON, JACQUES. *Mallarmé et les mots anglais.* Montreal: University of Montreal Press, 1978.

MONDOR, HENRI. *Histoire d'un faune.* Paris: Gallimard, 1948.

———. *Vie de Mallarmé.* Paris: Gallimard, 1941.

MONTAL, ROBERT. *René Ghil: Du symbolisme à la poésie cosmique.* Brussels: Labor, 1962.

MORIER, HENRI. *Dictionnaire de poétique et de rhétorique.* Paris: Presse universitaires de France, 1975.

NATTIEZ, JEAN-JACQUES. "An Analysis of Debussy's *Syrinx.*" *Toronto Semiotic Circle: Monographs, Working Papers and Prepublications* 4(1982.

NEWLIN, DIKA. *Bruckner, Mahler, Schoenberg.* London: Boyars, 1979.

NIETZSCHE, FRIEDRICH. *The Birth of Tragedy and the Case of Wagner.* Translated by Walter Kaufmann. New York: Random House, 1967.

ORDLEDGE, ROBERT. *Debussy and the Theatre.* Cambridge: Cambridge University Press, 1982.

ORTEGA Y GASSET, JOSE. *The Dehumanization of Art and Other Essays on Art, Culture and Literature.* Translated by Helen Weyl. Princeton: Princeton University Press, 1972.

OVID. *Metamorphoses.* Translated by Rolfe Humphries. Bloomington: Indiana University Press, 1955.

PANTLE, SHERRILL HAHN. *"Die Frau ohne Schatten" by Hugo von Hofmannsthal and Richard Strauss.* Las Vegas: Peter Lang, 1979.

PATER, WALTER. *Works of Walter Pater.* London: Macmillan, 1900.

PAZ, OCTAVIO. *Children of the Mire.* Translated by Rachel Phillips. Cambridge: Harvard University Press, 1974.

PEYRE, HENRI. *Baudelaire: A Collection of Critical Essays.* Englewood Cliffs, NJ: Prentice-Hall, 1962.

POWERS, HAROLD S. "Language and Musical Analysis." *Ethnomusicology* (January, 1980) 1–60.

PRAWER, S. S., ed. *The Penguin Book of Lieder.* Baltimore: Penguin, 1964.

RICHARD, JEAN-PIERRE. *L'Univers imaginaire de Mallarmé*. Paris: Editions du Seuil, 1961.
RILKE, RAINER MARIA. *Nine Plays*. Translated by Klaus Phillips and John Locke. New York: Ungar, 1979.
————. *Sämtliche Werke*. Frankfurt: Insel, 1861.
ROSEN, CHARLES. *Classical Style*. New York: Norton, 1972.
————. *Schoenberg*. New York: Viking, 1975.
RUWET, NICOLAS. *Langue, musique, poésie*. Paris: Edition du Seuil, 1972.
SCHAEFFER, R. MURRAY, ed. *Pound and Music*. New York: New Directions, 1977.
SCHER, STEVEN PAUL. *Verbal Music in German Literture*. New Haven: Yale University Press, 1968.
SCHERER, JACQUES. *Le "Livre" de Mallarmé*. Paris: Gallimard, 1957.
————. *The Structural Functions of Harmony*. New York: Norton, 1954.
SCHOPENHAUER, ARTHUR. *Die Welt als Wille und Vorstellung*. Leipzig: Broadhaus, 1888.
————. *Parerga and Paralipomena*. Translated by E. Payne. Oxford: Clarendon Press, 1974.
————. *The World as Will and Idea*. Translated by R. B. Haldane and J. Kemp. London: Paul, Trench, Trubner, 1964.
SCHORSKE, CARL E. *Fin-de-Siècle Vienna*. New York: Random House, 1979.
SCHRADE, LEO. *Beethoven in France*. New Haven: Yale University Press, 1942.
SHATTUCK, ROGER. *The Banquet Years*. new York: Random House, 1968.
SHAW, GEORGE BERNARD. *Music in London, 1890–94,* 4 vols. London: Constagel, 1932.
————. *The Perfect Wagnerite*. New York: Dover, 1967.
————. *The Sanity of Art*. New York: Tucker, 1908.
SILZ, WALTER, *Early German Romanticism*. Cambridge: Harvard University Press, 1929.
SONDRUP, STEVEN. *Hofmannsthal and the French Symbolist Tradition*. Berne: Lange, 1976.
SPITZER, LEO. *Classical and Christian Ideas of World Harmony*. Baltimore: Johns Hopkins University Press, 1963.
STAIGER, EMIL. *Musik und Dichtung*. Zurich: Atlantis, 1959.
STEIN, JACK M. *Richard Wagner and the Synthesis of the Arts*. Westport: Greenwood, 1973.
STRINDBERG, AUGUST. *Six Plays*. Translated by Elizabeth Sprigge. New York: Doubleday, 1955.
SUHAMI, EVELYNE. *Paul Valéry et la musique*. Dakar: University of Dakar Press, 1966.
SYMONS, ARTHUR. *The Symbolist Movement in Literature*. New York: Dutton, 1958.
TOVEY, DONALD FRANCIS. *Essays in Musical Analysis*, 6 vols. London: Oxford University Press, 1972.
URBAN, G. R. *Kinesis and Stasis: A Study in the Attitude of Stefan George and His Circle to the Musical Arts*. The Hague: Mouton, 1962.
VALÉRY, PAUL. *Écrits divers sur Stéphane Mallarmé*. Vol. 12, *Oeuvres de Paul Valéry*. Paris: Gallimard, 1950.

VERLAINE, PAUL. *Oeuvres complètes.* Paris: Vanier, 1907.

——. *Oeuvres en prose complètes.* Paris: Gallimard, 1972.

——. *Selected Poems.* Translated by C. F. MacIntyre. Berkeley: University of California Press, 1948.

WAGNER, RICHARD. *Gesammelte Schriften und Dichtungen.* Leipzig: Siegel, 1900.

——. *Richard Wagner's Prose Works.* Translated by William Ashton Ellis. London: Paul, Trench, Trubner, 1897.

——. *The Ring of the Nibelung.* Translated by Andrew Porter. New York: Norton, 1976.

WEBERN, ANTON. *The Path to the New Music.* Edited by Willi Reich. London: Universal, 1960.

WENK, ARTHUR. *Claude Debussy and the Poets.* Berkeley: University of California Press, 1976.

WHYTE, LANCELOT LAW. *The Unconscious before Freud.* New York: St. Martin's Press, 1978.

WILSON, EDMUND. *Axel's Castle.* New York: Scribner, 1931.

WINN, JAMES ANDERSON. *Unsuspected Eloquence: A History of the Relations between Poetry and Music.* New Haven: Yale University Press, 1981.

YEATS, WILLIAM BUTLER. *Autobiographies.* London: Macmillan, 1966.

——. *Essays and Introductions.* New York: Collier, 1961.

——. *The Variorum Edition of the Plays.* Edited by Peter Alt and Russell K. Alspach. New York: MacMillan, 1957.

ZUCKERKANDL, VICTOR. *Sound and Symbol.* Translated by Willard R. Trask. New York: Pantheon, 1956.

Index

Numbers in italic refer to pages with musical figures.

David Michael Hertz is Assistant Professor of Comparative Literature at Indiana University, Bloomington. He formerly taught at New York University, where he held a Mellon Postdoctoral Fellowship in the Humanities during the 1983 academic year. A composer and pianist, he holds degrees in both music and comparative literature and frequently gives lecture/recitals on the interrelations of the two arts.